Historic
New Brunswick

Dan Soucoup

Pottersfield Press
Lawrencetown Beach
Nova Scotia, Canada

Canadian Cataloguing in Publication Data
Soucoup, Dan, 1949 –
    Historic New Brunswick
    ISBN 1-895900-09-3
1. New Brunswick — History.   I. Title.
FC2461.S68 1997   971.5'1   C97-950162-8
F1043.S68 1997

1

Pottersfield press gratefully acknowledges the ongoing support of the Nova Scotia Department of Education, Cultural Affairs Division, as well as the Canada Council for the Arts and the Department of Canadian Heritage.

Printed and bound in Canada.

Pottersfield Press
Lawrencetown Beach
83 Leslie Road
East Lawrencetown
Nova Scotia, Canada B2Z 1P8

THE CANADA COUNCIL | LE CONSEIL DES ARTS
FOR THE ARTS | DU CANADA
SINCE 1957 | DEPUIS 1957

To the great popular historians of the province —
William O. Raymond
William F. Ganong
J.Clarence Webster
and
Esther Clark Wright

The author acknowledges the assistance of ...
Provincial Archives of New Brunswick
Halifax Regional Library and Reference Department
Thanks Mac for those books.

Contents

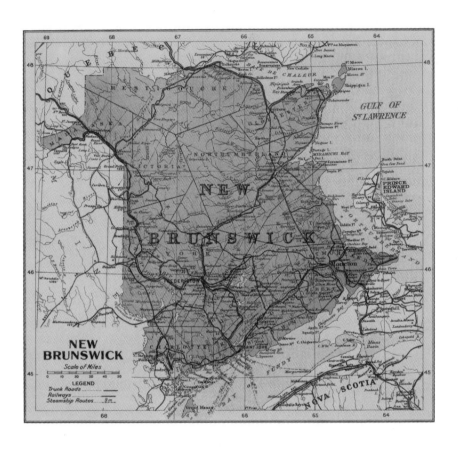

Introduction

"The history of New Brunswick is no less interesting and fascinating than that of many European countries but tangible evidences in the shape of forts and early buildings are scanty, owing to the fact that they were mostly constructed of wood and have consequently disappeared."

J. Clarence Webster
Historical Guide to New Brunswick

As a child, I can remember a dark object that stood by the highway at Frosty Hollow, just outside Sackville. As I discovered years later, the object wasn't the Frosty Hollow troll but the work of one of New Brunswick's most important historians, J. Clarence Webster. And my introduction to Maritime history was the Beaubassin-Ancient Indian Portage cairn, erected by the Historic Sites and Monuments Board of Canada during the time Dr. Webster had served as the chairman of the national board.

History-makers shape events that, in retrospect, we often cite as the key ingredients of the epoch or decade that determined a people, a region, or even a province. The events and people mentioned here are no exception, and give some sense of the distinctive history and traditions that developed in New Brunswick.

Distinctiveness — a place apart. This theme comes to mind when one thinks of the political birth of the province in 1784. Carved out of the old British colony of Nova Scotia, New Brunswick, with its vast forests and waterways, was indeed a very different place than other parts of the Maritimes, and its history was bound to develop separately.

New Brunswick's uniqueness did not begin with the Loyalist vision of a separate province but rather at the beginning of human history. We know that prior to European contact, a separate Aboriginal nation, the Maliseet people, appeared along the St. John River. The French period also saw

7

northern Acadia develop independently from the Acadian peninsula, where colonization took place almost a century ahead of its northern neighbour.

As the only official bilingual province in Canada, New Brunswick's dualism is enshrined in its past as two European nations played a vital role in the development of the province. Dualism is also at the core of its geography with two great river systems, the St. John and the Miramichi, extending over a majority of its land mass. Yet New Brunswick's history is also one of conflict that can be seen in terms of a north-south division, characterized by rural and urban, poor and prosperous, neglect and privilege, Catholic and Protestant, French and English. This tension has given rise to many of the events described within. I hope the reader will take from these pages some sense of the sweep, diversity, and human ingenuity that has characterized New Brunswick's past.

Chronology

10,000 B.C. Early Aboriginal People Appear
1534 A.D.   Jacques Cartier at Baie des Chaleurs
1604 -   First Winter for Europeans — Saint Croix Island
1611 -   First White Settlement on the St. John
1631 -   Conflict in Acadia: La Tour & d'Aulnay
1643 -   Coal Mining in North America
1659 -   Earliest English Fort
1668 -   Nicholas Denys
1672 -   The Seigniorial System: Failure in Acadia
1672 -   Acadia Expands to Chignecto
1674 -   Dutch New Brunswick
1677 -   Jemseg, Capital of Acadia
1689 -   John Gyles, A Maliseet Prisoner
1690 -   First Dry Dock
1692 -   Acadian Headquarters at Naskwaak
1695 -   New Brunswick's First Saw-Mill
1698 -   Acadians at Shepody Bay
1700 -   Northern Acadia: One Century of European Presence
1710 -   Permanent British Presence in Acadia
1717 -   The Meductic Church
1733 -   Acadians Resettle the St. John
1740 -   Maliseet Abandon Meductic
1749 -   Le Loutré Arrives at Chignecto
1751 -   Fort Beauséjour is Constructed
1751 -   Another Fort at Baie Verte
1753 -   The Spy of Beauséjour
1755 -   The Expulsion of the Acadians
1756 -   Boishébert and the Defense of the Acadians
1757 -   Beaubears Island, National Historic Site
1758 -   Monckton Builds Fort Frederick
1760 -   The Battle of the Restigouche

9

1828	-	Old Government House
1829	-	King's College
1830	-	Johnny Woodenboat
1830	-	St. Stephen, Sawmill Capital
1830	-	The Seaman's Hospital
1830	-	William End's Gloucester County
1834	-	Marriage Monopoly Ends
1836	-	The Westmorland Road
1837	-	First Triumph of the Assembly
1837	-	The Aroostook War
1839	-	A Church Burning on Grand Manan
1839	-	Restigouche County Established
1839	-	The Penny Paper
1842	-	A Geologist & A Museum
1842	-	First Provincial Art Exhibition
1843	-	The Baron of Dorchester
1843	-	The Miramichi's Fighting Election
1843	-	Mount Allison Established
1844	-	The Great Military Road Project
1844	-	The Leper Colony
1844	-	Perley's Indian Report
1845	-	The Celestial City
1845	-	The Early Steamboats
1846	-	The Steeves' Dynasty
1847	-	The Good Samaritan
1847	-	The Quarantine Island
1847	-	The Woodstock Riot
1848	-	Responsible Government
1849	-	First Female Educator
1849	-	The Orange & Green Confrontation
1850	-	Shipbuilding: The Golden Age
1851	-	Grand Manan & The Fisheries Act
1851	-	Madawaska Boundary Settled
1851	-	The Railway Era
1853	-	The Milltown Timber Baron
1854	-	Reciprocity Begins
1854	-	Rise of the Smasher Party
1855	-	New Brunswick's First Town
1856	-	Prohibition Becomes Law
1857	-	Collapse of the Moncton Shipyard
1858	-	New Brunswick's Last Duel
1858	-	Andrew Bonar Law

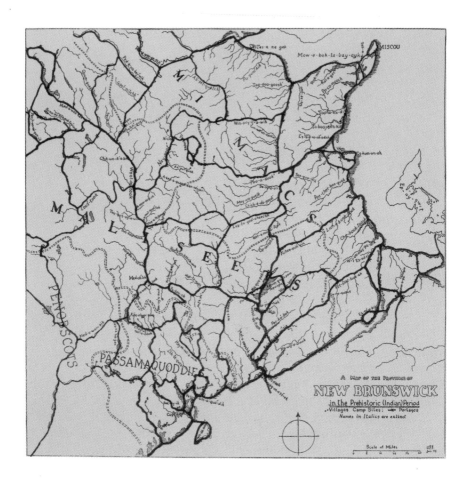

Ancient waterways and Aboriginal regions of the pre-contact period. Known campsites, Aboriginal names, and portage routes are also shown. W.F. Ganong, 1899.

Ancient Sites and Waterways
of the First Peoples

10,000-500 Years Ago
Pre-Contact Period

The pre-contact era in New Brunswick is loosely divided into three periods. The Early Period, about ten thousand to six thousand years ago, is characterized by scarce archaeological evidence within the provincial boundaries; however, at Debert, Nova Scotia, as well as in Maine and Labrador, artifacts have been found that place a people called Palaeo-Indians throughout the Maritime region, although little is known of their culture.

The Middle Period lasted from six thousand to three thousand years ago. Evidence exists, especially from around four thousand to three thousand years ago, to suggest a number of different peoples or traditions inhabited the region. The Laurentian people moved into the St. John River area from Maine and established many temporary hunting and fishing campsites but did not move further east or south into the coastal areas. The Susquehanna people appeared about four thousand years ago along the coast of the Bay of Fundy but did not venture offshore into the Bay.

The other known tradition of the Middle Period included the Maritime Archaic people and actually dates from the Early Period. These coastal people hunted and fished in large sea-going canoes and their coastal sites were semi-permanent villages, yet they also travelled far distances throughout the region.

The Late Period lasted about 2,500 years, from three thousand to five hundred years ago when European contact began. Of the two major traditions from the period, the Maritime Woodland tradition of the Maliseet and Mi'kmaq nations most closely resembled the Aboriginal culture recorded by Europeans about five hundred years ago. Another group of

15

people followed what has been called the Middlesex tradition and arrived in New Brunswick from the Ohio River valley about 2,400 years ago. Their best known custom was constructing large burial mounds and, of the known Middlesex sites in the region, the Augustine Mound at Red Bank on the Miramichi River is by far the best preserved.

3,000-500 Years Ago
Distribution of the First Nations

The Maritime Woodland tradition developed into the predominant culture of the region populated by the ancestors of today's Maliseet and Mi'kmaq. By the end of the Late Period, Europeans encountered two distinct nations occupying the land with well established borders based on the principal rivers and harbours of the region.

The Mi'kmaq people occupied the coast from the Gaspé to Nova Scotia and inland, along the main rivers that flow into the Gulf of St. Lawrence. The upper reaches of the Bay of Fundy was considered Mi'kmaq territory, with the dividing line at Martin Head near the western end of the present Fundy National Park. Inland, the headwaters of the principle rivers provided a natural boundary for the Mi'kmaq nation, as the southeastern boundary remained close to the Northumberland Strait but the northern division swung far west as the vast Miramichi and Restigouche River systems extend deep into the interior.

The Maliseet with their close allies, the Passamaquoddy, occupied the western area, and their territory extended southeast to include the headwaters of the Canaan River in present day Westmorland County, and the Salmon River of Kent County. The entire St. John River system was considered Maliseet territory as well as the Bay of Fundy between Martin Head and Point Lepreau, the latter being the coastal dividing line between the Passamaquoddy and the Maliseet.

The Passamaquoddy did not extend inland much further than Magoguadavic Lake and were bordered on the west by their allies, the Penobscot nation who occupied the territory along the Penobscot River. To the north, both the Maliseet and Mi'kmaq nations were bordered by their traditional enemies the Mohawk, whose occasional invasions into the east coast region created havoc for the Maliseet and Mi'kmaq. During the pre-contact period, it's doubtful that any permanent Mohawk settlements were established in the region.

3,000–200 Years Ago
Ancient Waterways & Portage Routes

The remarkable geographic fact about New Brunswick that produced such a splendid travel system is that all navigable waters of the province are easily linked to the great St. John and Miramichi River systems that extend through almost the entire region. The river systems were interlinked by a series of well-known streams or overland portages that allowed for easy passage by the most perfect of all Aboriginal inventions — the birch bark canoe.

Cut from the white birch tree, the lightweight, highly versatile birch bark canoe could carry people and freight through narrow streams of less than two feet, drawing only a few inches of water while moved along by means of a light pole. Yet the same vehicle was adaptable for coastal travel or when fitted with the Maliseet invention of slats, or "canoe shoes," could be dragged over dry river beds or wet rocks.

At the centre of the ancient river routes of the region was the St. John with hundreds of miles of smooth, unobstructed water and only one major portage at Grand Falls. Like a huge waterwheel, the St. John River allowed fast and safe passage south to the Bay of Fundy and Nova Scotia, across short portages to the Miramichi and points east, north into Quebec or over the famous Eel River portage to New England. Indeed most rivers of the region offered relatively smooth waters for canoe travel that allowed for ease of communication among the First Nations peoples throughout the area and into northern New England. Except for the rivers of Charlotte County, the upper waters of the Miramichi, and the Nepisiguit, few rivers are impassable due to dangerous rapids or falls. During the dry season when waters became too low for fast travel, much of the region could be navigated by coastal waters. In winter the same routes were travelled by snowshoes and tobaggans, as the frozen rivers and snow-covered paths allowed for ease of travel.

While the universal engine of transportation was the canoe, portage paths were the bridges whereby pre-contact travellers changed river systems, and then continued voyages that could take them through endless waterways deep into the continent or back to villages or camp sites. Between the headwaters of the principle rivers, the portage routes followed ancient paths that were named for the direction in which the traveller was headed. Travelling overland from Nictau Lake to the Nepisiguit would be called the Nepisiguit portage, while the other way would be cited for its destination at Nictau. New Brunswick is full of place names such as Portage Vale, Portage River, Portage Island or Portage-Du-Lac. Today many of the original portage routes are still intact winding through remote wilderness areas, while others are part of our provincial road systems.

St. John–St. Lawrence

While many canoe routes led from the St. John to the St. Lawrence, the most travelled route to Quebec led from the far northern point of the St. John, up the Madawaska River to Lake Temiscouata and across an extensive portage to Rivière-du-Loup. This ancient portage became the main communication link between Quebec and Nova Scotia during the historic period of French and English conflict, when Aboriginal messengers travelled the entire 720 kilometres (450 miles) during spring runs from Quebec to Saint John in five days. A post road was cut along the portage route during the first years of New Brunswick's birth as a province and the present highway follows much of the same route.

St. John–Restigouche

The Green River to the Kedgwick River offered a difficult and treacherous route to the Restigouche, so the most popular route was up the Grand River to the Wagan Brook, where a five kilometre (three mile) portage ends at the Wagansis Brook that winds into the Restigouche. As the Restigouche is a smooth flowing river with few rapids or dangerous falls, the Grand River route became the main canoe route for all traffic from the Baie des Chaleurs to the St. John. During the dry season the entire fifteen kilometres (nine miles) of brook travel was sometimes portaged. This route was also often considered a better way to travel to the St. Lawrence from the Restigouche, rather than going overland via the Gaspé.

St. John–Nepisiguit

The journey from the Tobique River to Nictau Lake, with a short four kilometre (2.5 mile) portage to Nepisiguit Lake, is one of the most difficult canoe routes across New Brunswick. Rich in big game and fish, the Tobique–Nictau–Nepisiguit area was a popular route but quite challenging as the swift Tobique River demanded strength and endurance. The Nepisiguit, which is thought to mean a "hard river" in Mi'kmaq, contains treacherous rapids and a number of dangerous falls that must be portaged, especially Indian Falls, but also the Narrows and Grand Falls. Due to the difficulty of this route, travellers in a hurry often chose the Grand River–Restigouche route to the Nepisiguit.

St. John–Miramichi

Many routes were available to the Miramichi, including a difficult and rarely used route from the Tobique River to Long Lake and across a thirteen kilometre (eight mile) portage to the Little Southwest Miramichi Lake. Another route, actually the shortest distance between the two rivers but a difficult portage, leaves the St. John at the Shikatehawk River, which is considered unnavigable for most of the twenty-four kilometres (fifteen miles) until the South Branch of the Miramichi at Foreston took the paddler to the main river. This route was the most direct to the Miramichi and undoubtably the most popular. In the dry season, both the Southwest Miramichi and a more southern route near Napadogan to the Taxis River, could be treacherous until reaching Boiestown.

Another route to the Southwest Miramichi was up the Nashwaak River to Cross Creek and across a portage to the Taxis and the Miramichi. To the east of this route, a road was eventually built from Naskwaak Bridge to Boiestown. The most southern route from the St. John to the Miramichi involved paddling up the smooth and lazy Gaspereau River at the top of Grand Lake, and hiking a ten kilometre (six mile) portage over quite level terrain to the Cains River. From the Cains, an easy voyage to the Miramichi made this route a long but popular trip.

St. John–Penobscot

The upper St. John River routes into the territories of the Penobscot and Kennebec nations were known to the early Maliseet and Mi'kmaq, and included a portage at the head of the Allagash River to the Northeast Branch of the Penobscot. The same branch of the Penobscot River could be reached from the Aroostook River, where a coastal route could be taken to the Kennebec River or an overland portage route via the Sebasticook River would take a traveller to the heart of the Kennebec region.

The most important of all routes to New England was the Meductic–Eel River to North Lake route that formed the major waterway south to Passamaquoddy Bay as well as west to the Penobscot River. This famous and ancient portage route was the path that brought the Maliseet boy-prisoner John Gyles to Fort Meductic, and it was on this portage that Abraham Gesner claimed to have found rocks worn down from centuries of moccasin traffic. The old Maliseet portage begins four miles above the Eel River.

The Eel River is unnavigable near the St. John; the Meductic portage begins near the old Maliseet village at Meductic and cuts across to where Benton begins. Here Eel River is navigable to First Eel Lake, where at the lower end an Aboriginal portage of about five kilometres (three miles) still leads to North Lake approximately where the current highway cuts between the two lakes. North Lake empties into Grand Lake which forms part of the Chiputneticook Lakes that now separates Maine from New Brunswick.

Heading south from Grand Lake to Passamaquoddy Bay involved another portage at Mud Lake near Forest City, as well as numerous falls and rocky rapids while descending the rough St. Croix River. Portages west from the St. Croix led to the Machais River and also to the Penobscot, but the main portage route to the Penobscot River led from Davenports Cove on Grand Lake, four kilometres (2.5 miles) southwest to the Baskahegan River above Danforth. Down the Baskahegan would lead to the Mattawamkeag River that emptied into the Penobscot River, and at this junction stood the main Penobscot Indian village and palisaded fort. West to the Sebasticook River and one short portage led to the Kennebec village and fort at Norridgewock. This ancient route of waterways and portages was widely used for centuries and became an important highway for conducting warfare during the early era of white encroachment in New England.

St. John–Passamaquoddy Bay

In addition to travelling via the Eel River portage, the coastal route was always a possibility, especially during the warm summer months. The only portage for travellers canoeing down the lower St. John was at the mouth of the river where the Reversing Falls allowed for passage only during slack water on each side of the tide. At Marble Cove, a portage route ran over the neck to Saint John harbour opposite Navy Island.

Another route to Charlotte County exited from the St. John along the Oromocto River and journeyed to the Magaguadavic River. That route led to the coast, or across again to Lake Utopia and Passamaquoddy Bay. From the headwaters of the South Branch of the Oromocto River, a hard portage route led to the Lepreau River but most of the rivers of Charlotte County are difficult to canoe and portage routes are still over very rough and rocky terrain.

St. John–Richibucto

At the top of Grand Lake a paddler could turn off the Salmon River to the Gaspereau and the Miramichi, or continue up the Salmon until the river swung past the Cordy Brook. Here an easy portage of less than five kilometres (three miles) connected the traveller to the Richibucto River where Highway 116 first meets the river. The Salmon River is one of the smoothest rivers for canoeing in the region and this route was much travelled in previous times because of its speed and comfort.

St. John–Petitcodiac

A portage route from the Kennebecasis to the Petitcodiac River via the Anagance area was sometimes used by travellers from the lower St. John but the main route to the Petitcodiac was along the Canaan River. From Washademoak Lake to the Petitcodiac was one of the most travelled routes from Quebec to Beauséjour, and involved following the Canaan River just past Nevers Brook where one of the longest portages in the area intersected the North River, a waterway that is not navigable most of the year. The portage continued overland and met the Petitcodiac River two miles east of the present village of Petitcodiac. The nineteen kilometre (twelve mile) portage could be reduced to about 12.5 kilometres (eight miles) if the North River were passable down to the Petitcodiac, where early travellers could then meet the Fundy tides at Salisbury, and coast down to the Bay.

Many early French travellers mentioned this main route of communication between the St. Lawrence and eastern Acadia, and this route was also the passage that New Englander Jonathan Eddy used to reach the Chignecto area to attack Fort Cumberland in 1776.

Petitcodiac–Missaguash–Baie Verte

The Frosty Hollow Valley passage was another important portage route in the historic link between Quebec, the eastern Acadian region of Beaubassin and the Missaguash River. From the Petitcodiac River, an Aboriginal or Acadian messenger could paddle around the dangerous Fort Folly Point and across the mouth of the Memramcook River, or could portage from Fox Creek to the head of the Memramcook River, and down to Dorchester, where an ancient portage led for five kilometres (three miles) to Frosty Hollow and Westcock. From Frosty Hollow (named for its early frost), the Tantramar or Aulac rivers led into the marshlands, or a coastal route took paddlers to the Missaguash River and the Acadian area of Beaubassin.

The Missaguash River was also a vital passage way for historic travel across the Isthmus of Chignecto, and into the Gulf of St. Lawrence or southern Acadia. A tidal river to above Point de Bute, the Missaguash turns into a meandering stream through small lakes and bogs that in earlier times was navigable for canoes until five kilometres (three miles) from Baie Verte, where a portage trail began just past Halls Hill. The initial hill of this portage was called Portage Hill, where the headwaters of the Gaspereau River began flowing towards Baie Verte, named for the salt-water grasses that sprout each summer. Franquet's map of 1752 chartered this canoe route just before a French road was constructed from Baie Verte to Fort Beauséjour, which allowed the waterway to fall into disuse.

Baie Verte–Restigouche

The sea route along the Northumberland Strait to northern New Brunswick had few inland portages as the Mi'kmaq sea canoe with its "hogged" centre, allowed for efficient travel in open water. From Baie Verte, a ten kilometre (six mile) portage went overland to Shemogue and cut off a long paddle around Cape Tormentine. Another portage of similar length connected the Petitcodiac at Fox Creek (near Moncton) to Shediac, while a six kilometre (four mile) trail linked the Memramcook River to the Scoudouc River, which also led into Shediac Bay.

Above Richibucto, Point Escuminac was often avoided due to high winds and in Kouchibouguac Bay, a traveller could head up Portage River to its source, where a short portage led over a large peat plain to a favourite campsite for paddlers called Coffee Island. The portage then entered Two Mile Brook which flows into Gullivers Brook that in turn, leads to Bay Du Vin River and Miramichi Bay. This portage route was an important passage way for Mik'maq and Acadian travellers between the Miramichi and Fort Beauséjour during the struggle for control of northern Acadia.

North of the Miramichi to Baie des Chaleurs, the sea route was most tempting since above Burnt Church, a series of islands and sand lagoons protected paddlers from off-shore winds. Yet a number of inland routes were also possible, including the most popular route to the head of the Northwest Miramichi, where another of the numerous Portage Rivers led to a short portage to Gordon Meadows Brook. This brook ferried canoes for some twenty-two kilometres (fourteen miles) before another short portage around some very difficult rapids brought a traveller to the Nepisiguit River and into Bathurst harbour.

Both Nicholas Denys and Chrestin LeClercq mentioned this Miramichi to Nepisiguit portage in their writings, but except for a hunter's route from the Nepisiguit across to the Upsalquitch and down the Restigouche, all early travel above the Nepisiguit River was done along the sea-coast. From the Restigouche, the St. Lawrence could be reached by a number of passages including heading up the Restigouche and over to the St. John, or across to the Metapédia River on the Gaspé, where a portage to the Matane would eventually lead down to the St. Lawrence.

1534 – 1700
White Exploration and Settlement

1534
Jacques Cartier at Baie des Chaleurs

In July of 1534 explorer Jacques Cartier, on his first voyage to North America, encountered Mi'kmaq travellers in nine canoes as his ships lay anchored in the Baie des Chaleurs (Bay of Warmth). The Mi'kmaq traded furs for iron utensils including knives, and while this exchange was not the first European meeting with people of the New World, it did mark the beginning of France's claim to Acadia and New France.

Cartier provided some of the earliest written descriptions of North American Aboriginal culture in *The Voyages of Jacques Cartier*, where he also recorded geographical features of the eastern coastline for future expeditions. With religious conflicts dividing France, it would be more than sixty years before the French would attempt a settlement effort in the New World.

Cartier's *Voyages* is the first written European account of sailing in waters off New Brunswick. While Cartier explored Kouchibouguac Bay, Point Escuminac, and Miramichi Bay before anchoring in Baie des Chaleurs, scholars agree that his first Mi'kmaq encounters took place on the Gaspé side (north shore) of the bay near Port Daniel.

1604
First Winter for Europeans — Saint Croix Island

The first European settlement in Acadia, and the first north of Florida, was on a small island in the mouth of the St. Croix River. Pierre du Gua de Monts, accompanied by geographer Samuel de Champlain, left

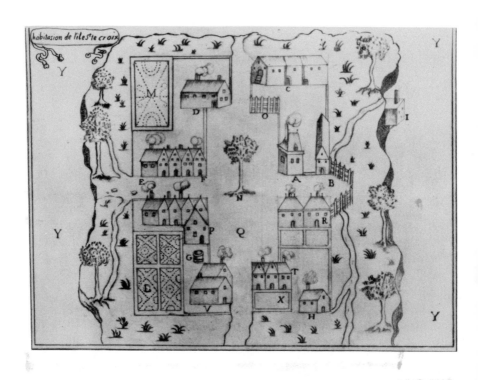

Champlain's view of de Monts' St. Croix settlement, 1604 (New Brunswick Provincial Archives)

France in a convoy of two ships during the spring of 1604. After exploring the coast of Nova Scotia, they sailed into the Bay of Fundy arriving in the harbour of a large river on Saint-Jean-Baptiste Day (June 24). The small party then moved west and, due to their fear of attack from the Passamaquoddy, selected a two-hectare (five acre) island site in the St. Croix River to establish a safe haven for the coming winter. They erected dwellings, storehouses, a wooden chapel and several gardens but snow arrived early that fall. The winter was extremely severe and without insulation or spring water on the island, the settlement suffered greatly through the long winter freeze-up. Of the original seventy-nine settlers, thirty-five died, mainly from scurvy. By spring only eleven men were healthy enough to hunt for provisions. When French supply ships arrived in June, the party decided to abandon the island for more hospitable grounds and sailed across the Bay of Fundy to the Annapolis Basin and established the Port Royal Habitation opposite Goat Island.

Above the island, two coves met the river to form a cross so de Monts named the site Saint Croix Island; later the name changed to Dochet's Island. Its location was in dispute until a New Brunswick excavation team, led by Robert Pagan and Saint John Loyalist Ward Chipman, uncovered the remains of Acadia's first pioneer settlement in 1797. The Webster–Ashburton Treaty line of 1842 established the island to be on the west side of the New Brunswick–Maine border, and consequently part of the United States. Yet its historic significance as the first North American winter settlement of Europeans above Florida has given the island international recognition as the birthplace of Acadia.

1611
First White Settlement on the St. John

After de Monts established the Port Royal colony, near present day Annapolis Royal, Nova Scotia, he was unable to continue to finance the tiny colony. His successor, Baron de Poutrincourt, with his son Charles de Biencourt, attempted to control the entire fur trade and fisheries of Acadia from their headquarters at Annapolis Basin. In defiance of Poutrincourt, a rival party of fur traders and fishermen from St. Malo, France, established a European settlement on an island at the top of the Long Reach section of the St. John, thirty-four kilometres (twenty-one miles) above the river's mouth.

Named Ile Emenenic by the French under the command of Captain Merveille, the settlement also included Robert Gravé de Pont, the son of one of the original founders of Port Royal. The sea captain and fur trader

25

reportedly attacked or held hostage a young Maliseet woman, threatening the delicate relations between Acadian settlers and the Maliseet. Biencourt was dispatched with soldiers and the Jesuit priest Biard to discipline the young Gravé de Pont and, after some initial resistance, overcame the upstart colony. Father Biard celebrated mass on the island and the settlers submitted to Port Royal's authority.

It is unknown how long the settlement remained on the St. John. But it is possible that the raiding party led by Samuel Argall, the Jamestown, Virginia freebooter, destroyed the colony in 1613 since the raiders burned the few remaining structures on nearby Saint Croix Island. By 1618 Gravé de Pont had given up his trading post on the St. John for an expedition to the East Indies, where he died at sea. Besides organizing the first permanent European settlement in New Brunswick, Gravé de Pont also became the first white to learn the Maliseet language and culture. After the expulsion of the Acadians, Ile Emenenic, near present-day Brown's Flat, was renamed Caton's Island as Isaac and James Caton were granted the site prior to the arrival of the Loyalists.

1631
Conflict in Acadia: La Tour and d'Aulnay

When de Monts became seigneur of Acadia, he acquired many rights including a monopoly on all fur trading in Acadia. Poutrincourt and Biencourt inherited the title and after Biencourt died, his friend Charles de La Tour, who had been at Port Royal since about 1610, acquired the fur trading rights for Acadia. Dissatisfied with the fur trade on the Nova Scotia peninsula and fearing that rival representatives of the King of France would soon be dispatched to Acadia, La Tour built a fort at Saint John harbour called Fort Sainte-Marie and developed a sizeable fur trading business along the St. John River.

La Tour's rival, Issac de Razilly was appointed supreme Commander of New France and became Governor of Acadia, with his Lieutenant Charles de Menou d'Aulnay second in command. In 1635 d'Aulnay succeeded de Razilly as Governor of Acadia and soon a bitter rivalry broke out between d'Aulnay and La Tour, largely due to La Tour's success at fur trading in Saint John and his reluctance to accept d'Aulnay's authority over the entire Acadian region.

After a series of conflicts and intrigues, in which d'Aulnay attempted to have La Tour sent back to France and forfit the northern trade to his control, d'Aulnay attacked La Tour's settlement. He did not succeed in capturing the fort until 1645, when La Tour was in Boston attempting to acquire assistance. Despite heroic resistance under the command of Françoise Marie Jacquelin, La Tour's wife, Fort La Tour was captured and destroyed and the entire garrison was hanged by an angry d'Aulnay. Madame La Tour was forced to witness the executions and died a few weeks later. Thus the wars of the rival leaders of Acadia ended — with d'Aulnay the supreme ruler, while the rebel Charles de La Tour, stripped of his power and possessions, became an outcast wandering for a time between Boston and Quebec.

Not content to accept defeat, La Tour sailed to France in 1650 after hearing of d'Aulnay's death and convinced the king to appoint him Governor of Acadia. To further consolidate his position and avoid another civil war, he returned to Acadia and married d'Aulnay's widow, Jeanne Motin. At Saint John, La Tour secured the fort that d'Aulnay had built on the west side of the harbour opposite Navy Island. He remained at Saint John until an English expedition under Major Robert Sedgwick forced him to surrender. By 1656, La Tour's fort was in the hands of two English traders, William Crowne and Colonel Thomas Temple. La Tour retired to his old residence at Cape Sable, Nova Scotia, where he died in 1667 having lived in Acadia for more than fifty years.

The remains of the two historic Saint John forts are now gone. In fact d'Aulnay's original site served as the foundation for a number of later French and English forts including Fort Martignoon, Governor Villebon's Fort St. Jean, Fort Managoueche, and the 1758 Fort Frederick.

1643
Coal Mining in North America

The Grand Lake area near Minto is the earliest recorded site for coal mining on the North American continent. Governor John Winthrop of Massachusetts left a record in his published journal of receiving a load of coal in Boston in 1643 from the north side of Grand Lake.

Governor Winthrop agreed to assist Charles de La Tour in his struggle with d'Aulnay for control of the St. John River valley. In August of 1643 he furnished La Tour with one hundred men in four Massachusetts ships. La Tour sailed to Saint John where d'Aulnay's ships were blocking the harbour and forced d'Aulnay to return to Port Royal. One of the New England vessels then sailed up the St. John, through the Jemseg River to the northern side of Grand Lake, where North America's first load of surface coal was loaded and shipped to Boston.

1659
Earliest English Fort

Colonel Thomas Temple founded the earliest English trading post in northern Acadia at Jemseg, along the St. John River, in 1659. Sir Thomas had established England's sovereignty over Acadia in 1654 after capturing Port Royal and La Tour's fortress at Saint John. By 1657 Sir Thomas had been named governor of Acadia and, after repairing La Tour's fort, moved up river to trade with the Maliseet and construct a fort on a knoll near the junction where the Jemseg River meets the St John.

From his headquarters at Jemseg, Sir Thomas was safe from coastal attacks and remained in control of Acadia until Charles II restored the territory to France by the 1667 Treaty of Breda. Removing himself to Boston, where he prospered in real estate and trade, Temple continued to challenge France's right to Acadia until the French governor, De Grandfontaine, took control of the trading post in 1670.

1668
Nicholas Denys

A controversial and colourful character in early Acadia, Nicholas Denys is considered the first white settler on the Baie des Chaleurs. Although misfortune plagued him most of his life, Denys managed to remain active in Acadia for more than fifty years.

Around 1645 Denys built the first known fishing and trading fort on the North Shore at Miscou Harbour. But Governor Menou d'Aulnay, who had chased him out of mainland Nova Scotia, refused to accept his right to fish and trade along the Gulf of Saint Lawrence and expelled him from Miscou. After d'Aulnay's death, Denys was still trading in Cape Breton and built another trading post at present-day Bathurst. In 1654 he was appointed Lieutenant Governor of the Gulf of St. Lawrence region, which included Cape Breton to the Gaspé, Prince Edward Island and Newfoundland. Denys became heavily engaged in commercial operations throughout the area as he attempted to establish fishing and fur trading monopolies.

Less than successful at establishing fur trading or fishing colonies, Denys became hopelessly in debt to his partners in France. In 1668, burned out of his Cape Breton headquarters at St. Peters, he moved to Bathurst (then also known as St. Peters) and erected a habitation with an enclosed eighteen-foot-high stockade. At Baie des Chaleurs, Denys, who was now seventy years old, wrote one of the most important accounts of seventeenth century life in Acadia. Especially of interest was Denys' de-

28

scription of the Mi'kmaq way of life and his account of the cod fishery. *The Description & Natural History of the Coasts of North America* was published in Paris in 1672 but, like his other enterprises, it failed to advance his financial situation.

He was reported to have been penniless in Paris in 1685 but he returned to the Baie des Chaleurs area, where he died in 1688 and reportedly was buried near his habitation at Pointe au Père in Bathurst harbour. While historians have been unable to confirm his burial site, which also was known as Ferguson's Point, J. Clarence Webster's research revealed that a large willow tree had been planted by his son after Denys' death and remained there until the early twentieth century.

1672
Acadia Expands to Chignecto

The Isthmus of Chignecto, the geographical centre of the Maritimes, was first settled by the Acadians when, in 1672, well-to-do farmer and surgeon Jacques Bourgeois and four other families from Port Royal moved to the upper reaches of the Bay of Fundy. On a grassy slope near the south bank of the Missaguash River, between present-day Aulac and Amherst, Bourgeois, along with Thomas Cormier and Pierre Arsenault, established the little community of Beaubassin.

This new settlement, on the Nova Scotia-New Brunswick border at the head of the Cumberland Basin, flourished because of the rich soil, the largest marshland in eastern North America, a good fishery and a new source of furs, as well as its close proximity to the Northumberland Strait, Quebec and the trading routes of the Atlantic. Apple trees were brought from Port Royal and a small chapel, Notre Dame de Bonsecours, the second in Acadia, was constructed nearby at Butte à Roger.

Within a few years the small village became the administrative centre of Acadia when Michel Leneuf de La Vallière de Beaubassin settled nearby on an elevated section of the marsh called Ile de Vallière, subsequently named Tonge's Island. Awarded a seigneury grant of about 2,590 square kilometres (one thousand square miles) by Frontenac, La Vallière was named commandant of Acadia in 1678 and later governor. Except for a year's residence at Port Royal, La Vallière administered Acadia from Beaubassin until 1684.

Initially Beaubassin seemed immune from the coastal attacks that had plagued Port Royal and the St. John but in 1696, and again in 1704, raids from New England under Benjamin Church destroyed much of the community. Despite numerous attacks from British forces and New Eng-

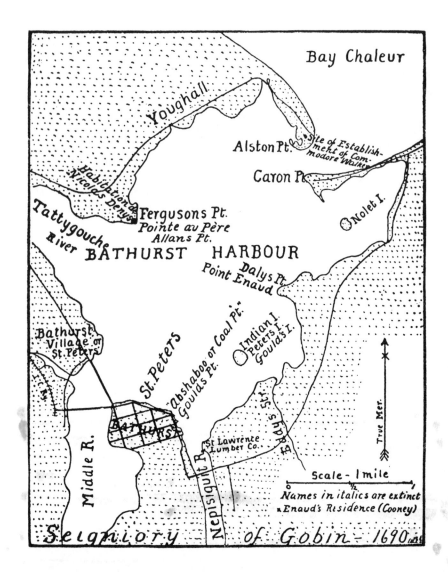

Bay Chaleur

Youghall

Alston Pt.
Site of Establish-
ment of Com-
modore Walker

Caron Pt.

Habitation
Nicolas Denys

Nolet I.

Tattygouche
River

Fergusons Pt.
Pointe au Père
Allans Pt.

BATHURST HARBOUR

Point Enaud

Dalys Pt.

Bathurst
Village or
St. Peters

St. Peters

Abshaboo or Coal Pt.
Goulds Pt.

Indian I.
Peters I.
Goulas I.

Bathurst

Middle R.

St. Lawrence
Lumber Co.

Nepisiquit R.

Dalys St.

True Mer.

Scale - 1 mile

Names in italics are extinct
Enaud's Residence (Cooney)

Seigniory of Gobin - 1690

W.F. Ganong's historical map of Bathurst harbour. Nicholas Denys' fort is situated on the north side of the harbour.

30

land privateers, Beaubassin was rebuilt and continued to grow until the middle of the eighteenth century when the French authorities decided to claim all territory west of the Missaguash River. The historic battle line had been drawn. In 1750, under the leadership of Father Germain and the mysterious Abbé Jean Louis Le Loutre, the Acadians were ordered to burn Beaubassin and resettle on the northern side of Chignecto. The same year, British soldiers from Halifax erected Fort Lawrence on the ruins of Beaubassin and across the Missaguash French troops constructed Fort Beauséjour, as the struggle for control of North America continued.

1672
The Seigniorial System: Failure in Acadia

While de Razilly, La Tour, and others received huge land grants under the French regime, the seigniorial land grant system actually began in 1672, when Acadia came directly under the control of the French crown and influential men were awarded significant lands in return for certain obligations.

In exchange for land title and fishing, hunting, and trading rights, a seignior was obliged to attract settlers, clear land, administer justice and pay homage to the crown. By 1700 about thirty-five seigniories were granted in the region that would become New Brunswick, including five on the St. Croix River and more than fifteen on the St. John. Only La Vallière at Beaubassin was able to attract settlers and develop a community similar to those established in Quebec. Unlike Quebec, the Acadian seigniorial system ended in failure as the war with Britain prevented French settlement efforts in the late seventeenth century. By 1700, other than at Chignecto, northern Acadia was virtually empty of Europeans as the seigniorial system could not protect the French settlers and the tiny inland agricultural communities disappeared.

1674
Dutch New Brunswick

During its first 150 years as a European colony, Acadia continued to move back and forth between French and English control; however, a unique situation occurred in 1674 when a Dutch sea captain named Jurriaen Aernoutsz conquered Acadia for Holland.

Both France and England were at war with Holland and Aernoutsz sailed to North America planning to attack their colonies. Arriving at New York, Aernoutsz discovered that England and Holland had ceased hostilities

31

upon signing the Treaty of Westminster, so his attention shifted to the northern French colony of Acadia. The Dutch commander with his ship, *Flying Cloud*, first captured the French fortress at Pentagouet on the Penobscot River, taking prisoner the Governor of Acadia, Jacques de Chambly. He then sailed eastward to the St. John River, capturing Fort Jemseg under the control of Chambly's lieutenant, Pierre de Joybert de Soulanges. Now a Dutch possession, Acadia was named New Holland and New York Dutch merchant Cornelis Steenwych was declared governor.

Aernoutsz remained in Acadia for a short time. A number of his men attempted to impose exclusive trading terms in the region, which upset the commerce between Massachusetts and the natives. The New England authorities, unwilling to suffer any trading restrictions with Acadia, denounced the Dutch as pirates. Aernoutsz's men were banished from Acadia by force. Boston had no interest in occupying it and the French were gradually able to re-occupy Acadia. Jemseg would again become the centre of French power under the new French governor Villebon.

1677
Jemseg, Capital of Acadia

By the late seventeenth century, Acadia and its centre at Port Royal had been sacked and captured so often that the new inland settlements on the St. John became increasingly attractive to the French. Close to Quebec and their Indian allies and safe from the raiding parties along the Bay of Fundy, Jemseg became the first inland seat of French power in the region. By 1676 Pierre Joybert de Soulanges had been set free (he had been captured and imprisoned by the Dutch raiding party under Aernoutsz) and was granted a number of seigneuries between Jemseg and the Nashwaak River, totalling almost 160 kilometres (one hundred miles).

The next year Joybert was named administrator of Acadia by Governor Frontenac of New France and he established headquarters at Jemseg, where considerable time and effort was spent repairing the fortress. Joybert died in 1678 and Michel Leneuf de La Vallière, his successor, moved the capital to the new Acadian colony at Beaubassin. Joybert's widow, the daughter of the Attorney-General of New France, began to spend more time in Quebec than on the St. John. This meant that Joybert's land grant along the St. John lapsed as the settlement and farming requirements were not fulfilled.

1689
John Gyles, A Maliseet Prisoner

One of the earliest written accounts of life in seventeenth century New Brunswick is John Gyles' remarkable autobiography of his nine years as a prisoner living among the Maliseet and the French on the St. John River. Abducted at age nine from his New England home at Pemaquid by a Maliseet raiding party, Gyles was taken along the ancient inland portage route of the Penobscot River to the Eel River and over to the Maliseet's fortified headquarters on the St. John River at Meductic. Here, the first English-speaking resident of what is today the province of New Brunswick became a slave, first to the Maliseet and later to a French seigneur's family at Jemseg, experiencing numerous adventures and conflicts involving the three peoples of the disputed region.

Set free in 1698 by Sieur de Chauffours, in exchange for assisting the seigneur to save his estate from Major Church's raiding party, Gyles returned to New England and later recorded his story — including his observations on the life and customs of the Maliseet people. Fluent in Maliseet and Mi'kmaq as well as French and English, Gyles proved a valuable asset to the struggling New England colony serving as translator, advisor, and negotiator in prisoner exchanges and other matters of war. As a British officer, Captain John Gyles commanded a number of New England forts as his reputation for predicting Aboriginal and French military behaviour grew. He ended his days in Roxbury, Massachusetts, having lived to see the destruction of the French fortifications in Acadia during the 1750s. John Gyles' historical journal served as the basis for the publication *The Ordeal of John Gyles* by Stuart Trueman.

1690
First Dry Dock

An unusual and little known aspect of early French settlement efforts at Chignecto was the creation of the first dry dock in Canada, and possibly North America. At the confluence of the La Coupe and Aulac Rivers, about five miles inland from Cumberland Basin near today's High Marsh Road, Acadian settlers built an ingenious dry dock in the late seventeenth century.

Prior to the control of the Fundy tides by means of the aboiteaux — a simple device that blocked the incoming tides from passing above the dyke but allowed fresh water to escape — much of the Chignecto marshlands was flooded by tidal action. The rivers contained deep canyons banked by red mud. The tide would have averaged forty feet at the mouth of the Aulac and about twenty feet inland at the dry dock site. These great tides created an inland shelter for sea-going vessels, safe from the almost continuous warfare of the Fundy Bay. The hidden site was ideal for the slow, meticulous ship repair work of the period that required extensive use of hand tools and rudimentary materials.

Boats floated up the Aulac on a rising tide and as the dry dock gates were opened the vessel was placed over the selected resting place. After the gates were closed, a flap valve would allow water to escape but not to re-enter. As the maximum draft for Fundy vessels of the period was around thirteen feet, the re-fitted vessel could always be refloated down the Aulac during a high tide.

Today the remains of this unique and clever invention remind us of the Acadians' remarkable ability to use tidal action to transform the Fundy marshlands into a prosperous agricultural community. Evidence of huge timbers and earth works seemed to point to some sort of dry dock on the La Coupe River, but its existence was not fully established until the 1920s when J. Clarence Webster did an extensive study of the Chignecto region. His research, aerial views and surveys established conclusive evidence that the dry dock was built over three hundred years ago.

1692
Acadian Headquarters at Naskwaak

Joseph Robinau De Villebon was a talented military officer, as well as adept in acquiring Maliseet assistance against English forces. In 1690 he arrived at Port Royal only to find the fort destroyed and Governor Meneval a captive in Boston. Fearing more attacks on Port Royal, Villebon moved to fortified French quarters at Jemseg. The next year, he returned from France with an appointment as the Commandant of Acadia, a position he maintained until his death in 1700.

Determined to establish a stronger fort close to his Maliseet allies at Meductic, Villebon built Fort St. Joseph, or Fort Nashwaak (Naxoat) as it became known, on the upper side of the mouth of the Nashwaak River across from present day Fredericton. Surrounded by a line of heavy palisades and a ditch, the fort was sixty-one metres square (two hundred feet square) with a bastion at each corner where eight guns were mounted. The small garrison at Fort Nashwaak comprised about forty soldiers, a gunner, armourer and a surgeon, but Villebon's strength lay in his ability to mobilize the Indians bands of the region. From this strong fortification, and with encouragement from Governor Frontenac at Quebec, Villebon began to successfully wage war on the New England colonies to the south with the able assistance of the Maliseet, Mi'kmaq, Passamaquoddy and Penobscot peoples.

Villebon captured the New England stronghold at Pemaquid, Fort William Henry, in 1696, capturing almost a hundred soldiers and conducting a brilliant military campaign of hit and run tactics that created terror throughout coastal New England. A retaliatory expedition under Colonel Hawthorne and Benjamin Church destroyed Beaubassin but failed to dislodge Villebon from Fort St. Joseph where the New Englanders were rebuffed.

Two years later Villebon abandoned his Naskwaak stronghold and re-established himself at d'Aulnay's old fort at the mouth of the St. John, where French ships were beginning to load lumber for the masting industry in France. At Menagoueche, as Saint John was then called, Villebon traded freely and governed Acadia until his death. While Villebon spent little time actually governing Acadia, he was perhaps the most accomplished military officer in the French colonial ranks.

1695
New Brunswick's First Sawmill

According to the 1695 census at Naskwaak, Sieur de Chauffours was seignior of a large tract of land around the mouth of the Naskwaak River that included Fort St. Joseph. Here de Chauffours had a house and thirty acres of land under cultivation and is reported to have operated a sawmill along with his brother the Sieur de Freneuse. This reference to an existing lumber mill is often cited as the pioneer mill of an industry that is now the largest commercial activity in the province.

1698
Acadians at Shepody Bay

While French interest in Northern Acadia continued to stagnate during the late 1600s, the growing Acadian population continued their settlement efforts along the upper tidal marshes of the Bay of Fundy. Despite little or no immigration into Acadia from France, the Acadian people managed to increase their population through large families and some intermarriage with the Aboriginal population. The first Acadian farmer on the Petitcodiac was Guillaume Blanchard, who settled at today's Hillsborough in 1698 where a thriving community soon developed called Village-des-Blanchard. Esther Clark Wright in her book, *The Petitcodiac*, also cites other pioneer farmers from Port Royal, Pierre Thibaudeau and his sons who established saw and grist mills at the mouth of the Shepody River in 1700. With a British garrison enforcing English colonial law on the Acadian peninsula, the Shepody Basin became a favourite area for new Acadian settlements. The population reached an estimated 1,200 by 1750. About 1733, further up the Petitcodiac at the bend in the river, three families from the Grand Pré area — Babineau, Breau and Thibodeau — became the first Europeans to settle the Moncton region, which was then known as Terre-Rouge.

1700
Northern Acadia: One Century of European Presence

Unlike the Nova Scotia peninsula, where well over one thousand Acadian settlers had established themselves along the Fundy marshlands, the northern region of Acadia was largely the same wilderness in 1700 that de Monts and Champlain had witnessed in their arrival almost one hundred years earlier. Except for a few newly arrived Acadians on Shepody Bay and on the Tantramar at Chignecto, little permanent development had occurred above the Missaguash River, which today marks the New Brunswick-Nova Scotia border.

Along the St. John River where fur trading, prime lumber, and rich soil made the river valley an excellent choice for European settlers, French settlement efforts had little effect. France, preoccupied with its European pre-eminence and the immense inland potential of Quebec and the St Lawrence, had little interest in undertaking expensive new settlements in Acadia. England's interest lay to the south, with the expanding colonies of Viriginia, New York and Massachusetts. Massachusetts considered Acadia part of its territory, not for settlement purposes but to harvest its rich fishery and to trade for furs with the Acadians, the Maliseet and the Mi'kmaq.

The Maliseet and Mi'kmaq were still largely in control of the northern territory, with their villages and camp sites intact and their travel routes along inland waterways and portages unaffected by European conflict. While southern Acadia had a significant agricultural community by 1700, with its disruptive effect on Maliseet and Mi'kmaq society, the wilderness above the Bay of Fundy remained largely undisturbed.

By this time, European religions, technology, disease, and hunger for fur was having a significant negative impact on First Nation societies throughout eastern North America, but the northern Acadian region was still one of the least affected. A pestilence that was probably European in origin did wipe out more than one hundred St. John River Maliseet beefore 170, bt,t overall, the northern area of present-day New Brunswick had not yet begun to experience the intensive settlement patterns that would overwhelm and dispossess the original Maritime peoples.

1701 – 1760
Conflict and The Expulsion

1710
Permanent British Presence in Acadia

As had happened many times before, Port Royal was captured by British and New England regulars in 1710 under Francis Nicholson. But this time the victors remained in Acadia, renamed Port Royal Annapolis Royal and attempted to hold the fortification with a garrison of 450 men under the able command of Paul Mascarene.

Three years later the Treaty of Utrecht officially ceded Acadia with her "Ancient boundaries" to Britain but France chose to interpret the treaty to mean Port Royal and the Nova Scotia Atlantic coast — exempting Cape Breton, northern Nova Scotia and the entire Gulf of St. Lawrence region. Despite France's determination to hold on to the northern land mass of Acadia, approximately two thousand French-speaking Acadians now resided in British-held territory. Britain had no immediate settlement plans for Acadia and over the next forty years the centre of French Acadia moved east, as the new communities of Minas and Chignecto grew to contain the majority of Acadians. By mid-century an all-out struggle for supremacy would break out all over Acadia — with the Isthmus of Chignecto becoming a major battle ground.

1717
The Meductic Church

The Maliseet constructed their stronghold at Meductic on the St. John as protection against warring bands, especially the fierce Mohawk whose ventures into the St. John River Valley from the St Lawrence were always dreaded by the Maliseet. Meductic was a crossroads, a rendezvous point on the canoe highway of eastern North America. Located below Woodstock, Meductic anchored the inland route to New England via the Eel River to the Penobscot and Kennebec Rivers in Maine. Canoes heading to the Bay of Fundy, east to the Miramichi or the Petitcodiac also had to pass by Meductic. Described by the French as "le premier fort de L'Acadie," the Meductic fortress had a ditched earth wall surmounted by a wooden stockade with a heavily constructed cabin within. Cornfields stood nearby in the rich flat-land of the riverbank.

In 1717 the Maliseet erected a church, probably only the second built in Acadia above the Missaguash River, while the French missionary Jean Loyard was priest of the Mission. The first missionary to live among the Maliseet was Simon Girard de la Place, who had taken up residence at Meductic in 1685. The Maliseet later abandoned the village and established a new centre at Aukpaque. About 1794, Kingsclear became the main Maliseet village and a church was constructed that today houses the historic church bell from the Meductic chapel.

1733
Acadians Resettle the St. John

During the first fifty years of the eighteenth century, the majority of European settlers in present-day New Brunswick were Acadians continuing to expand up into the Chignecto Basin, where the Fundy marsh lands were familiar sights to sons and daughters of Annapolis and Minas Basin Acadians. But the French had also encouraged settlers to move up into the St. John valley, claiming that all land north of the Bay of Fundy had not been granted to the British by the Treaty of Utrecht.

By 1733 at least twenty families had established farms on the old French estates at Jemseg, Maugerville, Grimross (Gagetown), Nashwaak, and the largest at St. Anne's Point (Fredericton). However, the tiny communities did not grow, as the French directed their resources away from the St. John to maintaining the Quebec–Chignecto–Louisbourg military network that sought to contain British power in mainland Nova Scotia. In 1748 Abbé Le Loutre wrote that "There are fifteen or twenty French families on this river," but after 1750 Acadians began to move into the St. John River area to escape the conflict at Beaubassin. Acadians escaping the Expulsion in 1755 attempted to remain in these settlements as refugees, but a British force under Colonel Monckton burned all river villages as far as Aukpaque (Springhill) forcing Acadians to flee north into the Madawaska region.

1740
Maliseet Abandon Meductic

No one is quite sure of the reason but after Father Jean-Baptiste Lo-yard's death at Meductic in 1731, the Maliseet began to abandon their river fortress and move downriver to a cluster of islands and riverbanks below the falls at Kingsclear called Aukpaque. The move occurred at the same time that Acadian settlers began to resettle the fertile land between Jemseg and St. Anne's Point. Trade with the Acadians may explain the move but the new missionary for the entire St. John River, Jean-Pierre Daniélou, may have also encouraged the relocation as an attempt to prevent English claims to the lower St. John River.

By 1767 Meductic was abandoned for Aukpaque as the Maliseet were granted the islands and intervales above Fredericton (now called Springhill) but later the Loyalists settlers claimed the rich soil for their farms and pastures. By 1794 the Maliseet had been pushed to unwanted land beside the Kingsclear Falls and received title to land adjacent to the river, which became the Kingsclear Reserve.

1749
Le Loutre Arrives at Chignecto

One of the most intriguing figures in Acadia was L'Abbé Jean Louis Le Loutre, who began his career in Acadia as missionary to the Mi'kmaq at Shubenacadie in 1738. When France and Britain declared war in 1744 over the issue of the Austrian Succession, North America was again part of the conflict and Le Loutre, while officially a neutral priest, became heavily involved on the French side. By 1745 he was a de facto military leader — inciting the Mi'kmaq to attack British garrisons, participating in raiding parties and serving as a liaison between French military authorities and the Acadian settlers. Governor Cornwallis reacted to the attacks by placing a £50 reward on his capture, dead or alive.

While British efforts were directed towards establishing their new centre at Halifax, Le Loutre built his headquarters and a church on the west side of the Missaguash River and induced many Acadians to abandon their homes at Beaubassin and join him. According to the French, British territory ended on the east bank of the Missaguash and when Major Lawrence arrived at Chignecto in 1750 he discovered Le Loutre had burnt the village of Beaubassin. The Acadian settlers had been evacuated to the Tantramar marshland. French forces under Louis de La Corne were encamped just west of the Missaguash and prepared to defend Beauséjour Ridge as

French territory. Forts were quickly constructed and tension mounted when an English officer, Edward How, was killed under a flag of truce. British officials cited Le Loutre as instigating the murder.

A cold war lasted five years as British and French forces looked at each other across the Missaguash, yet Le Loutre was working feverishly to dyke the lowlands around the Aulac and Tantramar rivers to supply farmland for the reluctant Acadians he had enticed to leave British soil. Le Loutre's vision was to contain British power by force in mainland Nova Scotia while expanding the Acadian settlements and French military might in northern Acadia. While present at Fort Beauséjour during the seige, he escaped via the St. John River to Quebec and sailed to France, only to be captured at sea and held prisoner in Britain until the peace treaty of 1763 ended hostilities between the two warring nations.

Le Loutre's controversial presence in Acadia is still the subject of much debate, since some historians see his partisan role as one of provoking Lawrence to order the deportation of the Acadians. As a French nationalist and a charismatic leader, Le Loutre mixed religion and politics to further the cause of French Acadia but was overcome by the overwhelming forces of the British and their New England allies.

1751
Fort Beauséjour is Constructed

Unwilling to accept the Isthmus of Chignecto as the beginning of French territory in Acadia, Governor Edward Cornwallis sent a small force under Charles Lawrence to Beaubassin, where they encountered a hostile French force under Louis de La Corne. Officially at peace with France, Lawrence withdrew to the Minas Basin area but returned in the fall and began construction of Fort Lawrence on the Beaubassin ridge.

To counter the fortification, the Governor-General of New France, Jacques-Pierre de la Jonquière ordered the construction of a similar fort two miles to the west at Pointe-â-Beauséjour, overlooking the Missaguash River and Cumberland Basin. Vital in maintaining French interests in eastern North America, the strategic Chignecto region linked Quebec with Île Royale (Cape Breton) and allowed Acadian produce and livestock to move through Baie Verte and feed the sprawling town of Louisbourg.

Named after an early settler, Laurent Chatillon, Sieur de Beauséjour, Fort Beauséjour was begun in April 1751 by Lieutenant Gaspart-Joseph de Léry and comprised palisade walls in the shape of a pentagon with five-metre high earthwork and bastions at the angles. By 1754, Fort Beauséjour was a much more substantial structure than Fort Cumberland with four in-

Fort Beauséjour in 1755 as seen from Fort Lawrence. Tonge's Island is on the left. From an original map by English engineer Winckworth Tonge. (New Brunswick Public Archives)

side casemates, a powder magazine, barracks, officers quarters, and capable of housing eight hundred men. Surrounding the fortress stood homes, storehouses, a hospital and Le Loutre's church modeled after Quebec's Basilica.

Less than two hundred soldiers, about 250 Acadians (of the approximately three thousand living above the Missaguash) and a number of Mi'kmaq were inside Beauséjour when two thousand New England soldiers, under Lieutenant-Colonel Robert Monckton, landed at Chignecto on June 2, 1755. Under orders from Governor Lawrence and Massachusetts Governor Shirley to dislodge the French from Chignecto and armed with heavy artillery, Monckton's army surrounded Fort Beauséjour within ten days. After continual bombardment by cannon fire, a number of Acadians were killed and on June 16 Commander de Vergor surrendered the fort. The Acadians and Mi'kmaq were released without their weapons and, according to the terms of surrender, the captured soldiers were sent to Louisbourg.

Renamed Fort Cumberland, Beauséjour was greatly strengthened and maintained by British forces as a base for military operations into northern Acadia against French forces. The strategic fortress again saw military action during the Eddy Rebellion of 1776 but was abandoned in 1835 and allowed to fall into ruins, before being restored in the 1920s to become one of the province's most important historic sites.

1751
Another Fort at Baie Verte

By 1750 the British navy controlled much of the Atlantic Ocean and the Bay of Fundy, with Annapolis Royal and Halifax as the military centres of English Acadia. French military and supply ships concentrated along the Gulf of St. Lawrence as their landing and departing at Baie Verte was vital to French power at Quebec, Louisbourg and Chignecto. To block English expansion into northern Acadia, the French constructed Fort Gaspereau at the mouth of the Gaspereau River near the head of Baie Verte in 1751, the same year Fort Beauséjour was started. Measuring over thirty-three metres (one hundred feet) per side, the square fort contained number of military buildings, and a two-storey block-house at each corner, with a cannon on the upper floor.

Communication with Fort Beauséjour, seventeen miles away, was first maintained via the old portage route through a chain of lakes and down the Missaguash River but in 1754 a roadway was cut between the forts.

After the capture of Fort Beauséjour, Colonel John Winslow took Fort Gaspereau, commanded by Captain Villeray, and renamed it Fort Monckton. The English garrisoned it for about a year, until nine soldiers were killed in a battle with Mi'kmaq warriors. The slain men were buried in the nearby graveyard. The fortress was destroyed in 1756 but the graveyard, with nine headstones, was preserved and cited by William F. Ganong in 1899 as the oldest existing burial-ground in New Brunswick.

1753
The Spy of Beauséjour

After Benedict Arnold, New Brunswick's most notorious traitor was the mysterious scribe and spy, Thomas Pichon. Educated in Paris, Pichon served with the French army in Europe and in 1751 became secretary to Governor Jean-Louis de Raymond at Louisbourg. Two years later he arrived at Fort Beauséjour where he acted as chief clerk for stores and, more importantly, served as scribe to the officers editing their correspondence. Pichon even helped Le Loutre with his letters and writings.

After working for Le Loutre, Pichon seemed to have developed a dislike for the radical missionary and the Roman Catholic religion and it is here that we may find a motive for Pichon's betrayal of his country. However, many historians point to the money he received for providing Captain George Scott and other officers at Fort Cumberland with copies of official French documents, the Acadian census, military plans and warnings of French attacks. Pichon even outlined the steps necessary to secure the fort, which Monckton later used in capturing Fort Beauséjour.

Robert Monckton's army was of such significance that Fort Beauséjour would have fallen without Pichon's duplicity, but the information certainly hastened the fort's capitulation since Pichon also encouraged Commander de Vergor to surrender. After the fall of Beauséjour, Pichon continued his spying in Halifax and later in London, under the name of Tyrell. He wrote several books and developed a further reputation for duplicity, this time as a seducer of young women.

He published a book about his experiences in Cape Breton that received some praise as a plausible account of eighteenth century life at Louisbourg but Thomas Pichon has been almost universally condemned for his treason, greed and promiscuity. He died in 1781 in broken health. J. Clarence Webster wrote and published Thomas Pichon's story in 1937 called Thomas Pichon, "the Spy of Beauséjour," an Account of His Career in Europe and America.

1755
The Expulsion of the Acadians

In July of 1755 one of the most significant events in the history of the region occurred — Governor Charles Lawrence and his council issued an ultimatum to the Acadians: "they must now resolve either to take the Oath without any Reserve or else quit their lands, for that Affairs were now at such a Crisis in America that no delay could be admitted."

The oath of allegiance requested by Lawrence included the duty as English subjects to bear arms for the English king and the reluctant Acadians, who feared French and Aboriginal reprisals for not remaining neutral, felt compelled to refuse the oath. Lawrence's council issued the order to expel the Acadians on July 28 and over the remaining summer most Acadians in British territory below the Isthmus of Chignecto were confined and transported south to the American colonies.

In total almost eight thousand Acadians were expelled. But at Chignecto and the Memramcook and Petitcodiac regions, where more than three thousand Acadians resided, only about one third were deported. The remaining Acadians escaped to the St. John River valley, the Miramichi, the Restigouche region, Quebec and Île Saint-Jean (Prince Edward Island) where they experienced many hardships avoiding English forces.

By 1761 most Acadians in present-day New Brunswick had been captured by the British authorities and transported out of Acadia. Two years later the Treaty of Paris ended the Seven Year's War and dashed France's colonial dreams in North America. But the Acadians were gradually allowed to return and re-establish settlements in new villages on the least productive lands in Acadia.

1756
Boishébert and the Defense of the Acadians

During the Deportation more than two thousand Acadians fled north into present-day New Brunswick but were pursued by British forces, especially those commanded by the victor at Beauséjour, Lieutenant-Colonel Robert Monckton. The great stretch of rivers and forests between the Bay of Fundy and the St. Lawrence had escaped European attention during the first half of the eighteenth century as Britain and France fought over southern Acadia.

However, events unfolded quickly after the 1748 Treaty of Aix la Chapelle returned Cape Breton to France but failed to address the question of who owned the northern coast of the Bay of Fundy. Captain Gorham and his Halifax Rangers were immediately sent to Saint John to claim the region for Britain. In 1749, the French Administrator of Canada, Count de la Galissonnière, sent Lieutenant Charles Deschamps de Boishébert to the mouth of the St. John to re-establish a French military presence and enforce the French claim to all of Acadia above the Bay of Fundy.

Boishébert and his troops initially established their headquarters sixteen kilometres (ten miles) up the river, at a stronghold situated at the mouth of the Nerepis River. Now called Woodman's Point, Fort Nerepis became Boishébert's base of operations to frustrate British efforts to control the Acadian settlements along the St. John. While Britain and France were still officially at peace, Boishébert began to rebuild Villebon's old fort at Saint John. On its completion, Fort Nerepis was abandoned.

Despite an overwhelming difference in strength and resources — English colonists numbered about 1.2 million in North America in 1750, while there were sixty thousand French-speaking settlers — Boishébert, with assistance from the Maliseet, managed to defend the St. John River from British encroachment. A capable military officer, Boishébert, who had been part of the force that defeated the British at Grand Pré in 1747, later joined a military excursion to the Ohio Valley. He returned to command French forces at Saint John. Upon the capture of Fort Beauséjour, a large British expedition headed to the mouth of the St. John to attack his troops. Outnumbered, Boishébert burned his fort and began a campaign of guerrilla warfare. A British force under Major Frye attacked Acadian settlements at Shepody Bay, devastating the village at Shepody but on September 3, 1755, Boishébert defeated Frye upriver near Village des Blan-

44

Shipbuilding during the nineteenth century at Beaubears Island. The site on the Miramichi also hosted French refugees, Aboriginal villages, English pioneer settlements, lumber operations and a salmon fishery. (NBPA)

chard (Hillsborough) after a desperate battle, and returned to the St. John with thirty destitute Acadian families.

1757
Beaubears Island, National Historic Site

Boishébert continued to attack and harass British troops attempting systematic deportations of the Acadians, despite scarcity of supplies and limited assistance from Quebec or Louisbourg. He wintered at Cocagne during 1756 with a group of fugitive Acadians on a site along the south shore of the bay. Today that site is called Le Camp de Boishébert. He also plotted an expedition against Fort Monckton (Fort Gaspereau), but Boishébert's most important accomplishment was establishing a settlement on Beaubears Island on the Miramichi River.

In January 1757 he arrived on Beaubears, where he attempted to establish fortifications for the estimated 3,500 Acadians refuges that were clustered around the island. Boishébert developed a refugee centre opposite

45

Beaubears Island that today is part of The Enclosure Park. Located at the tip of the mainland that separates the Northwest and Southwest branches of the Miramichi, Boishébert's safe haven for refugees became known as Camp de l'Espérance. It was protected by a battery as well as two down-river lookout sites, at French Fort Cove on the north side and at Canadian Point on the Chatham side. Along with Father Charles Germain, Boishébert was able to provide temporary protection for the Acadians but many died of starvation and disease.

Boishébert was present at the fall of Louisbourg in 1758, and assisted in relocating a number of Acadians to Beaubears Island, but Wolfe's expedition to the Miramichi in 1758 destroyed the entire settlement while many Acadians were killed, captured, or fled to the Restigouche area. The same expedition burned Pointe de Village, a French settlement on the north side of Miramichi Bay that included an Acadian church, and hence became known as Burnt Church. Beaubears Island was later settled by English-speaking pioneers and became an important fishery and shipbuilding centre during the nineteenth century. Joseph Gubbins' *New Brunswick Journal* of 1813 makes reference to a French stone chapel but today little remains. A National Historic Site, Beaubears Island is one of the Miramichi's most important locations.

1758
Monckton Builds Fort Frederick

After the fall of Louisbourg, General James Wolfe suggested immediate expeditions to northern Acadia to destroy the Acadian settlements and the remaining French forces. Wolfe himself sailed to the north shore of the Gulf of St. Lawrence, while Lieutenant-Colonel Lord Rollo was dispatched to Île Saint-Jean (Prince Edward Island), and Brigadier General Robert Monckton assembled a force of more than two thousand men and a dozen vessels and set sail for the St. John River.

Monckton's fleet met with little resistance upon arriving in Saint John harbour since Boishébert's force, along with the French priest Germain, had withdrawn to Quebec. The old fort of d'Aulnay was rebuilt and renamed Fort Frederick, after one of the princes of the House of Brunswick. After spending about a month erecting the fort, Monckton proceeded up the river to attack Acadian settlements, losing a large man-of war, *Ulysses*, to the hostile tides of the Reversing Falls. All settlements up to and including Grimross (Gagetown) were burned with all cattle and crops destroyed, but the largest community at St. Anne's Point (Fredericton) was spared since Monckton's ships began running aground on the river's shoals.

While many Acadians fled to Quebec, some wintered at St. Anne's Point hoping to escape hostilities. But the community came under attack during the winter by troops from Fort Frederick, who had travelled the St. John on snowshoes. The destruction of St. Anne's Point, together with the fall of Quebec, sealed the fate of the remaining Acadians on the St. John. By late 1759, the last two hundred Acadians had surrendered at Fort Frederick and were removed to Halifax. The lower St. John River valley came under permanent English control in early 1760, when the Passamaquoddy and Maliseet nations agreed not to attack the English, nor aid their enemies, in exchange for erecting a truck-house for trade at Indiantown. The disputed lands of Acadia, fought over for 150 years, were finally resolved, and virtually no Acadians remained on the marshlands of their beloved Baie Française (Bay of Fundy).

1760
The Battle of the Restigouche

With Louisbourg and Quebec captured, only Montreal remained in French hands when in the spring of 1760 France finally sent a six-ship naval force under Captain La Giraudais to Canada. Only one day out of Bordeaux, the fleet encountered British ships and only three French vessels, including the flagship *Machault*, reached the Gulf of St. Lawrence. Despite capturing a British ship, the French were unable to reach Montreal due to a superior British squadron on the St. Lawrence River. La Giraudais took shelter on the Restigouche River and sent messengers overland to Montreal to receive orders from Governor Vandreuil.

Meanwhile word of the French squadron had reached British commanders at Louisbourg, and a British naval force under John Byron, father of the poet Lord George Gordon Byron, was dispatched to Baie des Chaleurs.

"Mad Jack" Byron's superior force — which included the *Fame* with seventy-four guns, the *Dorsetshire* with seventy, and a number of frigates — attacked La Giraudais a few miles west of Campbellton on June 22. The French fleet fought with such determination that the sporadic battles and maneuvering did not end for seventeen days. Overpowered and with defeat inevitable, La Giraudais ordered the *Machault* abandoned and scuttled. The other two French ships, the *Bienfaisant* and the *Marquis de Malauze* were also sunk. The last naval battle of the Seven Years War in North America ended with the loss of the remaining French fleet and Montreal eventually captured by British forces. A number of artifacts have been recovered from the famous frigate, after the *Machault* was located underwater and surveyed.

1761 – 1782
The English Period

1761
Resettlement at Chignecto

With the expulsion of the Acadians virtually complete, Governor Lawrence issued his celebrated proclamation in 1758 offering free land and favourable terms to any English-speaking New Englander who would move to Nova Scotia and cultivate the lands seized by the French.

Three years later, twenty-five families mainly from Providence, Rhode Island, arrived on the Chignecto marshlands at Sackville (then called Tantramer Township) and established the first English settlement above the Missaguash River. The Public Archives of Nova Scotia still has the list of "subscribers for the Township Lying on Tantramer River" that included many well-known names from the region such as Estabrooks, Foster, Cahoun, Robinson, Seaman, and Parker, as well as names that are no longer part of any of the Chignecto communities.

The first town meeting took place in 1762 and initially the settlement thrived, with eighty families listed in the Chignecto region by 1765 that included the townships of Cumberland, Amherst and Sackville. Sackville's population was listed in a 1766 census as 349. The first Baptist congregation in Canada arrived in Sackville from Swansea, Massachusetts in 1763 under Rev. Nathan Mason and two years later, the first Sackville land grants were made when two hundred lots of five hundred acres each were divided.

The Chignecto region was also the site of one of the earliest Methodist congregations in Canada that owes its origins to the Yorkshire emigrants of 1772. The settlers erected the second oldest Methodist church in Canada at Pointe de Bute in 1788. The early immigration of English-speaking settlers to Chignecto seemed to stall after 1766 and even suffer a population decline. By the time the Yorkshire pioneers arrived at Sackville in 1772, one report claimed that only three families remained in the township. This decline is explained in part by the removal of the Fort Cumberland garrison to Halifax, which would have meant the loss of a major market for the settlers produce and less security for the region. Yet when the Loyalists arrived a decade later, the Chignecto marshlands were mainly settled and large numbers of Loyalists were unable to permanently remain in the area.

1762
Simonds, Hazen, White and Company

A Massachusetts group, headed by Captain Francis Peabody, Jonathan Leavitt, and James Simonds arrived in Saint John in the summer of 1762 to establish the first permanent English-speaking settlement. Fort Frederick served as their home the first night on land and a child was reportedly born at the fort to Hugh and Elizabeth Quinton.

Francis Peabody moved to Maugerville but young James Simonds along with cousins William Hazen and James White formed a partnership to create a trading company, after the restrictions on the fur trade were removed in 1763. Simonds and Hazen had been active in trade and the fishery at Indian Island in Passamaquoddy Bay, where they had operated a trading post but they sensed less competition and more opportunity further east.

James Simonds was the leading partner in the company while initially William Hazen remained in Massachusetts and handled the re-distribution of the shipped goods throughout New England. Besides furs and the fishery, the partnership operated a general store and was active in lumber, shipbuilding, hay, lime and especially in liquor and food staples. In 1764, thirty Massachusetts tradesmen arrived in the upper cove section of the harbour where the company began to expand rapidly.

Simonds and Company acquired a land grant of more than 2,024 hectares (five thousand acres) within present-day Saint John but most of the company's activities were centred at Portland Point, near the present National Harbour Board site. Commercial activities included a tidal mill for lumber and shipbuilding at Mill Pond, a trading store, and, nearby at Lilly Lake, a grist mill. A limestone quarry and four kilns for burning lime thrived and during the first ten years more than 3,500 hogsheads of lime were shipped to Massachusetts. Acadians employed by Simonds constructed an aboiteau at nearby Marsh Creek and soon reclaimed more than 242

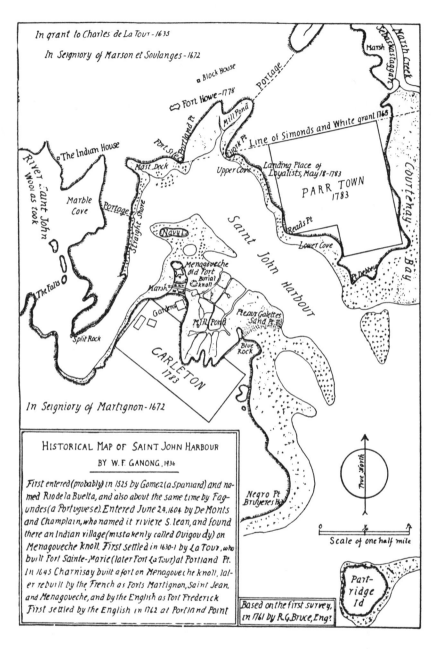

In grant to Charles de La Tour - 1635

In Seigniory of Marson et Soulanges - 1672

□ Block House

Portage

Fort Howe - 1778

Mill Pond

Line of Simonds and White grant 1765

Fort Spur

Portland Pt

York Pt

The Indian House

Mast Dock

Upper Cove

Landing Place of Loyalists, May 18 - 1783

PARR TOWN 1783

River Saint John
Wool as took

Marble Cove

Portage

Straight Shore

Navy I.

Saint John Harbour

Reads Pt

Lower Cove

Courtenay Bay

Pt Debbus

Menagoveche Old Fort Burial knoll

The Falls

Marsh

Gardens

Mill Pond

Fleaur Galettes Sand Pt

Split Rock

Blue Rock

CARLETON 1783

In Seigniory of Martignon - 1672

Negro Pt
Bruyeres Pt

Marsh
Sebaskastagan

Marsh

HISTORICAL MAP OF SAINT JOHN HARBOUR

BY W. F. GANONG, 1936

First entered (probably) in 1525 by Gomez (a Spaniard) and named Rio de la Buelta, and also about the same time by Fagundes (a Portuguese). Entered June 24, 1604 by De Monts and Champlain, who named it riviere S. Jean, and found there an Indian village (mistakenly called Ouigoudy) on Menagoveche knoll. First settled in 1630-1 by La Tour, who built Fort Sainte-Marie (later Fort La Tour) at Portland Pt. In 1645 Charnisay built a fort on Menagoveche knoll, later rebuilt by the French as Forts Martignon, Saint Jean, and Menagoveche, and by the English as Fort Frederick. First settled by the English in 1762 at Portland Point

True North

0   ½   1
Scale of one half mile

Partridge Id

Based on the first survey, in 1761 by R.G.Bruce, Eng.r

Map of Saint John harbour based on R.G. Bruce's 1761 survey. W.F. Ganong, 1936 hectares (six hundred acres) for hay production. The first known ship to be built entirely on the St. John River, a schooner called *Betsy*, was constructed by this firm. In 1769 the company paid shipwright Michael Hodge about twenty-four shillings per ton to build the vessel from local wood, although the rigging was imported from Newburyport, Massachusetts. On one trading voyage to the West Indies, the *Betsy* returned to Saint John with a reported ninety-eight thousand gallons of rum.

Massachusetts currency (L.M. for Lawful Money of Massachusetts) was the official trading currency on the St. John River until the end of the American Revolution, but cash was scarce and beaver skins were used as barter throughout the firm's early years. Of course, rum was another trading commodity with almost universal appeal. The beverage was used by both Aboriginals and whites to the extent that the estimated annual consumption for every adult male was twenty gallons.

While Simonds, Hazen and White were officially sanctioned as traders, they did not enjoy a trading monopoly and competed for the river trade with John Anderson at Nashwaak and Captain Issac Caton, whose trading post was located at Brown's Flat. The Simonds Company employed agent Benjamin Atheton to construct a post at St. Anne's Point, which was rebuilt on a site near Old Government House when an ice jam destroyed the first structure.

On the eve of the American Revolution, the firm had a lucrative trade with New England but this commerce was suspended during the Revolution and Yankee privateers attacked and plundered the trading post at Saint John. Still Simonds and Company managed to develop a Caribbean trade and continued to prosper after the arrival of the Loyalists. The driving force behind the company's success was James Simonds, who moved to Maugerville once Saint John was left unprotected from coastal raiding parties but he continued to play an active part in the commercial affairs of the growing seaport.

1763
The Maugerville Planters

New Englanders established three significant communities in the early 1760s in what later became the province of New Brunswick — the Chignecto settlements, Saint John, and the Maugerville Township on the St. John River. Governor Lawrence's famous proclamation calling for New Englanders to settle in Nova Scotia had appeared in the *Boston Gazette*, creating huge interest in the free farmlands to the north. As early as April, 1762, a group of Massachusetts Puritans, led by Captain Francis Peabody, began meeting to plan the new settlement that originally was called Peabody's in honour of its founder.

Maugerville was planned in 1762 by surveyor Israel Perley, who had first attempted to lay out a town site at St. Anne's Point but was driven off by the Maliseet at Aukpaque. The new township extended on the north side from Mauger's Island (Gilbert Island) twenty kilometres (12.5 miles) upriver to present-day Lower St. Marys. Approximately eighty families arrived the following year. While the exact number of Massachusetts pioneers who made the voyage is unclear, 292 people appeared on the 1766 census, including new arrivals and infants. Each of the initial sixty-four land grants consisted of 202 hectares (five hundred acres) and the flourishing agricultural community with its rich soil (the result of the river flooding its banks each spring) almost doubled its population within ten years. Eventually one hundred grants were issued but the little settlement remained south of Oromocto Island, since the Maliseet village above St. Anne's Point remained hostile to the settlers encroachment.

One of the more controversial aspects of pre-Loyalist New Brunswick was the government's land grant policy. After the arrival of the settlers at Maugerville, King George III proclaimed that all land grants would be restricted to military officers and soldiers as a reward for their services during the Seven Years War. Residency was not initially required, so a great land grab immediately took place with immense tracts of land given out as the authorities were deluged with requests. One speculator, Colonel Alexander McNutt managed to reserve over 404,858 hectares (one million acres) on the St. John.

Land speculation and attempts to establish a tenant system, as in Britain, followed the King's proclamation but ultimately these attempts ended in failure, as the promise of settlement without free-hold land offered little incentive to pioneers. Like the French seigniorial system a hundred years prior, the tenant system complete with absentee landlords did not work in New Brunswick due to the lack of willing settlers. With the arrival of the land-hungry Loyalists, most large estates were confiscated for failure to fulfil conditions and given to the new settlers. In her book *The Petitcodiac*, Esther Clark Wright writes about this attempt to impose a feudal system: "But that was the old proprietary game over again, and once it failed: absentee landlords in New Brunswick could remain absentees but not landlords."

The Maugerville settlement had pre-dated King George's decree and Nova Scotia's agent in London, Joshua Mauger, successfully argued the Maugerville settlers' case before the Colonial Office. The Massachusetts colony was allow to remain intact on the St. John and, in appreciation, the settlement was renamed Maugerville. The pioneers were Congregationalists in religion and built the first Protestant church on the St. John River in 1775 near Oromocto Island. A land dispute, three years later, resulted in the church being pushed down the frozen river to Sheffield, where it was rebuilt in 1840 largely from the original lumber.

1765
William Davidson and the Masting Industry

Far removed from Halifax and the Bay of Fundy, the Miramichi and the North Shore did not receive the attention in New England, nor the settlers, that the St. John River valley received. However, after the Expulsion of the Acadians William Davidson from Inverness, Scotland and his Aberdeen partner John Cort, managed to acquire a 40,485 hectare (100,000 acre) grant extending some twenty-one kilometres (thirteen miles) on either side of the Miramichi. The grant, that began at Beaubears Island, included both fishery and timber rights. In 1766, Davidson employed twenty-five New England workers as he began shipping furs and fish to Europe and the West Indies. Soon white pine was also being exported and Davidson built the first ship on the Miramichi, a schooner called *Miramichi*, that unfortunately was lost at sea on its maiden voyage.

The Revolutionary War made Davidson's Miramichi operation susceptible to coastal raids and he moved to Maugerville in 1777. Two years later he managed to convince the Halifax authorities of his ability to supply the Royal Navy with masts, yards, and other timbers. White pine masts were especially valuable to the British navy during wartime and any mast exceeding thirty-three metres (one hundred feet) usually sold for over £100 sterling. Nova Scotia had no such timber. While the French had been known to have shipped St. John River masting timber to France about 1700, Davidson certainly pioneered the industry north of the Bay of Fundy during this period. He rafted the masts to the mouth of the St. John where the British navy would convoy the prize cargo to England under heavy guard. Davidson was exceedingly successful and soon a bitter feud broke out with the firm of Simonds, Hazen and White, who had begun a rival enterprise.

At the close of the American Revolution, Davidson returned to the Miramichi and soon employed more than thirty workers in his fishery, shipyard and sawmill operations. But the Loyalist influx to New Brunswick had created demand for land and Davidson's original grant was expropriated by the new Loyalist-dominated government, since he had not fulfilled the settlement condition of his 1765 grant.

William Davidson did attract some settlers to the Miramichi and developed the first English-speaking community in the region. However his genius was as a man of industry and energy. He continued to develop the

53

lumbering industry on the Miramichi, until his death at age fifty in a severe snowstorm while snowshoeing on the river.

1765
The Petitcodiac Settlements

The Petitcodiac River valley received its first non-Acadian settlers in 1765, when several German families from Pennsylvania arrived at Hopewell, near the head of the Shepody River. The twenty Philadelphia families were among the 159 persons counted in the following year's census; once cattle arrived from Boston the community began to thrive and export. Producing lumber, grindstones, and plaster of Paris, the tiny settlement also recorded the first known exports of food from the region, mainly potatoes and cheese. A small amount of hay may have been shipped from Saint John to Boston prior to 1767, but the German farmers were known to have shipped a number of hundred-weights of cheese to Philadelphia and London, as well as a quantity of potatoes. Massive land grants to absentee military officers and influential Halifax officials were normal for the era and the German settlers were really tenants and not pleased with their initial settlement terms. They successfully sued the Shepody Bay proprietors and their agent, Thomas Calhoun, and gradually were able to own property.

A similar suit for unfulfilled promises was successfully launched a few years later by settlers further up the Petitcodiac at The Bend, which had previously been known as Le Coude by the Acadians. Captain Hall's ship had left Philadelphia with five families in 1766 and settled the Moncton Township. While Henry Stief (Steeves) moved down river to homestead at Hillsborough, Jacob Trites, Charles Jones, and Michael Lutz remained at The Bend and managed to challenge the wealthy land speculators, including the famous American statesman Benjamin Franklin. Trites and his group managed to acquire about 2,429 hectares (six thousand acres) in what is today part of the city of Moncton. Gradually these "foreign Protestants," Germans who had fled to Pennsylvania from Saxony to escape religious persecution, settled much of the Petitcodiac River valley, including above the tidal line at Salisbury and throughout Albert County.

1767
Memramcook: Rebirth of Acadia

Details of the exiled Acadians return to Acadia are sketchy but in 1764 the British Lords of Trade informed Lieutenant Governor Wilmot that the Acadians could now return to Nova Scotia, provided they swore an oath of allegiance and resettled in small numbers. By 1766 Acadian exiles from Massachusetts had settled on the St. John River above the Maugerville township, especially at St. Anne's Point, but had no title to their land and soon were pushed up into the Madawaska region with the arrival of the Loyalists.

The Acadians at Madawaska were officially recognized as New Brunswick residents after the Loyalists settled in 1787 and eventually received title to about eighty-one hectares (two hundred acres) per settler. Permanent settlements were established in 1768 on the Baie des Chaleurs around Caraquet, at Cocagne and on the Petitcodiac. But the Memramcook River valley is usually regarded as the original site where the Acadian families returned after the Expulsion.

While seven Acadian families at Cocagne received the first land grants in 1772, the Memramcook valley is known as the Birthplace of New Acadia because it was the only major Fundy marshland region that the Acadians were allowed to resettle. Refugees from Fort Beauséjour, prisoners from Fort Edward and other French-speaking exiles began arriving about 1767 and the dykes were soon restored on the west side of the river. In 1780, the Acadians built a church, l'Église de la Montain, and the following year, the region became the first religious parish to be founded after the Deportation through the efforts of Bishop Briand of Quebec. Father Joseph Thomas Leroux arrived in 1782 and soon Memramcook was considered the spiritual centre of the New Acadia as the Memramcook Acadians again cultivated the fertile tidal marshlands and recreated the agricultural achievements of their ancestors.

Without political power the Memramcook Acadians had two drawbacks to contend with — the advancing English and German settlers, and the members of the Halifax ruling council who also laid claim to much of the best agricultural land. Nova Scotia Provincial Secretary Richard Bulkeley had arranged an 8,097 hectare (twenty thousand acre) grant for himself at the mouth of the Memramcook. Joseph DesBarres and others also had large holdings that forced the Acadians to work as tenants. Once New Brunswick separated politically from Nova Scotia, Acadian and English-speaking settlers successfully contested Bulkeley's claim but the Acadians ended up receiving the less fertile land. On the west bank of the Memramcook, DesBarres' land claims were upheld and Acadians were required to pay rent to the DesBarres heirs well into the nineteenth century.

By 1775, 261 Acadians were recorded in the census at Memramcook, and in 1803, 3,700 New Brunswick residents were estimated to be French-speaking. Yet the New Brunswick Acadians did not exceed the Nova Scotian Acadian population until well into the nineteenth century. Nova Scotian Acadians were given voting rights in 1789, but as Catholics Acadians above the Bay of Fundy did not receive the same right until 1810 and full political power came much later, well over two hundred years after the Deportation.

1770
Tenant System at Campobello

In 1767 a Welshman, Captain William Owen, was granted the outer island of Passamaquoddy Bay and took possession three years later, along with thirty-eight indentured servants who, in exchange for free passage out of Liverpool, had agreed to work for Owen for several years without wages. A colourful lieutenant in the British navy Owen, who had lost an arm in India and an eye in England during an election riot, ran Campobello as a military affair, complete with prison stocks and a whipping post.

A few New England settlers had arrived prior to Owen, including Robert Wilson who had settled without title at Wilson's Beach in 1766. Owen and his heirs considered all non-sanctioned settlers as squatters and the Wilson Beach settlement was called "the Wilson Encroachment." Unlike other New Brunswick settlements, only a few Wilson Beach pioneers won title to their land and all other settlers on Campobello became tenants of the Owen clan. Forty years later a visitor described the conditions on the island as "feudal-like."

William Owen left the island in 1771 and was killed at Madras, India in 1778. A number of the homesick settlers attempted to return to England but were lost at sea. A nephew, David Owen, inherited the island but New Englanders began to comprise the majority of the island's population and eventually Campobello became a popular vacation resort, especially for Americans.

1772
English Immigration to Chignecto

In 1772 about a thousand British settlers from Yorkshire began arriving at Halifax with the majority destined for Chignecto, largely through the efforts of Lieutenant Governor Michael Francklin who owned vast tracts of land and was desperate for tenants. The Yorkshiremen were anxious to leave England since the British economy was in a downturn after the Seven Years War, land prices were rising, and land enclosure was preventing small farmers from accessing common grazing rights.

These British immigrants were valuable settlers since they were aware of advanced farming practices and had knowledge of dyke building from the Yorkshire lowlands. Drawn to the Chignecto marshlands, these hard-working immigrants were only interested in becoming temporary tenant farmers until such time as they were able to purchase farms for themselves. Approximately eighty families settled throughout the Isthmus of Chignecto, becoming valuable allies for British interests during the American Revolution when the New England settlers of the region began expressing their pro-American sentiments.

1776
Civil War: The Eddy Rebellion

Although not a full scale war, the Eddy Rebellion was a serious challenge to British authority, pitting those sympathetic to the American Revolution against those settlers loyal to Britain. Both sides attempted to secure support from the Aboriginal people. By 1775, Nova Scotia was actually a colony of both England and New England. However northern Nova Scotia's two major communities, Maugerville and Cumberland, were composed of a majority of New England planters sympathetic to the republican cause of the United Colonies and both townships, except for the Yorkshire settlers at Cumberland, openly sided with the American rebels.

Yankee privateers from Machias delivered the first blow in August, 1775, burning the undefended Fort Frederick at Saint John and capturing a British supply ship. The next spring a similar invasion occurred at Saint John but this time the privateers sailed upriver to Maugerville where 120 citizens declared their allegiance to the Government of Massachusetts. Openly defiant of British rule, the St. John River settlers posed a challenge to the Nova Scotia authorities at Halifax, but the rebellion at Chignecto was more advanced with rebel commander Jonathan Eddy actively planning an uprising.

Born in Massachusetts, Jonathan Eddy participated in the expedition against Fort Beauséjour in 1755. He later moved to the Chignecto area and represented Cumberland County in the Nova Scotia House of Assembly but the Stamp Act heightened anti-British feeling, as Eddy and his Scottish-born friend John Allan became leaders of the revolutionary movement at Chignecto.

With the outbreak of the American Revolution, Eddy was unsuccessful in convincing George Washington to send troops to Nova Scotia. Eddy managed to recruit a rag-tag group of twenty Machias men and set off for Chignecto, against the advice of Allan who felt the force was not sufficient. Despite acquiring additional rebels at Passamaquoddy Bay, Maugerville, and Chignecto, Eddy had less than two hundred men when he attacked

Fort Cumberland on November 14, 1776. A reinforced Fort Cumberland under Lieutenant-Colonel Joseph Goreham easily rejected Eddy's attacks and the arrival of British troops on November 27 drove the invasion force into disarray. Eddy eventually returned to Machias. Despite pro-American sentiment at Chignecto, Eddy's small band had been too weak to seriously affect the British presence and Eddy began to concentrate his efforts on securing Machias and eastern Maine for American possession.

Meanwhile John Allan had attempted to secure the assistance of the eastern Native tribes to fight the British and convinced Maliseet rebel chief Ambroise Saint-Aubin to back the American effort, at least temporarily. A British naval force operating on the St. John River under Major Gilford Studholme, along with British Indian Commissioner Michael Francklin, pacified the St. John Maliseet and regained the loyalty of the Maugerville settlers. Too remote from New England, northern Nova Scotia remained in British hands mainly because American Revolutionary forces had no navy and could not commit land forces away from the main battlefields of the Thirteen Colonies. Allan was effective in securing eastern Maine for the Revolutionaries and spent his last days trading in the Passamaquoddy area around Lubec.

1777
Construction of Fort Howe

With no garrison and Fort Frederick in ruins from Yankee raids, Saint John's harbour area lay open to attacks by sea. By 1777, Machias privateers had plundered the small settlement so often that all trade had come to a standstill. Rebel John Allan had incited the St. John River Maliseet to threaten the white settlements above the harbour mouth so that the entire region lay exposed to the revolutionary cause. But the stores of Simonds, Hazen, and White had suffered the most, and through the efforts of William Hazen, Major Gilford Studholme was dispatched to Saint John with orders to either rebuild Fort Frederick or construct a new fort.

Studholme, a capable Irish-born army officer, had defended Fort Cumberland from Eddy's raiders and had also been involved in military campaigns along the St. John, including commanding a company stationed at Fort Frederick. He chose a new location, a ridge overlooking Portland Point and began building Fort Howe. The blockhouse was originally built in Halifax, shipped to Saint John, and reassembled. The fortress included a blockhouse with barracks for eighty men within a palisade and abatis, along with another blockhouse towards the east end of the ridge. Eight six-pounders were mounted and later a stone magazine was erected.

Fort Howe, with Major Studholme in command, became headquarters for the British military and established security for the Saint John area, as well as serving as the first civil jail. Although the fortress did not fire a shot in defense of the harbour, it was an important security installation for maintaining civil order during the transformation of Saint John into a major centre during the turbulent Loyalist era. Fort Howe was manned and re-armed during the War of 1812 and remained a military reserve until 1914.

1778
The First Treaty with the Maliseet

At the outset of the American Revolution, the area that became New Brunswick in 1784 was viewed by New England revolutionaries as northern Massachusetts, and by the British authorities at Halifax as northern Nova Scotia. Both sides saw Aboriginal support as crucial to securing the region. Soon the Mi'kmaq and Maliseet were caught in a dangerous game of determining who to support in order to ensure their own safety and survival. With their hunting and fur trade in decline, they were facing new hardships yet colonial neglect and settler encroachment made the British unlikely allies. The Massachusetts Bay colony had virtually wiped out a number of New England Aboriginal settlements and were also considered untrustworthy.

With the defeat of French power and the Acadian Deportation, Maritime Aboriginals who fought on the losing side were forced to travel to Halifax in 1761 and pledge their loyalty to the British Crown in the "Burying of the Hatchet" ceremony. In 1775 Maliseet chiefs Ambroise Saint-Aubin and Pierre Tomah declared their support for Massachusetts in a gathering at Bangor and, the following year, signed a treaty with the Americans promising an army of six hundred warriors in exchange for their own truck house at Machias. The balance of power had shifted in favour of the Republican cause when Saint-Aubin and Tomah joined rebel John Allan in his attack on Fort Cumberland in 1777.

However the British soon gained the upper hand by repelling Allan's attack and sending a sloop of war, *HMC Vulture*, to the St. John River where Major Studholme erected Fort Howe and proceeded to enforce British military authority on the river. Unsure of gaining any benefits from entering the conflict on either side, the Maliseet soon developed a rift within their community — as Pierre Tomah entered into peace talks with the British while Ambroise Saint-Aubin fled to Machais with many of his own band members. Saint-Aubin remained committed to Allan and the Republican cause until his death in 1780.

59

Halifax merchant-politician Michael Francklin had been appointed Superintendent of Indian Affairs in 1777. In September of 1778 he travelled to Fort Howe, where his assistant James White and Major Studholme convened the first British–Aboriginal peace treaty held north of the Bay of Fundy in order to ensure the loyalty of the Maliseet and Mi'kmaq. More than twenty years prior, Michael Francklin had been held captive by Aboriginals and knew their language and habits well. He also understood their anti-British sentiments were due in part to British authorities denying them access to Catholic priests. Francklin imported the Acadian priest Joseph-Mathurin Bourg to the Fort Howe conference. Bourg promised to become the resident missionary to the St. John tribe and also revealed a letter from the Bishop of Quebec threatening to excommunicate anyone who fought against the British. Francklin promised to build them their own trading post above the Reversing Falls at a site now called Indiantown.

Signed on September 24, 1778 by Pierre Tomah, the supreme Sachem of the Maliseet, the Peace and Friendship Treaty effectively ended the Maliseet threat to British power along the St. John River. In September of 1779, the Mi'kmaq bands of eastern New Brunswick were forced to travel to Windsor, Nova Scotia and sign a similar treaty promising to remain loyal to British interests in the region. By 1780, the wars were effectively over throughout the Maritime region as British military power became supreme. With the arrival of the Loyalists three years later, the Aboriginal way of life was permanently disrupted as settlers poured into the territory.

1780
Fort Hughes Blockhouse

On the west side of the Oromocto River, near its mouth, a blockhouse was built to ensure protection for settlements against American raids and to allow communication by couriers along the St. John to Quebec. Log huts were constructed about a day apart between Oromocto and Quebec (two weeks or longer in winter) and a demanding trip between Fort Howe and Quebec could pay a courier as much as one hundred dollars. A few soldiers under Lieutenant Constant Conor were stationed at Fort Hughes, named after the Lieutenant Governor of Nova Scotia. Once the American threat died down, the fort was allowed to fall into ruins and was not restored.

1783 – 1799
The Loyalist Province

1783
The Arrival of the Loyalists

With the close of the American Revolution, Britain was unable to protect those Americans who had remained loyal to the crown. After their property was confiscated, most Loyalists escaped to New York, where Sir Guy Carleton arranged to transport them to British-controlled territory. In the spring of 1783, the first fleet of about twenty vessels left New York and arrived at the mouth of the St. John River, where many of the approximately three thousand refugees disembarked on May 18. Over the next six months, about one thousand Loyalists arrived in the Passamaquoddy area where St. Andrews was established, and a number of Loyalists also settled in the Chignecto area. But the vast majority of the twelve thousand Loyalists who left New York for New Brunswick settled throughout the St. John River valley, instantly creating the city of Saint John, the town of Fredericton, as well as villages along the river, including Kingston, Gagetown, and many others. A Fall Fleet carried the regiments of loyal American troops, who were given the rich intervale lands and islands above Fredericton. Overall, the massive resettlement was poorly planned and much suffering occurred among the Loyalists as they waited for their promised land in cold, damp quarters.

John Parr, Governor of Nova Scotia, was unprepared for such an invasion and was reluctant to confiscate the best tracts of unsettled land held by his Halifax friends. Consequently many Loyalists waited in temporary structures in Saint John without legal title to any property. Suffering was intense the first winter at Fredericton, where Loyalists arrived at St. Anne's Point late in the year and many were unable to build log huts before the snow arrived in early November. Colonel Van Buskirk's New Jersey Volunteers pitched their tents below the town, near the river at Salamanca, where some died from exposure and lack of supplies. They were buried nearby in the Loyalist Cemetery, originally called the Royal Provincials Burial Grounds.

Unlike Saint John where Loyalists were forced to fight for prime lots after they had landed, the Loyalists at St. Andrews avoided chaos by drawing lots before embarkation and dividing the town into 430 land grants. Soon homes and other buildings in the town numbered in the hundreds with about a thousand permanent residents. At Saint John, the final transports arrived in December and many of the disbanded regiments finally drew for the remaining lots in the Lower Cove district. Yet wintering in huts in such a harsh climate produced much dissatisfaction and created bitterness within Saint John that would resurface for years to come.

1784
A New Province

Governor Parr and his Nova Scotia administration at Halifax had not been especially helpful in relocating the Loyalists north of the Bay of Fundy. So it was not surprising that in early 1784, a decision was made in London to create a new province out of the mainland portion of Nova Scotia. The new governor was a military officer, Colonel Thomas Carleton and, instead of the proposed New Ireland, the name New Brunswick was chosen in honour of the German House of Brunswick, whose dynasty ruled Great Britain. A provincial seal was granted with a ship sailing up a river beside a new settlement under pine trees and included the motto, She Restored Hope (*Spem Reduxit*).

Unrest and confusion continued among the Loyalist refugees in Saint John. Carleton and a group of well-placed Loyalist gentlemen including Edward Winslow, Ward Chipman, Jonathan Odell and George Ludlow, sailed from London for Saint John with plans to install a model British colony, which Winslow promised would be the most "gentlemanlike" government on earth. While the Loyalist elite expected great things to happen once this new aristocratic colony was established, New Brunswick would disappoint this ruling gentry since little wealth had been created out of the remote wilderness. The rank and file Loyalists seemed less willing to accept such a vision of a privileged society with a social order designed to benefit a chosen few.

August 16 became the official day of the birth of the new province, yet Governor Carleton did not arrive at Saint John until November. The province was divided into eight counties with twenty-six elected members forming an Assembly; however, the real power was retained by Carleton and his appointed Legislative Council. Men over twenty-one could vote but Blacks and Aboriginals were excluded, and the Acadian vote in Westmorland was disallowed in the first election of 1785. Serious trouble occurred in Saint John where an election riot broke out. Troops from Fort Howe were called out when a discontented group headed by Elias Hardy claimed an election fix after their own poll station was closed. They attacked the government's polling station at the Mallard House causing havoc, but lost the election when Sheriff Oliver reversed the results, and declared the pro-government candidates the winners. The first meeting of the Legislature was held on January 3, 1786, at the Mallard House.

Borders for the new province remained uncertain in the north. In the western region, Britain's claim of the St. Croix River was countered by New England's insistence that the historic separation between Acadia and Massachusetts was the tiny Magaguadavic River. Much to the dismay of the Halifax authorities, Nova Scotia lost about two-thirds of the vast Chignecto marshlands as New Brunswick's eastern boundary was set at the Missaguash River.

1784
Ward Chipman: Portrait of a Loyalist

Ward Chipman was typical of the Loyalist leaders that arrived in Saint John with Governor Carleton to promote a "restoration" of the northern wilderness to the Loyalist ideals left behind in the United States. A Massachusetts native, Chipman had been educated at Harvard and was part of Howe's evacuation of Boston that arrived in Halifax in 1776. After returning to New York, he turned up in London in 1783, and along with Henry Edward Fox and Edward Winslow in Saint John, comprised the partition lobby intent on dividing Nova Scotia into two provinces.

While a hard working and talented lawyer, Chipman's expectation for preferential treatment and government employment was never far from his mind as he helped Carleton establish the new province. A wave of protest occurred when Chipman and his group of fifty-five Loyalists signed a petition requesting land grants of 2,024 hectares (five thousand acres) each, when the average Loyalist was slated to receive eighty-one hectares (two hundred acres). As Solicitor General, he acted as crown prosecutor in all the major criminal cases before the court and together with eight other lawyers formed the first New Brunswick Bar in 1785, ensuring that only

63

Ward Chipman, a prominent Harvard-educated lawyer and a leading Loyalist in the new province of New Brunswick. (NBPA)

prominent Loyalists entered legal practice. Among Chipman's most prominent clients was the famous chameleon Benedict Arnold.

Besides drafting the charter for the new City of Saint John, Chipman assisted Edward Winslow in establishing the provincial legal system, which became noted as an extremely conservative code. Despite a number of important democratic reforms that had been enacted in Britain and the American colonies, Chipman chose to ignore the improvements. Chipman was not popular in New Brunswick since he fought any challenges to the status quo, including a controversial case that restricted public fishing rights in Saint John harbour in order to benefit his father-in-law, William Hazen.

The exception to Chipman's spirited defense of the privileged few was his mysterious challenge to the institution of slavery in 1800. While it was not fully successful, the Slavery Trial did manage to crack the Loyalist belief in the legality of slavery and helped end the practice two decades later. Some historians have argued that Chipman's motivation was to impress anti-slavery sentiment in Britain, yet he defended slaver Stair Agnew five years later. Chipman may have been genuinely interested in the plight of minorities since he assisted a number of Black immigrants acquire land around Loch Lomond, and successfully prosecuted a white soldier accused of murdering an Aboriginal.

Ward Chipman helped establish King's College, the Bank of New Brunswick, and built the most opulent resident in Saint John, but his lasting legacy to New Brunswick was his brilliant contribution to the historic boundary dispute with the United States. Certainly the most important of the founding fathers of Loyalist New Brunswick, Chipman worked tirelessly in many areas of the new province's development, but saw little distinction between benefitting himself and his adopted colony. His death in 1824 marked the end of the first generation of Loyalist leaders in New Brunswick.

1784
Elias Hardy: Portrait of a Reformer

Elias Hardy opposed Ward Chipman throughout his career and, for over ten years, fought the entire Loyalist elite in New York, London, and New Brunswick in their attempts to establish an oligarchy throughout British North America. Hardy studied law in England and emigrated to Virginia, where his criticism of the American revolutionary Tom Paine inflamed republican sentiment. He escaped to New York where he practiced law and became involved in Loyalist politics. Hardy was one of the leading opponents of the famous "Fifty-Five" petition group that included

Ward Chipman. The group had requested large land grants for themselves in order to adequately settle in New Brunswick. Hardy drafted a counter-petition signed by six hundred ordinary Loyalists. Despite receiving assurances that the best land would be equally divided among all Loyalist exiles, Hardy arrived in Saint John in 1783 and encountered massive discontent as the well-connected Loyalists were busily awarding themselves the choicest properties.

Elias Hardy soon became the leader of the rank-and-file Loyalist faction that feared they would became tenants of the more well-to-do Loyalists. Despite being described as a "viper" and leader of "undeserving people," he was able to petition Governor Parr to take seriously the widespread grievances occurring at Saint John. However Hardy's group was finally out-foxed, and New Brunswick was soon firmly in the grip of a Loyalist elite that would remain in control for many years. While Hardy did not run in Saint John during New Brunswick's first election, he was the leader of the anti-government slate, called the Lower Cove Party, that defeated Ward Chipman's candidates. However violence at the polls was cited as justification for reversing the results, and the Loyalist nominees headed by Chipman and Jonathan Bliss were declared the winners. Through the efforts of William Davidson, Hardy was elected to represent Northumberland County and became a voice for reform in the new Assembly.

Elias Hardy's politics were viewed by most as reasonable and well founded and his reputation for legal counsel grew to equal Chipman's, as the two often faced each other on opposing sides of a legal question. Hardy's most famous case was defending Munson Hayt against charges of slander by Benedict Arnold, who was represented by Chipman.

While not part of New Brunswick's inner governing circle, Hardy was no hot-headed radical and became well respected in Loyalist society for his sophisticated efforts to extend the elected Assembly's role from merely rubber-stamping decisions made by the Governor's Council. His most important political contribution to New Brunswick was establishing the Assembly's role in originating revenue bills. Hardy died in Saint John in 1798, less than a wealthy man and was buried in an unmarked grave.

1785
Benedict Arnold: Portrait of a Traitor

In addition to accepting Loyalists from the United States, New Brunswick also received a number of Loyalist outcasts who had been unsuccessful at establishing themselves in England and who returned to British North America seeking opportunity. After having fought for both sides in the

66

American Revolution, Benedict Arnold arrived in Saint John from England intent on developing a West Indies trade.

Unhappy with his position in the American military command and motivated by personal gain, General Arnold defected to the British side in 1780, and was awarded £6,315, plus a pension. Accused of greed and mocked as a traitor throughout his life, Arnold saw his prospects diminish in Europe throughout his four-year stay in London, and arrived in Saint John in late 1785 only to have his vessel shipwrecked in the harbour. The new American Republic was excluded from the carrying trade to the Caribbean by the British navy and Arnold soon had a three hundred ton ship, *Lord Sheffield*, constructed by Maugerville shipwrights. A lucrative trade with the West Indies soon developed, and at Lower Cove near Broad Street, Arnold along with his partner, Connecticut Loyalist Munson Hayt, erected a wharf, warehouse and general store. A warehouse was also built in Fredericton and another at Campobello as Arnold's business initially flourished. Eventually Arnold became widely unpopular as his overbearing manner and reputation for dishonesty inflamed the small Loyalist community.

Benedict Arnold began lawsuits against a number of people involved in his affairs, including one of the most controversial cases of the period. Arnold sued his ex-partner Munson Hayt for slander over Munson's charge that Arnold deliberately set fire to their general store to collect the fire insurance. New Brunswick's two best lawyers, Ward Chipman and Jonathan Bliss, represented Arnold against Hayt's counsel of Elias Hardy. While the judge determined that the fire was accidently set and found Hayt guilty of willful slander, Arnold was awarded only twenty shillings in damages. A mob of Hardy's supporters sacked Benedict Arnold's mansion on King Street in Saint John the next day, while Arnold's effigy bearing the word "Traitor" was burned outside. Arnold had enough and after six years in New Brunswick returned to London, writing an angry letter to lawyer Jonathan Bliss declaring "I cannot help viewing your great city as a shipwreck from which I have escaped."

Benedict Arnold never returned to New Brunswick, leaving his sons in charge of his commercial interests, but his view of Saint John would change during the French Revolution. With war throughout Europe, he wrote to Jonathan Bliss declaring him "certainly fortunate to be placed in a snug corner." Arnold spent his remaining days attempting to become rich through trade and privateering. He also sought to repair his damaged reputation as a traitor "for money not conviction," and fought a duel in England during 1792 over an attack on his character. He died in 1801, after receiving a large land grant in Upper Canada that he was unable to exploit. Arnold's friend and New Brunswick's first Attorney General, Jonathan Bliss, occupied Arnold's Saint John residence at 32 King Street until 1810. The grand mansion was not torn down until just prior to the Great Fire of 1877.

1785
The Capital City

Governor Thomas Carleton's decision to move inland and establish a military centre at the old French village of St. Anne's Point dismayed the citizens of Saint John. Yet as a military officer, Carleton saw plenty of reasons to move upriver with his troops, including a more central location, better security and the need to try and prevent desertion among the garrison.

The first Loyalists disembarked in the fall of 1783 and while English-speaking settlers were already living at Maugerville, only three old French houses were reported standing at St. Anne's Point where an extensive Acadian village had been burned by New England Rangers in 1759. A miserable first winter took many lives but by 1785, when Carleton announced the new capital would be Frederick Town in honour of George III's second son, progress had been made, and the next year, Dugald Campbell surveyed the new town. Carleton acquired property, establishing his residence, Mansion House, on a site overlooking the St. John River where Maliseet and Acadians had previously lived. A fire destroyed Mansion House in 1825, and Old Government House was constructed three years later.

Not initially a commercial centre, Fredericton's dual role as provincial capital and military garrison surrounded by wilderness, meant slow growth with less than four thousand citizens after its first fifty years. Yet well situated alongside the mighty St. John River, Fredericton slowly became an important transportation, agricultural, and commercial centre for the surrounding region, as well as the educational and political capital of the province.

The governor's residence also served as Fredericton's first public building where Carleton met with his Council, entertained, and received petitions but the first meetings of the House of Assembly in Fredericton was held at the town's landmark structure, the British American Coffee House on Queen Street. The Coffee House and Inn was owned by innkeepers Van der Beck and Ackerman and had housed the Governor until his residence was completed in 1787. The historic building served many purposes and underwent a number of renovations but remained an important symbol of Fredericton's early years until it was demolished in 1961 to allow for the construction of The Playhouse.

1785
First Incorporated City

Governor Carleton moved the capital of the new province to Fredericton shortly after arriving at Saint John, and as a consolation, allowed Saint John to become the first incorporated city in British North America, complete with its own charter and a limited form of self-government. Carleton claimed that Saint John was too open to attack by sea and moved the seat of government inland, while the people of Saint John felt the Governor was less interested in mixing with sea-merchants and traders than the New England gentlemen who were establishing estates upriver. One possible motive for Carleton moving inland may have been his fear of troop desertion in a seaport, a common problem during the period.

Using New York's charter as a guide, ex-Boston lawyer Ward Chipman drafted Saint John's first by-laws and rules of trade. A city corporation was formed and the Royal Charter was printed by the city's only printers, William Lewis and John Ryan, who also published New Brunswick's first newspaper, the *Royal Gazette*. Chipman also suggested the name Saint John be used instead of the intended Saint John's.

On May 18, 1784, the two communities of Parr Town and Carleton were combined into Saint John with the first mayor, Gabriel Ludlow, appointed soon after by Carleton. Chipman was also appointed City Recorder and Deputy Mayor, but six alderman were elected to a civil city council with voting restricted to freemen defined as "The American and European white inhabitants." With well over 1,500 structures erected, the city grew rapidly and despite losing its political preeminence to Fredericton became the commercial centre of New Brunswick.

1786
Justice for the Maliseet

For a short period in 1786 a state of siege existed in the town of Fredericton, as Maliseet from upriver camped around the home of Judge Isaac Allen to ensure that justice was delivered in the case of two white men charged with the murder of a Maliseet. On May 20, two York County veterans of the Queen's Rangers, William Harboard and David Nelson, heard dogs barking and discovered some of Nelson's hogs missing while two dogs were mauling the remaining animals. They shot the dogs and went down the St. John River until they came across a boat containing Pierre Benoit and his wife. An argument took place and shots were fired by the white men, leaving Pierre Benoit dead.

New Brunswick's first murder trial was held in June in Fredericton with Chief Justice George Duncan Ludlow presiding and Solicitor General Ward Chipman prosecuting for the Crown. Tensions mounted as many Loyalists attended the trial, concerned that one of their own settlers could be tried for killing a Maliseet. Ward Chipman was equally determined to ensure that crimes against Aboriginals not go unpunished, and vigorously applied the criminal code. The celebrated case ended with the jury finding the accused guilty as charged and David Nelson, who fired the shot that killed Benoit, was hanged, while William Harboard was later pardoned. The execution of a white settler for killing an Aboriginal did much to ensure relative peace between Loyalist settlers and Maliseet during New Brunswick's early Loyalist period. While New Brunswick's civil code was seen as unresponsive to the public good and favouring the Loyalist elite, the criminal code was generally enacted equally without regard for race or social standing. More than anyone else, Solicitor General Ward Chipman had ensured that New Brunswick's criminal laws were enforced.

1787
The Anti-Loyalist James Glenie

Unlike the reformer Elias Hardy who challenged the Loyalist establishment and ended up one of the governing elite, the Scottish radical James Glenie was New Brunswick's first rebel to seriously challenge the Loyalist regime of Thomas Carleton. Glenie initially arrived in New Brunswick in 1785 attempting to acquire land grants for settlement purposes but was opposed by Governor Carleton, who had been part of the military board that determined his court martial for insubordination at Quebec in 1779. Carleton's role in Glenie's failed military career would later account for much of Glenie's opposition to Carleton and his Council, almost as much as Glenie's belief in the injustice of unelected government.

In 1787, Glenie and his family settled in the Oromocto area where he began to work in the masting trade, arranging to acquire, cut and ship large white pine to Saint John harbour. From Saint John, Glenie's partner Andrew Blair had arranged masting contracts with the British Admiralty that involved the navy shipping the squared timber in convoy to England. Carleton opposed Glenie's masting activities as discouraging agriculture in New Brunswick, but Glenie out-maneuvered the Governor by befriending the Surveyor-General of the King's Woods in North America, John Wentworth. Soon the Glenie–Wentworth alliance was formed and sought to protect the British navy's right to cut any white pine in New Brunswick, regardless of its location on private or Crown land.

In spite of Carleton's objection, Wentworth appointed Glenie Deputy Surveyor-General for New Brunswick, which meant that he could acquire the best timber for himself, while policing others from cutting too much timber. Elected in Sunbury County in 1789, Glenie began attacking the policies of the Loyalist elite and soon became a popular local figure as the pre-Loyalist population around Maugerville resented the Loyalist domination of provincial politics. Especially controversial was Carleton's decree that only Anglican ministers could perform marriages and other civil ceremonies, thereby ensuring the Church of England's predominance in New Brunswick. The Maugerville Congregationalists were not amused.

As an ex-military engineer and brilliant mathematician, Glenie was knowledgeable about military matters and ridiculed Carleton's decision to establish Fredericton as the military centre of New Brunswick. He argued that the Bay of Fundy was the natural line of defence against any threats to the province, whereas garrisoning troops far inland was a waste of valuable manpower. Within the elected Assembly, Glenie began attacking Carleton and his Council for denying the Assembly any role in provincial money matters. By 1794, Glenie led a loose coalition of elected Assemblymen whose grievances centred around the Executive Council's refusal to share political power. As the people's elected representatives, Glenie along with Robert Pagan, Samuel Denny Street, Stair Agnew, and others, began to challenge Carleton's authority as the sole governing power in New Brunswick.

The governing process ground to a halt in 1795 when Glenie stunned the Council by introducing and passing in the Assembly the Declaratory Bill, which sought enhanced Assembly power at the expense of Carleton's Council. Essentially the bill meant to bring New Brunswick's laws into correspondence with the laws of England, implying the right of New Brunswick's elected Assembly to assume the same role as Britain's Parliament. Glenie's goal was actually the censuring of the Council and the recall of Carleton, yet by 1802 the people of New Brunswick seemed tired of the legislative impasse and grew impatient over the lack of local improvements to their roads and other necessities. Glenie and Street were barely confirmed in the October election for Sunbury County while the remaining members of the anti-Carleton coalition were defeated.

Yet Glenie's shrill attacks had taken their toll on Carleton, who had been forced to defend his actions. He quit the province in 1803 while remaining Lieutenant Governor in absentia until 1817. With Carleton's departure, Glenie's political career began to decline but the Napoleonic Wars heightened British demand for New Brunswick timber and Glenie became preoccupied with his masting trade. During the winter of 1805, Glenie suddenly left New Brunswick never to return. With his wife left destitute in the province, Glenie wandered throughout the West Indies and Britain, dying a pauper in London in 1817, the same year that his arch enemy, Thomas Carleton, also died in England.

While Carleton is usually awarded a place of honour in New Brunswick's history, Glenie's role in the founding of the province is still the subject of much debate. While his career was typical of an era when self-interest and the public good were not readily distinguished, Glenie can certainly be considered the first New Brunswicker to seriously challenge the Loyalist elite, and also the first to successfully create a political movement that slowly began to wrestle political power away from the governing council of non-elected appointees.

1790
St. Andrews Rivals Saint John

By 1790, the infant community of St. Andrews had sprung to life and was thriving as a shipbuilding, lumber, and commercial centre that began to challenge Saint John as New Brunswick's chief seaport. The town's stunning growth was largely the result of one man, industrialist Robert Pagan.

Pagan and his three brothers, William, John, and Thomas, belonged to a successful Scottish merchant family that emigrated to North America in the late 1760s, establishing a large trading operation at Falmouth on the Maine coast near present day Portland. Branded as Loyalists, the Pagan brothers moved their operations to Castine at the mouth of Penobscot Bay, where a British garrison at Fort George protected the surrounding Loyalist community. Once the St. Croix River became identified as the probable US–British North American border, the Pagans and about 430 Penobscot families moved to the first peninsula east of the St. Croix and founded St. Andrews.

Unlike the chaos of the Saint John settlement, St. Andrews became a model Loyalist town. While William and Thomas Pagan eventually moved to Saint John, Robert Pagan assumed the throne as the commercial king-pin of St. Andrews and the entire Passamaquoddy region. Pagan's diverse activities included lumber, the fishery, importing dry goods and shipbuilding. He pioneered the use of Charlotte County black birch in building ocean-going vessels. With brother William, he established a weekly packet service between St. Andrews and Saint John. Also active in politics, Pagan represented Charlotte County in the House of Assembly for almost thirty-five years. And as a Scottish Presbyterian, he often sided with the radical James Glenie against the Fredericton Loyalist establishment.

By 1810, Pagan was one of the richest men in New Brunswick and helped found the province's first bank, as well as St. Andrew's first Presbyterian house of worship, the Greenock Church. He also assisted in unearthing de Monts' settlement on the St. Croix River, thereby ensuring the river as the site of New Brunswick's western boundary. Despite remaining wealthy until his death in 1821, Robert Pagan could not prevent St. Andrews' decline in economic prominence due largely to American success in acquiring the West Indies trade and the eclipse of the town in favour of St. Stephen as the region's lumber exporting centre.

1796
The Search for the St. Croix

The 1783 Treaty of Paris had intended to establish the western boundary between mainland Nova Scotia and the District of Maine (then northern Massachusetts) by agreeing to set the border at the St. Croix River, where de Monts had first established Acadia with his 1604 settlement. Yet an interesting problem remained — which river was actually the true St. Croix, since French names were no longer in use? Three rivers emptied into Passamaquoddy Bay, the Schoodiac (St. Croix), Digdeguash and the Magaguadavic, with the Americans claiming the most eastern river of Magaguadavic as the true boundary which would mean the loss of almost one third of New Brunswick.

Jay's Treaty of 1795 cleared up some questions regarding the boundary dispute but even existing maps were inaccurate, so the St. Croix Commission was formed to determine the boundary's location. The celebrated Loyalist Ward Chipman was appointed New Brunswick's agent, with the task of disproving the American agent James Sullivan's assertion that the Treaty's decision to accept the boundary at the first great river to the west of the St. John River fixed the international border down the middle of the Magaguadavic River. Chipman's approach was to establish beyond all doubt that de Monts and Champlain's settlement was the island in the Schoodiac River called Dochet's Island, thereby proving Acadia's historic boundary. During the summer of 1796, St. Andrews' entrepreneur Robert Pagan and surveyor Thomas Wright excavated Dochet's Island, discovering piles of cut stones and bricks which matched those described in Champlain's writings. New Brunswick's position was confirmed by the Commission after American efforts to find similar ruins on an island in the Magaguadavic failed.

The next step was to fix the source and the mouth of the true river in order to secure the entire boundary. Joe's Point, near St. Andrews, was

Sketch of The Monument marking the source of the St. Croix River and the western boundary of New Brusnwick. Drawn by Colonel Bouchette, 1817. (NBPA)

accepted as the St. Croix's mouth so islands below, including Grand Manan and Campobello, were considered part of New Brunswick's territory in the Bay of Fundy. (This was confirmed by a commission in 1817, except that the Passamaquoddy islands of Moose, Dudley and Frederic were awarded to the United States.) After continual disagreement about the upper river's source, two surveyors Samuel Titcomb and John Harris travelled up the north branch of the Schoodiac above the Chiputneticook Lakes and marked the river's source with a stake near the present Carleton–York County boundary. The surveyors marked their initials in iron: S.T. and J.H. 1797, and the site became known as The Monument.

While Robert Pagan and Thomas Wright contributed greatly to the resolution of the western boundary question. Ward Chipman is considered the mastermind of the province's strategy and earned a permanent place in history when the St. Croix Convention of 1798 ruled in New Brunswick's favour. However the Madawaska region remained in dispute until the Webster–Ashburton agreement of 1842 established the entire western Maine–New Brunswick border.

1800 – 1836
The Colonial Era

1800
200 Years of European Presence

In 1800, after two hundred years of European presence, about twenty-five thousand people lived throughout a large forested region called New Brunswick, with the majority clustered along the St. John River valley. Significant settlements had also taken root along the Passamaquoddy Bay in Charlotte County, the Fundy marshlands in Westmorland, the Miramichi, as well as Acadian communities on the north shore and Madawaska. Edward Winslow's census of 1803 noted that approximately fifteen thousand New Brunswickers lived within sight of the waters of the St. John River estuary.

At Saint John a significant urban community had not yet emerged; approximately four thousand people lived about the harbour's mouth. With the harsh environment, political uncertainty, and tiny, scattered settlements, New Brunswick's future did not look especially promising at the turn of the century. The Loyalist dream remained unfulfilled as labour shortages, poor agricultural land, and a fierce climate all conspired to keep the new province a marginal outpost of Great Britain's colonial empire.

Politically, the Loyalist ascendency was at its peak with the defeated Acadians isolated at Memramcook, Madawaska, and the coastal region from Shediac to Baie des Chaleurs. Maliseet and Mi'kmaq people were also being confined to marginal, unwanted lands, and the first reservations began to emerge as the British solution for a population unable to maintain its traditional way of life and now threatened with no livelihood or homeland. While it could be argued that New Brunswick was to remain a relatively unimportant British colony, few would deny that over the next sixty years, the province's growth was impressive. By 1860, the population would exceed

250,000 with New Brunswick's first city becoming the third largest urban centre in British North America comprising about forty thousand residents. Many factors influenced the stunning growth in industrial output and population during the first half of the nineteenth century but two events in particular contributed to the upswing in the province's prospects. The Napoleonic conflict and Britain's need for secure timber reserves fueled New Brunswick's early industrial expansion while the exodus of well over one million British immigrants to British North America on the returning timber ships fueled a second, more permanent expansion.

1800
Slavery: The Great Debate

Slavery existed in New Brunswick well before the arrival of the Black Loyalist "servants" in 1783. The 1760 Treaty that surrendered New France to Britain stated that any Blacks and Indians who were enslaved under the French would continue to be slaves under the British. But a large number of Black Loyalists, both freemen and slaves, had arrived by 1784 and one muster roll reported 1,232 servants in Saint John as well as 222 free Blacks. This number seems high since the majority of the three thousand Blacks who left New York landed at Shelburne, Nova Scotia but a fair number did end up in the Saint John area and were given marginal land near St. Martins and the Nerepis River.

Most prominent white Loyalists including Edward Winslow, Reverend Jonathan Odell, and Gabriel G. Ludlow, brought Black slaves with them to New Brunswick. Despite Britain's decision to discontinue slavery at home, many Loyalists were interested in continuing the institution of free labour in British North America. The only known exception to universal slavery in early Loyalist New Brunswick was at Beaver Harbour, Charlotte County, where a Quaker settlement prohibited slaveowners. Their Bay of Fundy settlement posted the following sign: "NO SLAVE MASTERS ADMITTED."

Blacks, including those freed in return for fighting for the British during the American Revolution, could not vote in early New Brunswick elections, nor could they become freemen of the new City of Saint John. Only freemen could practise a trade or sell goods within the city, so these restrictions were an important setback to acquiring a livelihood in early Saint John. While there was considerable public opinion against slavery and no laws that actually recognized slavery, many Blacks were still enslaved before 1800. Auction sales of cattle and household goods often included sales of slaves and while many slaves attempted to escape, if caught, the law would always support the white owner over the runaway.

Slavery was finally challenged in 1800 when a Black woman, Nancy Morton, protested her enslavement to Caleb Jones, a York County Loyalist. He claimed to have purchased her from another slave-owner, Stair Agnew. Judge Allen issued a writ directing Caleb Jones to bring Nancy Morton into court and justify holding her in slavery. As a test case, the issue was presented to the full Supreme Count Bench that included three judges who owned slaves and one, John Saunders, who did not. Solicitor General Ward Chipman and Samuel Denny Street presented the anti-slavery case, challenging the legality of the institution in New Brunswick. Defending the slave-owner was the remaining legal elite of the province, including Attorney General Jonathan Bliss, himself a slaver. Chipman masterminded the anti-slavery position by relying partly on the legal advice of his Nova Scotia friend, Sampson Blowers who was also attacking slavery in that province. Nova Scotia had refused to recognize slavery in 1787. Chipman was a clever legal scholar and was careful to leave out certain legal cases he knew would be damaging to his position.

New Brunswick's first slavery trial was complex because no laws existed on the subject in the province. Chief Justice George Duncan Ludlow and Judge Joshua Upham upheld the slaver's claims, while Judge John Saunders and Judge Isaac Allen ruled that slavery was illegal in New Brunswick since it was not recognized in British law. While Nancy Morton was returned to Caleb Jones, Judge Isaac Allen set his own slaves free and touched off a wave of protest. Slaver Stair Agnew challenged Judge Allen to a duel while Samuel Denny Street also challenged another pro-slaver lawyer, John Murray Bliss. After shots were fired outside the British American Coffee House on Queen Street in Fredericton, Bliss apologized to Street.

The net result of the split decision was that while slavery was not ruled illegal, it became an unpopular and unworkable institution. Many Blacks became indentured servants, whereby they agreed to serve their master for a number of years in exchange for their freedom. The courts began to rule more in favour of the slave after 1800, so slave-owners saw that the system could not be maintained and gave up on the practice. By 1822, the New Brunswick government claimed that no slaves were living in the province and twelve years later full emancipation was enacted. However it was well into the 1840s before Blacks were allowed full citizenship by receiving voting privileges.

1806
Trade and Wartime Prosperity

Benedict Arnold built one of the first ocean-going ships in New Brunswick that successfully exploited the American exclusion from the carrying trade to the British West Indies. But in attempting to appease American sentiment, Britain allowed Americans to re-enter the freight shipping business to the Caribbean in 1791. Very quickly the aggressive Yankees began to dominate the trade forcing New Brunswick ships to the sidelines.

This changed in the spring of 1806. Britain had defeated the French navy at Trafalgar and was able to claim the undisputed title as the world's marine superpower. With the Napoleonic blockade in effect, the British navy turned its attention to patrolling the sea lanes of the western Atlantic. The lethargic colonies of British North America needed a boost. A bounty was offered for all fish shipped directly from the Maritimes to the West Indies, which immediately stimulated shipbuilding and the fishery along the Bay of Fundy. When Britain acted further and outlawed all foreign salted produce in the markets of the West Indies, American reaction was swift. In an effort to hurt Britain's war effort against Napoleon, President Jefferson implemented the Embargo Act forbidding American ships to trade in foreign ports.

Although Britain and the United States were close to war, American raw materials and foodstuffs were needed by Britain while British woolens and hardware were in short supply throughout the American Colonies. With the New England free traders willing to risk their government's wrath by sailing into foreign waters, New Brunswick's prospects improved dramatically in 1807 when Britain passed the Free Ports Act. The Act allowed American shipping safe passage in Saint John as well as Halifax, Shelburne, and later St. Andrews. The four Maritime ports became major transshipping centres for the exchange of American and British goods. Together with fishing and timber exports, as well as a surge in shipbuilding, Saint John in particular experienced its first boom of wartime prosperity. But in 1812, New Brunswick would feel the chill of its own war as its great neighbour to the south declared war against Britain for the second time.

1807
A Timber Colony

New Brunswick's most important industry began with the French navy exporting masts to France around 1700. After the American Revolution closed American timber exports to Britain, a masting industry sprang to life along the St. John River. Tall white pine became a valuable commodity to harvest for the British Admiralty. While the majority of masts and other timber continued to be supplied from the Baltic region of Europe until 1807, New Brunswick's export became significant to Britain's needs, peaking in 1811 with 3,151 masts delivered to British dockyards.

Prosperity in the timber trade reached New Brunswick in 1807, when the Treaty of Tilsit, between France and Russia, effectively closed Baltic ports to British shipping. Napoleon's control of Europe meant Britain was locked out of its traditional source of timber just when its timber needs were increasing drastically in order to build new ships and feed its expanding industrial revolution. With import duties on Baltic timber forcing prices up, British North America became the new mecca for timber. New Brunswick's huge inventory of large pine trees was immediately attacked and soon there was an all-out stampede to cut all standing timber.

Farmers abandoned their fields and the fishery was postponed as New Brunswickers took to the woods in search of forests to cut. In 1807, 27,430 tons of timber were shipped to Britain and in 1815, 92,553 tons exited New Brunswick's ports for British timberyards. The authorities, including the King's Surveyor-General John Wentworth and his New Brunswick deputies, were unable to establish order in the forests since Britain's appetite for wood seemed unlimited. By 1835 all major stands of large timber that could be cut had been taken. First Charlotte County and the St. John River valley were depleted. Next the vast Miramichi stands were harvested, and finally, all sizable stands in northern New Brunswick were looted. Lumbermen then turned to Upper Canada and the St. Lawrence to fill their quota. While demand for timber and lumber products did not always remain constant, New Brunswick managed to continue to find ways to exploit its forests.

1811
An Englishmen's Tour

Lieutenant Colonel Joseph Gubbins was a British officer appointed to the post of Inspecting Field Officer of Militia for New Brunswick. In 1811, Gubbins was charged with helping to organize and train New Brunswick's local forces against possible American attack. Gubbins conducted two extensive tours of the province, inspecting the military readiness of the four thousand man force that made up the ranks of New Brunswick's Militia.

Gubbins lived at Chief Justice George Ludlow's estate in Springhill, just above Fredericton, and toured southern New Brunswick in 1811. A second tour in 1813 included Miramichi Bay and his surviving journals reveal interesting observations on a young province that was still largely a wilderness without reliable roads or basic amenities. However, more interesting still is the English gentleman's assessment of the province's people and their shortcomings.

Throughout his journals, Gubbins lamented that while most New Brunswickers were immediate descendants of the English, few displayed the British habits of religiosity, neatness, and frugality. He concludes that "in remote situations, such as poor new settlers have to begin upon, they degenerate very rapidly to a state of barbarism." For Gubbins this degeneration produced an upside down world where everyone had to work — including a gentleman who had to cut his own timber, another British officer who was reduced to keeping a lowly tavern, and even one brigadier who resorted to selling cabbages on the wharf in Saint John.

Gubbins saw the evils of colonial society as stemming from too much free land and not enough poor people, resulting in a situation where "officers of rank and other gentlemen are obliged to undergo all the drudgery of farming," which he claims further results in "the present rising generation certainly inferior to their parents." Even servants were unavailable and those that could be hired insisted on dining with the master. Gubbins saw further evil in the colonial province, where immigrants were unwilling to become tenants to the upper classes since they could acquire land grants for next to nothing. The fundamental problem for Gubbins was that "The poor are not educated to respect the rich as in Europe." He cited as evidence a situation in Westmorland, although he admitted that the militia there was perhaps the most efficient in the province. When a British engineering officer issued a written notice instructing the militia members to remove their hats when meeting him, the gentleman was ridiculed and threatened. The Westmorland locals were unwilling to remove their hats.

Joseph Gubbins saw these colonial shortcomings as part of the American disease of disrespect towards the ruling class. While visiting Eastport on the American side of Passamaquoddy Bay, he was shocked by what he saw as an America militia "marching about with a band of drummers and prostitutes." Gubbins also detested New Brunswick's famous mosquitoes and judged the evening parties where locals would gather for sing-songs to be "too bad even to laugh at."

Buried within the Englishman's journals are glimpses of an emerging society that even Gubbins admits was not what he expected. Almost all necessities were made at home by locals, except luxuries that could be had by cutting and selling lumber for cash. Largely self-sufficient in the rural areas, Gubbins notes that the province had few poor and marvelled at the kindness displayed when James Glenie deserted his wife and his financial obligations, yet her creditors refused to turn her out of house and home. Homes destroyed by fire were usually replaced by community-built efforts, and Gubbins noted a strange custom called a frolic. Locals, he claimed, often turned out to help a hard-up neighbour who, in turn, would offer food and gaiety to help celebrate the good deed. All in all, Joseph Gubbins' *New Brunswick Journals* is more about British disappointments at not being able to establish what Edward Winslow had predicted would be "the most gentleman-like government on earth," than about the real New Brunswick society of the early 1800s.

1812
The War of 1812: Friendship and Privateers

Due to trade interference at sea during the Napoleonic conflict, the United States declared war on Great Britain. Many thought New Brunswick would be a battleground but New England was generally opposed to the conflict, and American citizens in the St. Croix valley swore not to fight New Brunswick residents. The citizens of St. Stephen even agreed to share what gunpowder they possessed with their Calais neighbours in order to celebrate the American July 4th holiday. Unarmed American vessels were allowed into Saint John and throughout the conflict the two sides seemed more interested in trade than warfare.

The British encouraged private shipowners to outfit their ships and prey on the enemy in exchange for being allowed to keep the captured vessels. A license of this kind was called a "letter of marque" and during the conflict thirty-seven privateers sailed out of Maritime ports to capture more than two hundred prizes. The *Dart*, a privateer captained by John Harris, brought in eleven prize ships to Saint John. Harris' little vessel managed to capture a large brig in plain view of the American navy in Boston harbour, before being finally captured herself by Yankee privateers. Other famous Fundy privateer vessels included a captured American vessel renamed *The Brunswicker*, and Saint John's own *General Smyth*.

Near the war's end in 1814, British warships captured Eastport and nearby Moose Island, and controlled the coast as far south as Penobscot. But Britain gave in to American demands for a return to pre-1812 boundaries at the peace negotiations at Ghent and, gradually, the Bay of Fundy returned to its pre-war state.

81

1812
The Blockhouse and Tower

At the outbreak of the War of 1812, New Brunswick had little in the way of coastal defenses along the Bay of Fundy. Fort Tipperary had been erected above and behind St. Andrews in 1808, but during the conflict three blockhouses were constructed about the town's shoreline, one at Joe's Point, and others at Indian Point and today's Centennial Park. Built with local materials and mostly at local expense, the structures were erected with squared timbers that were dovetailed and chinked, and mounted mostly with four-pounder iron guns. The New Brunswick 104th Regiment patrolled during the first winter, until British regulars took over for the remaining war years. The defensive coastal structures remained important until about 1840 when they were allowed to decay.

Further east, on the highest site in West Saint John overlooking the city's harbour, is Carleton Martello Tower — a circular stone fort constructed during the War of 1812. The second oldest surviving Martello tower in Canada and one of over a hundred built throughout the British Empire, the tower is ten metres (thirty feet) high and composed of thick, round fieldstone and granite walls, designed to withstand cannon balls. A Napoleonic military innovation, the Martello fortresses were considered impregnable against attacks from the sea. Carleton Martello Tower became a crucial link in the defence of Saint John until the end of World War II and was continually updated and reinforced with new military technology.

1813
The Long March of the 104th

Unlike New Brunswick, the Upper Canadian colonies did experience invading American troops and in 1813 the New Brunswick soldiers of the 104th Regiment were sent to Canada to serve as reinforcements. Created by Thomas Carleton in 1793, New Brunswick's most famous regiment had been disbanded but quickly remustered to its full strength of a thousand men by 1810. Six hundred men from six companies, two from Fredericton and four from Saint John, were chosen and the first one hundred men under Colonel Halkett left Fredericton on February 16 with sleds and snowshoes. During the first week along the St. John River, the troops were housed in homes and barns but on through to Lake Temiscouata and the St. Lawrence, they had to build huts. Despite intense cold and deep snow, the 640 kilometres (four hundred miles) to Quebec were covered in twenty-four days and the entire march to Kingston was finished after fifty-two days, with no deaths along the way.

The long march of the 104th Regiment is considered one of the most remarkable in Canadian military history, since Benedict Arnold's much shorter march almost forty years earlier from Kennebec to Quebec resulted in almost three hundred deaths. A number of deaths did occur later at Kingston as a result of the march and the New Brunswick troops saw action against the invading Yankees and fought with distinction.

1813
The Rise of the Miramichi

By 1810, the St. John River valley had been stripped of large masting pine and other regions of British North America became important to Britain's timber demands. The Miramichi was one such region. The Glasgow firm of Pollok, Gilmour and Company sent Alexander Rankin and James Gilmour, aboard the brig *Mary*, to the great river where they established a small company town below Newcastle at Hutchison's Brook, called Gretna Green.

Soon wharves, a sawmill and a company store were erected as the young Rankin took charge and began shipping huge quantities of timber and lumber to Glasgow. The Miramichi firm of Rankin, Gilmour and Company prospered due to Alexander Rankin's hard work and his ability to control all timber activities on the Miramichi.

During the early 1820s, Rankin was challenged for control of the prime timber lands by Joseph Cunard, who had established a similar operation on the south banks of the Miramichi at Chatham. By 1824, the thriving Miramichi had exceeded Saint John in timber exports with yearly shipments of over 140,000 tons of squared timber exiting river ports. The next year, the Great Miramichi Fire destroyed nearly one-fifth of the entire province, and set back both Rankin and Cunard, as the tinder dry woods quickly burned throughout the entire river system in ten hours. An estimated 15,540 square kilometres (six thousand square miles) burned, including the outskirts of Fredericton. While Rankin's house was saved, he lost $40,000 in stores and merchandise. Indeed, most river settlements were destroyed, as well as many of the 150 vessels that were anchored or under construction in the river.

Despite this setback, the region flourished but suffered from lawlessness and roving gangs of displaced immigrants seeking opportunity and fortune. Law and order was attempted after 1822 when the 74th Regiment was stationed at Newcastle but the region was isolated and preoccupied with the feverish assault on the forests. Lieutenant Governor Sir Howard Douglas toured the burned-out region immediately after the fire, offering government assistance and in thanks Gretna Green was renamed Douglastown.

By 1830, both Rankin and Cunard were back with new operations, including the largest sawmills in the province. Together the lumber barons held timber licences for most of northern New Brunswick. Due to the fire, they expanded their activities outside the Miramichi with outlets at Bathurst, Dalhousie, Campbellton, as well as Kent County, Saint John and even Quebec. Their rivalry continued and spread into local politics and religion, but both companies suffered when timber prices fell after 1837. Rankin continued to dominate all aspects of life on the north bank of the Miramichi until his sudden death in England in 1852. Perhaps the most successful of all the New Brunswick timber barons, Rankin was almost as controversial as his rival Cunard, and while both men were cheered by their supporters, they were indeed feared by their enemies.

1815
The Black Refugees

The second wave of Black immigrants to New Brunswick arrived in Saint John harbour in 1815 aboard the *Regulus*. The 371 refugees were mainly escaped slaves from the Chesapeake Bay area, who had been promised their freedom and carried off by British ships to Bermuda during the War of 1812. Other shiploads of escaping Blacks had been sent to Nova Scotia, but by 1815 the Halifax authorities, alarmed at the number of possible refugees, asked New Brunswick to accept a share of the human exodus.

Temporary shelter and meagre supplies were handed out to the new arrivals but unlike Nova Scotia, where some provision had been made to settle the Blacks at Preston, New Brunswick made little effort to assist the immigrants. At the time, white settlers were receiving forty-one hectares (one hundred acres) per immigrant. Black refugees eventually received twenty hectare (fifty acre) lots in the Loch Lomond area near Saint John, but only after they petitioned the government's Executive Council and received the legal assistance of Judge Ward Chipman. In addition, the Blacks were expected to pay for the survey. They were not given clear title to the land, but were promised a "license of occuption" until such time as "sincerity and exertion had taken place." The food, clothing and shelter that had been given to white settlers, including the Loyalists, were denied to the Black refugees. Together with the denial of titled land grants, this meant that the plight of the Blacks in New Brunswick was guaranteed to worsen.

Unable to afford the initial costs of establishing a homestead in rural New Brunswick, the refugees were described as "hovering about Saint John in a very distressed state," and soon a number of the twenty hectare

84

(fifty acre) allotments at Loch Lomond were reassigned to white settlers. Black grievances were many but they received little assistance from the Emigrant Society of Saint John, and even a House of Assembly committee formed to resolve land title questions failed to act decisively on behalf of the Blacks. While slavery as an institution in New Brunswick was over, racial discrimination was not, and the failure of the Black settlement to prosper at Loch Lomond was largely the result of the treatment received. While the harsh northern climate and unknown farming techniques needed to prosper in New Brunswick also worked against these southern refugees, the land in Loch Lomond was unsuitable for agriculture purposes since the soil was only marginal, at best, for growing crops.

Despite claims by eminent historians such as Stewart MacNutt, the Black population of New Brunswick did not prosper since the first provincial census of 1824 listed 1,513 Blacks while the 1911 census counted only 1,071 Black New Brunswickers. While many factors contributed to the Black refugees becoming impoverished residents of the province, the initial decision to issue licenses of occupation instead of land grants seems crucial to the later problems of Black poverty and discrimination. The reason land titles were withheld from Blacks by the Loyalist-dominated Executive Council was never fully revealed, but fear that free-held land would imply voting privileges for Blacks was no doubt a concern, since Blacks did not receive the right to vote until the 1840s.

1820
First Chartered Bank

The great shipping merchants of Saint John and the colonial government at Fredericton were in desperate need of a financial institution, as well as a common currency, with which they could meet their obligations overseas, and pay their debts within the province.

With an initial capital of £50,000, the province's first bank was chartered in 1820 and the thirteen directors were selected from the political and commercial elite. City mayor John Robinson served as the Bank of New Brunswick's first president. With the new institution quickly able to hold most of the growing city's debt issue, the request for a banking monopoly throughout the province was granted.

Within ten years the bank's monopoly on provincial financial matters became controversial, as a small group of Saint John merchants owned a significant amount of the bank's stock and largely controlled lending decisions. Other business groups were unable to access funds and as the city's economy began expanding rapidly the need for additional financial institutions became apparent. Yet New Brunswick's first bank had powerful allies in government circles and, despite overwhelming opinion against maintaining the monopoly, both the Legislative Assembly and the Executive Council turned down a second bank. Only in 1834, after the Lieutenant Governor issued a Royal Charter over the Council's veto, did the Commercial Bank open. Later, a third, the City Bank, also received a charter.

The Great Fire of 1877 destroyed the original structure on Prince William Street, where chartered banking began in British North America. It was rebuilt and amalgamated with the Bank of Nova Scotia in 1913.

1821
Free Meeting House

The first major centres of Westmorland County were Sackville, Dorchester, and Shediac but today's largest community, Moncton, was barely a village in the early 1800s. In 1788 only twelve families were there and little growth had occurred by the time the first storekeeper, William Harper, moved to the Petitcodiac from Saint John in 1809. Shipping, roads, and later railways, made The Bend of the Petitcodiac into a sizeable town that was incorporated as Moncton in 1855. But its small population in 1821 may have been the reason why Ichabod Lewis and William Steadman decided to build what is today Moncton's oldest building, the Free Meeting House.

The land for the modest structure was acquired from William Steadman and it was built in the style of a New England Meeting House, without a steeple or bell. Designed to serve the needs of the entire religious community, the Free Meeting House is probably the best example in New Brunswick of early religious tolerance. The Baptist leader Rev. Joseph Crandall preached the dedicatory sermon but all denominations worshipped here until their own churches were built. A schoolhouse was said to have been erected nearby and a William Paton was reported to have taught the youth of the community the year Moncton's first public building opened.

The people of The Bend, and indeed Westmorland County, took their religion very seriously in the 1820s. So seriously that on Lieutenant Governor Sir Howard Douglas' first trip to the Petitcodiac in 1825, the Governor was arrested for attempting to travel on the Sabbath. Sunday travel was a Lord's Day infraction in Westmorland and His Excellency reconsidered his travelling plans and left by coach on Monday, but only after the Justice of the Peace dismissed the case.

New York Loyalist Ichabod Lewis and Solomon Trites were the original Trustees of the Free Meeting House; it continued to hold services and civic meetings until 1963. Renovated in 1892 by the Seventh Day Advent-

Early twentieth century photo of Moncton's 1821 Free Meeting House. (NBPA)

ists, Moncton's oldest existing building was again restored in 1990 as a city centennial project, and is again used for special events. More famous than the old structure was a three-hundred-year-old pine tree called "The Great Tree of the Bend," that stood nearby until it was taken down in 1920.

1824
The Great Crown Lands Debate

The most important issue during New Brunswick's colonial period was the question of who controlled access to Crown timber lands, almost fourth-fifths of the entire province. The cost of cutting these vast timber stands was also a point for conflict. Since prosperity had come to New Brunswick during the early years of the nineteenth century through an almost unrestricted assault on the forests, it was not surprising that tempers flared when a new reform Commissioner of Crown Lands arrived in Fredericton in 1824.

Thomas Baillie was an arrogant, but efficient, Irishmen with powerful connections in the Colonial Office in London. He was appointed, with a huge salary, to do two things in New Brunswick: raise revenue for the crown, and bring control to the wide-open timber trade. By this time, the Provincial Assembly had managed to wrestle the revenue collected from trade duties away from the Colonial Office and had turned the fund into an elaborate patronage system within the province. Baillie initiated a new timber tax, set at one shilling per ton of timber, and this tax was outside the Legislative Assembly's control. His high-handed methods in collecting this tax meant increasing conflict over the timber question.

Baillie was the classic outsider to New Brunswick's close-knit colonial society, his riding about Fredericton with his coach-and-four with outriders was considered obnoxious. His display of wealth caused a lot of public irritation, since it had been acquired through his appointment as the gatekeeper to the King's forests. When Baillie attempted to further increase revenues by auctioning large reserves to the highest bidder, he upset the powerful timber barons. Land speculation became widespread and when Baillie attempted to sell off the water-use rights to rivers and harbours political action against him began to mount.

Speaker of the Assembly, Charles Simonds became Baillie's greatest enemy, accusing him of corruption and mismanagement. A second enemy was the young York County lawyer, Lemuel Allen Wilmot, who led a delegation to London in 1836. Wilmot convinced Lord Glenelg that the monetary control and administration of New Brunswick's most valuable resource should be turned over to the people's representatives. Baillie was stripped of his authority and remained in the province for many years, but was financially ruined in 1839 over his investment in the peat moss industry.

The sale of Crown lands was significantly reduced after 1837 and revenues from the timber trade also began to fall as timber fees became the lowest in North America. Yet Britain's surrender of the Crown lands did much to appease the people of New Brunswick and when rebellion in the Canadas broke out over the lack of political reform, New Brunswick showed little interest in becoming involved.

1824
The New Governor

The 1820s are considered the high point in colonial New Brunswick's history, both in its relations with the mother country and in terms of its optimism about its own future. Certainly the most popular and capable British governor to appear in New Brunswick was Sir Howard Douglas. Described as the calm before trouble, the Douglas era began in 1824 when Sir Howard was appointed Lieutenant Governor and military commander-in-chief. With its prosperous timber industry in full gear, the province's mood was one of excitement as turbulent growth was taking place throughout the region.

Growth had finally come to regions outside the St. John River valley. Douglas was the first Lieutenant Governor to tour the eastern and northern ports, where he personally assessed damage from the Great Miramichi Fire of 1825. His fire-fighting actions during the great blaze earned him much respect among the ordinary citizens. Douglas's energy and capabilities were perfect for the young province. Described as "indefatigable," he improved roads everywhere, including designing the Broad Road from Fredericton to Saint John; established lighthouses around the province; stressed educational and agricultural advancements; and reorganized the military including the eleven thousand man provincial militia.

Howard Douglas's two greatest accomplishments were in the area of education and the long simmering western boundary dispute. A firm administrator, he somehow managed to convince the Legislative Assembly to devote £1,000 per year to support the College of New Brunswick. Douglas then became the driving force in erecting the Old Arts Building in 1829. He also acquired the Royal Charter for the institution, which was renamed King's College, and became its first chancellor in 1829. Douglas stood firm over the Maine–New Brunswick border dispute in Madawaska, arresting an American instigator and strengthening New Brunswick's boundary claim in arbitration hearings in the Netherlands.

Douglas had strong views about Britain's role in protecting British North American interests. When the anti-colonial Whigs came to power in 1831, Douglas resigned his New Brunswick position to return to England to argue for the extension of the colonial timber trade. While somewhat successful, Douglas's exit from the province was deeply regretted. His political career in England was unsuccessful since his conservative views were not popular, especially his opposition to the abolition of slavery. However New Brunswick was never again sent such a popular governor and relations with Britain became strained after his departure.

1825
Colonial Literature

In coming to New Brunswick, Loyalist writers had largely abandoned their craft in order to carve out a living in the wilderness. A Loyalist like Tory clergyman Jonathan Odell, who wrote prior to and during the Revolution, was unable to devote time to literary demands after fleeing to New Brunswick.

By 1825, the Napoleonic conflict and the resulting boom in provincial exports created the first significant provincial revenues — largely from the timber trade. Soon a tiny group with some leisure time began writing, and this early colonial writing became New Brunswick's first home-grown literature.

Peter Fisher, a Fredericton merchant, wrote the first English-language history of New Brunswick, published in 1825 by Henry Chubb and James Sears of Saint John. Entitled *Sketches of New-Brunswick: containing an account of the first settlement ... By an Inhabitant of the Province*, Fisher's account of the development and physical characteristics of the province was revised and reissued as *Notitia of New-Brunswick* in 1838. An earlier children's version of the history was also released as *The Fredericton primer*. Fisher wrote on all aspects of colonial society but championed the Loyalist ideal of an agrarian society. However his son would rise to lead the Smasher party's revolt against privilege thirty years later. Fisher's history remained the definitive account of the province until Abraham Gesner's work, *New Brunswick, with notes for emigrants*, was published in London in 1847. Fisher's *Sketches* was reprinted in 1921, and again in 1980.

Another important milestone in 1825 was the release of *The Rising Village* by the first native-born, English-language poet in Canada. Oliver Goldsmith was born in St. Andrews and his well known poem about Maritime village life was first released in London, but reprinted in Saint John by John McMillan.

The first novel to be written by a Canadian and published in Canada was Julia Beckwith Hart's *St. Urula's Convent; or, The Nun of Canada*. Written by the Fredericton teenager at age seventeen, the two-volume suspense novel was published in Upper Canada at Kingston in 1824 with only 165 copies issued. A more popular work, and one based on fact, was Kings County High Sheriff Bates' account of the exploits of the famous jailbreaker and horse-thief, Henry More Smith. *The Mysterious Stranger* was written by Walter Bates and published in 1817. Reprinted several times, Bates' straight-forward literary style helped make this fascinating story of the most remarkable prisoner ever held in a New Brunswick jail a publishing success.

While the literary quality of these early colonial writers was not exceedingly high or original, they at least provided an authentic and charming glimpse into the early days of New Brunswick.

1825
The Stone Construction Era

Wood was the construction material of choice throughout nineteenth century New Brunswick, since its cheap supply meant that reasonably priced homes and buildings could be adapted from English models of brick or stone construction. Yet during the 1820s, New Brunswick's first significant public buildings were constructed from stone, partly to reflect their importance in a colonial society, but also because, for the first time, excess stone was returning as ballast in the timber ships crossing the North Atlantic from Britain.

A number of military installations and a few private mansions in Westmorland County were constructed prior to the 1820s. Dorchester's Keillor House dates from this era and also the Bell Inn (c. 1811) which is considered one of the oldest existing buildings in the province. But New Brunswick's first public stone buildings were built in Fredericton and Saint John. In Fredericton the Old Arts Building was erected to house King's College and, near the river, Old Government House served as the residence of the King's representative in the province. In Saint John two great public buildings were also constructed, and because the structures were fashioned out of stone they withstood fires and are still standing today.

Constructed in 1825 out of British ballast, Saint John's first stone church remains today as one of the earliest examples of Gothic Revival architecture in North America. Lloyd Johnson designed Saint John's Anglican "Stone" Church, complete with its perpendicular Gothic tower, but its spires were added the following year by the celebrated architect John Cunningham. Cunningham built much of the city's early infrastructure, and his expertise of stone masonry was imported from Scotland where he spent his childhood. Cunningham's brilliant achievement in stone design and carving was well ahead of other North American stonemasons in producing Saint John's first stone landmark.

John Cunningham designed and built Saint John's most important early civic building, the Saint John County Court House. Completed in 1829, the Court House is in the British Neoclassical tradition with the building's fluted pilasters and a pediment on the upper floors reflecting a Doric influence. Ship's ballast brought the sandstone to Saint John. The Court House's most striking feature is the spiral staircase that contains forty-nine steps, each cut and fitted from a solid piece of stone. The stone staircase spirals three storeys without a central pillar and the legend goes that, in order to prove it safe, Cunningham had forty-nine men stand on the steps to ensure the structure's strength.

Completed in 1829, the Saint John County Court House was one of New Brunswick's earliest public buildings constructed of stone. (NBPA)

Judge Botsford presided over the first Supreme Court session. The building also contained a city court for civil cases and, initially, a city Common Council Chamber was installed since both justice and city affairs had been conducted in the cramped second floor quarters of Market Square. Despite being gutted by fire in 1919, the old Court House still remains the seat of justice for Saint John County.

1826
The Indian School Scandal

One of the most misguided and shocking periods in relations between whites and Aboriginals ended in 1826, with the closure of the Sussex Indian School. The London-based New England Company, which had moved to British territory after the American Revolution, opened the school for Aboriginal children in 1787. Composed of leading New Brunswick Loyalists, the company had as its goal the education and religious conversion of "the Indians."

Exploitation began quickly as residential schools were established at Meductic, Maugerville, and the largest at Sussex under schoolmaster and Anglican pastor Oliver Arnold. Attempting to "civilize" the "natives" by converting their children to Protestantism and to train them for trades, the New England Company bribed Mi'kmaq and Maliseet parents to consign their children to the Sussex boarding school. While in Arnold's custody, the children were used as free labour in the surrounding farms or as domestic help; many were sexually abused. Little instruction was given, while the well-endowed New England Company spent most of its funds on salaries to its board of management, including Ward Chipman, General John Coffin, and Jonathan Odell.

Arnold, in particular, benefited from his role as missionary and chief instructor by personally acquiring company funds, land, housing, and indenturing many of the children as slaves in his household, those of his two sons, and other leading Sussex-area families. A highly unfavourable report on the Sussex Indian School and its rector, commissioned by the New England Company, led to the closure of the school in 1826. Under public pressure, the whole experiment ended five years later. Board member John Coffin and treasurer George Leonard quarrelled with Arnold over the misuse of the school's money, but none of the whites involved questioned the cruel and flawed scheme of separating children from their parents for indoctrination purposes. The treatment of Aboriginal children and their wretched situation in New Brunswick would not be addressed again until Moses Henry Perley was appointed Commissioner of Indian Affairs in 1841.

1827
The Madawaska Conflict

A major dispute flared up in 1827 along the Madawaska settlements, when an American group under John Baker raised the US flag and would not allow the postman passage on his Fredericton to Quebec route. Madawaska settlers were mainly exiled Acadians who took part in New Brunswick elections and comprised part of the province's militia, but Americans were rapidly pouring into the rich timber lands, which the State of Maine now also claimed.

The western boundary dispute had been settled in the south. But the Treaty of Ghent had called for the border to run from The Monument above the Chiputneticook Lakes to the northern highlands, which had resulted in a stalemate since neither side could agree on what the "highlands" actually referred to. Maine's position was simple — a straight line to the St. Lawrence, which would ensure the entire Madawaska region as American soil.

Under orders from Lieutenant Governor Douglas, the Sheriff of York County arrested John Baker and took him prisoner to Fredericton, where he was tried by the New Brunswick Supreme Court and convicted of conspiracy and sedition. A fine and a two month jail term raised threats of war-like action from Governor Lincoln of Maine but, finally, authorities in Washington and London agreed to submit the dispute to the King of the Netherlands. The King recommended a compromise solution, which secured the north side of the St. John River for New Brunswick and allowed communication with Quebec but awarded 20,841 of the disputed 31,621 square kilometres (7,908 of the 12,209 square miles) of territory to Maine.

The Americans rejected the compromise and constructed a fort at Houlton; later, the British built a fort at Edmundston. The northern boundary conflict would remain unresolved for another ten years and erupt into another major crisis, the Aroostook War, before finally being settled in 1842.

1827
Fredericton's Military Compound

Fredericton began as a garrison town in 1785. The military were stationed in various places throughout the community until about 1810, when a two-block compound became more noticeable next to the river on Queen Street. General Symth complained about these wooden "huts by the river" and had them removed; but it was not until 1827 that permanent stone military structures began to be erected to house New Brunswick's largest military garrison.

In 1823 the celebrated artist and architect John Elliott Woolford became Barrack-Master General, and helped design a more extensive military compound as he remained the army's architect in Fredericton for the next thirty-six years. Built in 1827 to house more than two hundred troops, the three-storey stone Soldiers Barracks has since been renovated to reflect its original appearance.

A stone hospital with four six-bed wards was also constructed but was later replaced by the Justice Building. The 1828 Guard House contained a twelve-man Main Guard area and has been restored to include a Cell Block from 1848, Orderly Room (1829), and Guard Room (1866). A wooden Militia Arms Store from 1832 was built as part of the Military Compound and, besides housing weapons and ammunition, the building was also used as a military hospital, temperance hall, caretaker's residence, and liquor warehouse.

Nearby at Officers Square, the historic Old Officers' Quarters was built between 1839 and 1851. Its stone arches and iron handrails are quite typical of the construction designs favoured by the Royal Engineers during the colonial period. British regulars remained on site until 1869 and in 1883 the Military Compound became home to the first infantry unit of the Canadian Permanent Force, which became The Royal Canadian Regiment.

1828
Old Government House

Major John Elliott Woolford had submitted the winning design for a Royal Gazette tender to build a new Government House and on July 1, 1826, construction began on the new home for Lieutenant Governor Howard Douglas. Sir Howard's previous residence, Mansion House, had been burned beyond repair and the popular new Governor easily convinced the Legislature to spend almost £15,000 to build the splendid new vice-regal residence overlooking the St. John River.

The handsome stone structure became the official residence for New Brunswick's Lieutenant Governors for almost seventy years and was opened with a celebration ball on New Year's Eve, 1828. Pomp and ceremony were a constant feature at this architectural masterpiece, including entertaining visiting dignitaries and the nearby Maliseet, who gathered at Government House each New Year's Day.

Old Government House had an interesting history long after 1890, when it stopped housing Lieutenant Governors. Sir Leonard Tilley was the last to reside there but the building later served as the Deaf and Dumb Institute, a veteran's hospital and headquarters for the Royal Canadian Mounted Police.

1829
King's College

The 1820s produced two of the finest buildings in New Brunswick, both designed by J.E. Woolford. Besides Government House, Woolford was responsible for King's College first major structure, the Old Arts Building.

King's College began in 1785, when Loyalists petitioned Governor Carleton for an academy and a 2,429 hectare (six thousand acre) grant was issued on the hillside southwest of the new town of Fredericton. A local grammar school was established and in 1800 Carleton chartered a College of New Brunswick. It remained small as only two students managed to graduate in 1828.

Sir Howard Douglas was determined to upgrade the college and convinced the British government to release funds for construction of a new academic building from the timber revenue account (Casual and Territorial Revenue) and to commit £1,000 per year for the upkeep of the college. The Legislative Assembly agreed to the same financial commitment, provided the college would not remain an exclusive Anglican institution since many Assembly members were non-conformists.

Sir Howard's problem was to convince the British authorities, including the Archbishop of Canterbury, to grant funds and issue a Royal Charter while maintaining the college for all youth of the province, regardless of their religion. Despite pressure from Bishop Inglis of Nova Scotia to retain the college as an exclusive Anglican institution, Douglas persuaded British officials to exempt students from religious tests and subscription to the thirty-nine articles. Yet all college officials, including professors, were required to be Anglican clergymen and, consequently, the new King's College became essentially an Anglican denominational college supported by public funds. With a majority of non-Anglican politicians in the Legislative Assembly, criticism of the institution became a regular topic in the Assembly.

King's College (which would evolve into the University of New Brunswick) opened on January 1, 1829 and the Old Arts Building was declared the "finest building in the province" with Douglas installed as its first chancellor. The Georgian structure was built entirely of stone by master cutter John Murray and was designed for twenty students.

King's managed to graduate 111 students over its lifetime as a college, but Lieutenant Governor Colebrooke repealed the Church of England membership requirement for college officials and faculty in 1845. Amid a growing demand for an open provincial university beyond denominational control, the Governor had been forced to act. By mid-century with the rise of the Smashers and the disenchantment with Principal Jacob and his classical curriculum, King's College came under further attack with its future threatened.

1830
Johnny Woodboat

Gone from the St. John River for almost seventy years, the St. John River woodboat was a uniquely New Brunswick vessel, developed for lumbermen and farmers to ship wood products to Saint John. The woodboat's rig and hull was based on pre-revolutionary Massachusetts boats, mainly the Chebacco dogbody. It's unclear when the first woodboat was built, although the Saint John firm of Simonds, Hazen and White constructed two boats in 1783 to bring wood to market.

The Loyalists began building their undecked, two-crew Chebacco boats of approximately fifteen tons with a carrying capacity of eight cords. Between 1783 and 1815, the name woodboat gradually came into use, as the vessels developed into a distinct and versatile local craft, capable of hauling all sorts of freight throughout the St. John River. By 1830, the St. John River woodboat had evolved into its final form.

In all, about five hundred woodboats are thought to have been built, with Harvey Whelpley of Whelpley's Point near Saint John constructing the majority. Weighing around seventy tons, a typical woodboat was under twenty metres (sixty feet) in length and six metres (twenty feet) wide. Its hull was constructed of hardwood planking while above deck, softwood was usually the material of choice. Oakum was used throughout as caulking. Its bulldog bow gave the boat maximum cargo space but little speed, and its good buoyancy was countered by its odd look due to a cut-off stern resembling a dinghy. Its exposed sternpost included an external rudder that also contributed to its chunky look.

The woodboats were always rigged with two masts. Both the fore and mainsail were hooped to the masts and a small forty-ton boat would carry about 226 square metres (1,700 square feet) of canvas. Its bilge keel allowed the craft to sit upright when grounded in the huge tidal shifts around Saint John and it was able to haul large loads in shallow water upriver. The boats were developed to carry cordwood or deals from upriver sawmills to Saint John where ten or twelve woodboats were needed to fill a square-rigger for overseas markets. Although considered unfit to put to sea, many woodboats were used in the coastal trade throughout the Bay of Fundy and New England, where the Yankee nickname "Johnny Woodboat" was coined

A typical woodboat only lasted ten years. The fifty-six ton *J.A.H.* was the last constructed in 1917 and was equipped with a gasoline motor. The last to sail was the *Maggie Alice*, which was condemned in 1930 at Saint John. The schooner replaced the woodboat in the coastal trade and river freight began using the two-sail scow because it had less draw and better ability to maneuvre. Finally steamers or tugs were used on the St. John.

1830
St. Stephen, Sawmill Capital

During the first decade of the 1800s, British demand for masts and squared timber fuelled a great inland surge as timber crews cruised the backwoods, rivers and lakes, searching for the great white pines. Once the large straight trees were taken, the timber companies began harvesting smaller timber in the hopes of producing sawed lumber for overseas markets. By the 1820s, sawmills began springing up throughout the province, especially along Charlotte County's St. Croix River.

Penobscot Loyalists under Nehemiah Marks laid out St. Stephen in 1783. Three years earlier, the town's first white settlers, Daniel Hill, Jeremiah Frost, and Jacob Libbey built a water-powered mill near the mouth of Porter's Stream. Other early mills were constructed at Moores Mills and Milltown, but the small village of St. Stephen saw little growth during its first twenty-five years as Charlotte County's population was concentrated around St. Andrews and other coastal communities. But by 1810, demand for timber had resulted in hundreds leaving the Passamaquoddy Bay fishery to settle upriver at St. Stephen and engage in the forest trade.

By 1830, twenty-two sawmills were clustered around St. Stephen, with Charlotte County accounting for 20 per cent of all the lumber produced in New Brunswick. At its peak in the 1840s, 140 sawmills were operating along the St. Croix River with only the Miramichi and Saint John producing close to the 140 million feet of lumber exported annually from the St. Croix. At high tide, ships docked at St. Stephen to load lumber for overseas markets and eventually shipbuilding got underway as both ships and their contents were sold to British merchants.

Most sawed lumber was produced as deals, which meant that the piece was at least eight centimetres (three inches) thick, twenty-three centimetres (nine inches) wide, and three meters (ten feet) long. Planks were also measured at least 2.5 centimetres (one inch) by eighteen centimetres (seven inches) and three meters (ten feet) long, and small boards like ends, laths and shingles were also cut from white pine, but spruce and even hardwood were also exported.

As the first region to develop its lumber resources, Charlotte County was also the first to see its logs reduced in size during the 1850s. By the 1870s, the lumber boom was over, as the business collapsed and died out towards the end of the century. Yet St. Stephen had already turned to manufacturing to help offset the lumber decline. The cyclical lumber industry came back in the twentieth century, as the pulp and paper business created increased demand for wood. Once again, lumber became an important industry for Charlotte County.

1830
The Seaman's Hospital

New Brunswick's first hospital was erected at Saint John in 1822 and called the Kent Marine Hospital. But eight years later, a hospital for seamen was built at Douglastown to accommodate the large number of sailors who were manning the hundreds of timber ships serving the Miramichi. Plans were begun in 1826 and all three towns, Chatham, Newcastle and Douglas-town, attempted to have the hospital located in their community. Douglas-town was chosen for its central location, and also because of assistance from the town's best known citizen, Alexander Rankin.

Stone brought from Scotland, together with Miramichi sandstone, comprised its exterior structure which has remained largely intact since its construction in 1831. An interesting feature of the heritage building is a cupola standing on Grecian columns on the roof. Six large windows face the river, with a large two-storey front room originally used as the sick ward. Also still intact are the original kitchen and fireplace.

The upstairs was used as an isolation ward and the hospital was also used for town social functions and in 1860 as a vaccination centre for smallpox. The centre also served as a starvation relief centre for Irish and Scottish immigrants, as well as a smallpox relief station for the area's Aboriginal community. In 1921 the Seaman's Hospital was the last such health facility in the province and after ninety years of public service was closed. It soon reopened as the St. Samuel's Roman Catholic Church Hall.

1830
William End's Gloucester County

In 1827 the timber trade was flourishing throughout northern New Brunswick, as Northumberland County became divided into two additional counties — Gloucester and Kent. St. Peters became Bathurst, the shire-town for Gloucester with Loyalist merchant trader Hugh Munro appointed judge, justice of the peace, registrar, and the county's first representative in the Provincial Assembly. But Munro turned out to be a tyrant who controlled all public funds. He also bullied the Acadians and Irish immigrants in matters of trade. Unpopular with both the Acadian and Irish population, Munro was reported to be a cruel jailer capable of torture and imprisonment without cause.

In 1830 a young Irish immigrant who had practised law in Saint John and Newcastle, William End, successfully challenged Munro for the Gloucester seat in the New Brunswick Assembly by declaring Munro a tyrant and shouting throughout the streets of Bathurst: "The hour of liberty is come and the reign of tyranny is over." An eccentric and conservative member for Gloucester, End often sided with the Executive Council against the elected Assembly. Nonetheless, End served the people of Gloucester for twenty years and always championed the rights of the New Brunswick Acadians and the impoverished Irish immigrants.

William End was one of a number of English-speaking politicians who represented Acadians in the House of Assembly, since French-speaking New Brunswickers still had virtually no say in the affairs of the province. Yet End was successful in combining the Acadian and Irish population into a political majority in Gloucester that could not be ignored. He withdrew from politics in 1860 but became county clerk and magistrate and was involved in operating a Bathurst hotel. Twelve years later, End died in a fire deliberately set at his Douglas Avenue office. Young James Meahan Jr., whom End had previously sentenced to serve time at the county jail, was accused of his murder but managed to escape Sheriff Carter and his posse.

1834
Marriage Monopoly Ends

The early legislature of 1787 had established the Church of England as the official church of New Brunswick and had attempted to pass legislation that granted the Anglican clergy the sole right to perform marriages. Governor Carleton had granted exceptions to allow Roman Catholic, Presbyterian, and Quaker clergy to marry their own people, and, in remote areas, for justices of the peace to conduct the sacrament of marriage as a civil ceremony.

Bishop Inglis objected to this indiscriminate power arguing that British North America would soon degenerate into one of the irreligious Thirteen Colonies unless the legal powers of the Church of England were enforced. The Bishop of London agreed and the Marriage Act was enacted in 1791, which barred justices of the peace from performing the marriage ceremony and prohibited the growing Methodist and Baptist sects, from conducting their own marriages.

Ecclesiastical disharmony soon set in throughout the province, especially in remote areas where couples had to travel hundreds of miles to locate an Anglican clergyman able to perform the ceremony. Baptists in particular refused to submit to Anglican authority in religious matters and Walter Bates, High Sheriff of Kings County, claimed to have jailed more than one Baptist Minister for performing marriages. Religious leaders at

Maugerville and Westmorland County, where William Black had developed a strong vocal Methodist congregation, began to petition for revisions to the Marriage Act. But the Church of England, despite being outnumbered, managed to hold on to its privileged position.

By 1816 the elected Legislative Assembly was becoming a more powerful force in New Brunswick politics and cries of religious tyranny were being heard as the Anglican church came under increasing attack. Bishop Inglis' death weakened the Church of England but membership was already well in decline as headquarters were still centred far away in Halifax. Yet it was not until 1834 that the Dissenter's Marriage Act was passed, as the elected Assembly gained more control of constitutional matters. Finally licenses to perform marriages were extended to Baptists and Methodists, well over forty years after the restrictions were first enacted.

1836
The Westmorland Road

A passable coach road from Saint John to the Chignecto settlements at the Nova Scotia border had been the dream of the Loyalists since arriving in 1783, but the only known road east followed an old Indian trail south of the Kennebecasis Valley to the Hammond River, and south of Sussex Corner to the Petitcodiac. Known as the Cumberland Road, or the "short road," the circuitous route proved useless for the new settlements along the Kennebecasis, and in 1786, surveyor John Wetmore laid out a Great Road between Saint John and The Bend.

The new road, known as the Westmorland Road or the Main Road, followed somewhat of a straight line to Hampton Village, where it crossed the river by ferry, and along the north side of the Kennebecasis River to Apohaqui, then on the south side to Sussex, and on through Portage Vale to Petitcodiac. North around The Bend, the Westmorland Road headed east across the Memramcook River and south to Dorchester and Sackville. The Highway Act stipulated that all roads had to be at least four rods (five metres) wide, but the fundamental problem was lack of funds.

Private subscription in exchange for land grants raised £190 for the Westmorland Road, including £50 from Benedict Arnold, yet when surveyor Dugald Campbell made his inspection tour of southern New Brunswick in 1802, he reported that not sixteen kilometres (ten miles) were fit for wheel carriage. The road had been used so little that one stretch had been fenced across by a farmer. During the early 1800s most provincial travel was by river or coastal vessels, while winter travel was over the ice. Even surveyor Campbell's trip had been delayed by bad winds that had forced him to spend eleven days sailing along the Bay of Fundy in order to reach The Bend from Saint John.

By 1825, writer Peter Fisher claimed Kings County roads and bridges were good but he meant for walking rather than by coach. Eight years later, Judge Joshua Upham, travelling by horse and coach on his court circuit in Westmorland, complained about the terrible state of the main road. But in 1836, regular stage coach service began to operate between Saint John and Amherst. The Saint John Stage Coach Company offered two-day service at threepence a mile and left Saint John at 7:00 A.M. on Monday, staying at Petitcodiac for an overnight stop. The stagecoach arrived at The Bend around 9:00 A.M. Tuesday and reached Amherst early in the evening, but the roads still were less than ideal. Surveyor James Alexander reported a nasty spill outside The Bend at Boundary Creek that almost killed the passengers.

In 1837, all timber fees became part of provincial revenues and these new funds were partly devoted to building roads and bridges. Roads good enough for year-round wheeled traffic became the goal between Saint John, Fredericton and Sackville. Soon a regular mail packet coach became a reliable service and by the late 1840s, Charles Record and Daniel Caldwell were partners in the Saint John Stage Coach Company, operating stagecoach runs between Saint John and Nova Scotia. The Westmorland Bank's $30,000 gold reserve was brought from Saint John to Moncton by coach with the Bank's first president, Oliver Jones, riding shotgun to protect the cargo. With the establishment of railways in the late 1850s, horse and coach became obsolete especially for long range travel, but roads continued to be built throughout the province. By 1900 sixteen thousand kilometres (ten thousand miles) of roads and four thousand bridges had been constructed.

1837 – 1854
Growth and the
Self-government Struggle

1837
First Triumph of the Assembly

Until July 17, 1837, New Brunswick's wealth, which derived almost entirely from its forests, was controlled by the Governor and his Council. The Casual and Territorial Revenue came from duties on timber cut on Crown lands and also from the sale of Crown lands. These funds had grown enormously during the 1830s but were outside the control of the House of Assembly, and allowed the Governor to remain independent of the elected Assembly.

Finally in 1837, fearing a similar rebellion in New Brunswick to that occurring in the Canadas, Lord Glenelg of the British Colonial Office ordered Lieutenant Governor Campbell to surrender the Crown land funds. Visiting Assemblymen Lemuel Allan Wilmot and William Crane had assured Glenelg that the Assembly would assume responsibility for payment of the civil list, which amounted to the government's annual cost in salaries and expenses needed to run their affairs.

The so-called Civil List Bill received Royal Assent on July 17, 1837 and effective control of incoming revenue from Crown timber harvests passed from the Governor to the Assembly. For better or for worse, the purse strings of the province finally proceeded into the hands of the elected chamber. While disorder ensued as over-expenditures became common and parochial politicians spent provincial revenue unwisely, this passage marked the beginning of the ascendency of the House of Assembly in New Brunswick, and the first step in the development of Responsible Government.

103

1837
The Aroostook War

The final stage of the Maine–New Brunswick boundary conflict erupted in 1837, when both sides sent troops to a disputed timber region on the upper St. John River. Over the next three years, Maine militiamen faced British redcoats and the New Brunswick Militia. The British, under the direction of the old warhorse Sir John Harvey, who had just arrived in Fredericton as the new Lieutenant Governor, were adamant that no territory north of the St. John would be surrendered, although privately they had agreed to give up the Acadian villages on the south bank.

Governor Fairfield of Maine was equally determined to hold out for a favourable verdict. Although no serious fighting or deaths occurred both sides took prisoners, including Rufus McIntyre, Maine's land agent, who spent time in the York County jail. A drunken brawl between soldiers took place in a Houlton tavern but a truce was called, with both sides agreeing to joint jurisdiction until a new commission could decide the final boundary lines.

American statesman and orator Daniel Webster and Britain's Lord Ashburton finally settled the border in 1842, with the Americans securing the south side of the river and unrestricted access to float timber clear to the sea, while Great Britain secured the upper reaches of the St. John, including Lake Temiscouata and its portage route to Quebec. Unfortunately the Treaty of Ashburton divided the Madawaska people into two countries with two flags on opposite sides of the river. Ironically, the fierce American agitator John Baker ended up on the Canadian side where he prospered without ever becoming a Canadian citizen. He died in 1868 and was buried at St. Francis but in 1895, the State of Maine transferred the remains of this American hero to Fort Fairfield, Maine.

1839
A Church Burning on Grand Manan

Nicknamed the Emperor of Grand Manan, Wilford Fisher settled near Woodwards Cove in the early 1800s, establishing a smoked fish operation and other fishing ventures, as well as a retail enterprise. Soon Fisher was a magistrate, militia captain, and the most powerful man on the island with an appetite for complete control. His only vocal opposition came from clergyman John Dunn and on an October night in 1839, St. Paul's Church at Grand Harbour was destroyed by flames, while an effigy of a clergyman was found hanging in a nearby tree.

Evidence of arson pointed to Wilford Fisher and his followers, who were tried in the Sessions Court at St. Andrews. Acquitted due to the circumstantial nature of the evidence, the action by Fisher's group to try and silence John Dunn backfired. Islanders branded Fisher a church burner and refused to respect his authority. His repeated attempts to muster militiamen were refused, as islanders were in open revolt against his authority.

The church was rebuilt but provincial authorities still deferred to Fisher on island matters. His feudal control had been broken however, and for the next decade Grand Manan resembled the wild west. Without law enforcement, widespread drunkness and assaults became common occurrences. Rector John Dunn was transferred to a mainland church and his replacement was unable to challenge the corrupt Fisher nor organize the islanders into an effective opposition.

Guilt in the church-burning episode was never legally established yet Fisher's camp was certainly involved. Eventually Grand Manan became inflamed with evangelism and the temperance movement, as islanders grew to hate the effects of open lawlessness and vandalism. Still standing today at Grand Harbour is the tiny stone church, St. Paul's Anglican, built in 1840 after its wooden predecessor was torched.

1839
Restigouche County Established

Creation of the new county of Restigouche in 1837 can be attributed almost entirely to one man and his fear of losing his power. Robert Ferguson, known as the father of the Restigouche, ran the remote and sparsely populated region as his serfdom until challenged for political control by the young Irish upstart, William End.

Ferguson established himself at Martin's Point, which is now Campbellton, before 1800 and quickly became the leading merchant, exporting fish and timber. He constructed the area's only gristmill and sawmill, built wooden vessels, acquired large land holdings and, after 1813, became the leading political figure for northern Northumberland County. The Restigouche region became part of the newly created Gloucester County in 1827, but Ferguson's harsh treatment of the Acadians and Irish immigrants meant that the people's choice, lawyer William End, easily won a Gloucester seat in 1830, declaring Ferguson "a perjured old villain." The majority of north shore residents were now Acadians or Irish, yet Ferguson's influence over provincial officials meant that the rights of the Gloucester majority were often trampled for his own commercial gain.

Robert Ferguson's pre-eminence in the lumber trade was also challenged after the Great Miramichi Fire forced Joseph Cunard and Alexander Rankin north, in search of their own supply of timber. Ferguson allied himself with Rankin's companies, who by 1836 had well over 259 square kilometres (one hundred square miles) of Restigouche territory under timber license. With William End firmly in political control at Bathurst, Ferguson began lobbying Lieutenant Governor Archibald Campbell to carve another county out of northern Gloucester, where his influence and authority still remained. This was done in 1837, and Ferguson had his village renamed Campbellton in the Governor's honour. Despite being seriously challenged throughout the latter half of his career, the first merchant baron of the Restigouche retained much of his influence and political power until his death in 1851.

1839
The Penny Paper

George E. Fenety started the Maritimes' first penny paper in Saint John — the *Commercial News and General Advertiser*. With an initial circulation of five hundred copies, "the poor man's friend," as Fenety called his newspaper, began publishing tri-weekly out of Fenety's Canterbury Street office with the motto: "Reform and Responsible Government."

Fenety apprenticed with Joe Howe's publishing trade in Halifax and also worked in the United States before arriving in New Brunswick. Full of democratic zeal, Fenety saw his mission in life as implementing reformer ideas in New Brunswick politics. He supported the move to responsible government, vote by ballot, improved education, better working conditions for workers, as well as more help for New Brunswick's poor, especially for the impoverished Blacks around Saint John.

Circulation rose drastically as Fenety hammered away at the Family Compact's control of the province's political life. He also improved his paper by changing its name to the *Morning News*, and installing a telegraph line to report House of Assembly debates in Fredericton. Fenety's support of the reform ticket was rewarded in the 1850s when the Liberals were swept into power and he was appointed Queen's Printer. Fenety later sold his newspaper and moved to Fredericton, where he had a successful civic career as mayor of the capital.

1842
A Geologist and a Museum

Nova Scotian geologist Dr. Abraham Gesner arrived in Saint John in the spring of 1838 anxious to take up his new position as British North America's first provincial geologist. Sir John Harvey employed Gesner to undertake the first geological survey of New Brunswick to assess mineral potential. The province was especially interested in locating coal deposits.

For five years, Gesner travelled with Maliseet guides classifying the various rock formations, fossils, and other natural resources, enthusiastically describing the province's geology and its potential for mining. However Abraham had little practical experience in coal mining and his assessment of the Albert County coal fields were overplayed to the extent that mining companies spent huge sums on his overly optimistic advice and lost their investments. Angry reports flowed into the Legislative Assembly and Gesner's salary was withheld. Once Lieutenant Governor Harvey had been removed from office for overspending, Gesner was out of a job.

Abraham Gesner was one of the most gifted men of his day but misfortune followed him everywhere. His discovery of albertite, near the Petitcodiac River in Albert County, turned into one of the great disappointments and controversies of his career. The mineral was more like asphalt or petroleum than coal, and produced far more of his new invention kerosene than anything he had tested. The celebrated trial in Albert County in 1852 over the mining rights to the substance resulted in Judge Lemuel Allan Wilmot declaring that all mineral rights, including albertite, belonged to a prior mining lease owned by William Cairns. The decision cost Gesner two million dollars but the inventor of kerosene was involved in lawsuits and patent infringements throughout his career.

Before Gesner left Saint John in 1842, his terrible financial situation forced him to try and raise money by offering for public viewing his collection of 2,173 specimens gathered during his five years in New Brunswick. On April 5, a natural history exhibition opened at the Mechanics Institute on Carleton Street with Gesner in attendance. His collection remained at the Institute as part of its museum until 1870, when the institution was closed, but it later became part of the collection of the Natural History Society of New Brunswick.

Abraham Gesner published *New Brunswick with Notes for Immigrants*, a popular work on his travels and observations in New Brunswick, and his enthusiasm for the province's potential was well known. But it was as the inventor of kerosene that Gesner established his fame and he became one of the few Maritimers in the nineteenth century to receive recognition for his achievement during his lifetime.

1842
First Provincial Art Exhibition

The year 1842 was an important one for artistic pursuits in New Brunswick. English artist William Henry Bartlett's book, *Canadian Scenery*, containing numerous sepia drawings of New Brunswick scenes was published, and John Clow opened New Brunswick's first studio featuring the new daguerreotype photography. With almost thirty thousand citizens, Saint John was now a major urban centre with a burgeoning arts scene. In April, Abraham Gesner had created a stir at the Mechanics Institute with his display of exotic artifacts, but the Carleton Street centre was full of excitement in August at New Brunswick's first visual art exhibition.

Opened by Lieutenant Governor Sir William Colebrooke, the art exhibit featured a number of well-known provincial artists, including mechanical genius Benjamin Franklin Tibbets, whose oil, chalk, and pencil portraits displayed his proficiency and desire to become a professional portrait painter. Tibbets later abandoned his art to study steam power, and invented the world's first compound steam engine in 1845.

The exhibit also featured work from inventor and artist Robert Foulis, who conceived the idea for a steam fog horn. This artistic and mechanical genius had worked full-time as a portrait painter in Halifax, and four years earlier had established a School of Arts in Saint John. Fredericton artist Robert Parker's miniatures were on display. Fredericton's best known artist, Barrack Master General John Elliott Woolford also attended to show his work. Woolford's watercolours and paintings are still prominent today as are his most notable architectural achievements, the Old Arts Building on the campus of the University of New Brunswick and Fredericton's Old Government House.

Other artists included John Stanton, James Bell, and Arthur Slader. The paintings, described in a small pamphlet as "of sterling merit," were auctioned off at the end of the exhibition. Public art exhibitions became popular past-times for officers, merchants, and the growing leisure class of New Brunswickers. With the advent of New Brunswick's first provincial exhibition, visual art displays became an important source of revenue for artists and a vital medium for the exchange of artistic ideas.

1843
The Baron of Dorchester

Edward Barron Chandler began his long and lucrative legal career in Dorchester in 1823 and, the same year, began his equally extensive public career. Elected to represent Westmorland in the House of Assembly, he soon became an important member of the Assembly, and a strong advocate of Westmorland County interests. Despite his youth, Chandler represented New Brunswick in London in 1833 where he presented grievances to the Colonial Office. While an advocate for the Acadians of his riding, Chandler was at best a mild reformer and had little interest in the fashionable notions of political parties or responsible government.

In 1843, Lieutenant Governor Sir William Colebrooke appointed Edward Chandler to the Executive Council, New Brunswick's supreme governing council. He remained its leader until the Smasher victory of 1854. As an elected member of the House of Assembly and also spokesman for the Family Compact, Chandler tended to support the status quo and opposed the enactment of responsible government when it came to New Brunswick in 1848. However Chandler was a strong enough statesmen to be chosen leader of the new government that included, for the first time, two liberal reformers, Charles Fisher and Lemuel Allan Wilmot.

While the anti-establishment cries for full self government became Smasher slogans during the early 1850s, a strong economy allowed Chandler to manage an uneasy coalition that improved industry and trade by building railways and negotiating the Reciprocity Treaty with the United States. While he retained his Westmorland seat, the Smasher victory of 1854 ended Chandler's leadership role in provincial politics, yet he remained an influential public figure until his death in 1880. He supported Maritime Union, as well as some form of Confederation, and clashed with the "Lion of Westmorland," Albert Smith, over the province's future in British North America. Sensing the inevitability of Confederation, Chandler lobbied for a favourable deal for his native province.

Turning down a seat in the new Canadian senate, Chandler accepted an appointment as one of the commissioners in charge of the construction of the Intercolonial Railway from Halifax to Montreal. He succeeded in diverting the railway through his hometown of Dorchester, adding almost a half hour to the Sackville–Moncton route. Like most politicians of his era, Chandler saw no problem mixing self-interest with the interests of his community, and he lobbied hard for the federal penitentiary to be built in his shiretown. In 1879, he sold a piece of his own property, called "lot 6," that became the penitentiary's location.

Edward Barron Chandler remained an important conservative force in public life for almost sixty years, maintaining one of the longest public careers in New Brunswick's history. Considered a Father of Confederation, his final two years were spent serving the province as Lieutenant Governor.

1843
The Miramichi's Fighting Election

A fierce rivalry between the Miramichi timber bosses, Alexander Rankin and Joseph Cunard, caused their bitter clash over timber stands in the northwest Miramichi to become a political contest to determine who would be elected to the House of Assembly. Politics and the awarding of Crown timber reserves through the Crown Lands Office were quite interconnected during the period. At election time, Cunard and Rankin would often organize their lumber workers into political armies that would swarm the polling booths.

In 1830, Rankin and Cunard occupied the two Northumberland seats in the Assembly; but in 1837 Rankin and another Cunard enemy, John Ambrose Street, were elected to represent the north side, and William Carman, Cunard's candidate from Chatham, was outnumbered in the Provincial Assembly at Fredericton.

In December, 1842, Rankin was re-elected but Cunard's candidate John Thomas Williston defeated Street in a close contest that was protested for irregularities. The Assembly unseated Williston and new elections were called with both Street and Williston conducting inflammatory campaigns. Bloodshed broke out as pitched battles raged between the two factions in Newcastle and Chatham, involving gangs of five hundred to a thousand men who were attempting to keep rival groups from the polling stations. Cunard's Chatham men were beaten back across the river and the seige of Chatham was averted only after a cannon, loaded with scrap-iron and spikes, was discharged at Rankin's forces.

Troops were dispatched to maintain order after one person was killed while John Ambrose Street declared his life to be in danger. An inquiry, organized by Lieutenant Governor Sir William Colebrooke, cited both candidates for making provocative speeches but declared Street the winner. Joseph Cunard took this defeat in stride but his immense commercial achievements had overextended his resources and by 1848 he was unable to meet his financial obligations. One of the Miramichi's most colourful figures, Cunard stood over two meters (six feet) and galloped about on an enormous horse shouting orders. An angry crowd gathered outside his stores as rumours spread of his demise. With a pistol in each boot leg, Joseph Cunard rode through the mob declaring: "Now let me see the man that will shoot Cunard."

Cunard's failure threw hundreds out of work and depressed the region for several years, as many lumbermen headed to other regions of North America in search of employment. Although the Cunard family eventually paid the debts in full, Joseph Cunard left the Miramichi in 1849 and died in 1865 in Liverpool, England.

1843
Mount Allison Established

The Mount Allison Wesleyan Academy opened in Sackville in 1843, largely through the efforts and financial support of Charles Allison. Allison and his Sackville business partner, William Crane, ran a successful import-export business until the early 1840s. Allison, an Anglican, converted to the Methodist faith and retired to concentrate on establishing an educational academy for Methodists in the Maritimes.

Methodism had taken root in the Chignecto region around the time the Yorkshire settlers led by William Black arrived. Sackville's first Methodist chapel was only the second Methodist Church established in British North America. Under the influence of revivalist Reverend Smithson and John Bass Strong, Charles Allison's religious conversion in 1836 remained the dominant theme of his later life. "The Lord hath put it into my heart to give this sum towards building a Wesleyan Academy," uttered Allison at the initial meeting to establish the academy in 1839.

Allison not only pledged £100 per year for ten years but contributed greatly to the operations of the academy which began with seven students. He assisted in the opening of a branch of the academy for women in 1854. Twenty one years later the first woman graduate from a degree-granting college in the British Empire, Grace Annie Lockhart, received her Bachelor's degree in Science and English Literature. In 1858, Mount Allison received its degree-granting status as a college from the New Brunswick Legislature and thirty-seven years later the Owens Art Gallery, the oldest university art gallery in Canada, opened at Mount Allison.

1844
The Great Military Road Project

Britain ordered the construction of a military road across the heart of New Brunswick. It would provide a short, overland route between Quebec and Halifax for efficient transportation of troops and supplies during times of war. The sea route lay exposed to enemy attack and was frozen part of the year. While a post road existed between Quebec and Rivière-du-Loup, as well as from Halifax to The Bend, no direct route existed from the upper St. John across to Westmorland County, a distance of well over two hundred miles of unbroken forest.

In 1844, Sir James Alexander, an officer from Fort Henry at Kingston, arrived at The Bend with orders to hack out the most direct line through the wilderness to Boiestown and across the Miramichi. With axes, supplies, and a crew of ten men, Alexander headed northwest away from the Petitcodiac River, along what would eventually be known as Mountain Road: "I took my point of departure for the Military Road on the 28th of May, from a hemlock tree between the Free Meeting-house and school at the Bend, and we chained the road to the Mountain Settlement."

A trail existed over Lutes Mountain but beyond Steeves Mountain, Alexander encountered dense woods, swamps and numerous delays and only crossed the Westmorland County line twenty-five days later. A line was eventually blazed to Boiestown that crossed numerous rivers including the Canaan, Salmon, and Gaspereau, and a search was undertaken for a suitable site for a bridge across the Miramichi. Exploring west of Boiestown near Miramichi Lake, Alexander and his party became turned around in thick woods and almost starved before reaching the upper reaches of the Miramichi where food was located.

Another military crew cut through from Grand Falls to link up with Alexander's line at Boiestown. By the following year when the military road was slated for construction, railway fever had cast doubts on roads and their future. All attention was focused on a grand scheme to build a thousand kilometre (six hundred mile) trunk line along the east coast of New Brunswick to link Quebec with Halifax. The projected military road was cancelled in favour of the railway link, yet the Grand Trunk Railway was an immense construction project that would take over three decades to complete and cost millions. And even today, while Mountain Road heads north away from Moncton, no highway exists straight across the centre of the province.

New Brunswick's only lazaretto was established at Tracadie in 1849. (NBPA)

1844
The Leper Colony

New Brunswick's first Health Act was adopted in 1833 when Saint John acted to prevent infectious diseases from spreading throughout the port city. Leprosy had been found in Northumberland and Gloucester Counties since the first case was reported in 1817; by 1844 northern New Brunswick became alarmed as twenty cases of leprosy were reported in the Tracadie area.

Nineteenth century attitudes towards public health were quite laissez-faire as diseases were considered a natural cycle of living, but the most repulsive of inflictions, including leprosy, were thought to have Biblical as well as medical and social implications. In April 1844, the House of Assembly established a three-man Board of Health and appropriated £1,000 to erect a leper colony on Sheldrake Island, thirteen kilometres (eight miles) below Chatham in the Miramichi River. Since medieval times, segregation has been seen as suitable for the incurable disease, and eighteen lepers, ranging in age from eight to forty-six, were admitted to the island lazaretto.

113

Viewed by the inmates as more of a prison than a hospital, a high picket fence and two armed guards kept the lepers on the six-hectare (fifteen acre) island. Discontent among the afflicted became widespread as many of the lepers escaped the island and returned to their homes. The make-shift buildings were also burned, no doubt by the inmates themselves. Finally the Board of Health confirmed that they could not locate and confine all lepers and in 1849, they selected Tracadie as the site for a new lazaretto. Through the efforts of Tracadie parish priest François-Xavier Stanislas LaFrance, and the controversial French surgeon Charles-Marie LaBillois, conditions improved for the thirty-one patients who were transferred into the new Tracadie leper hospital. Tension remained, however, between the Board and the lepers over visiting privileges and their rights to remain in contact with the neighbouring community.

Finally in 1868, a landmark in the treatment of lepers was reached — seven nuns from the Religious Hospitallers of Saint Joseph in Montreal arrived in Tracadie to care for the sick. The Sisters instituted health reforms that included improved diet, hygiene, exercise and ventilation. By 1873, the agent of the infection, leprosy bacillus, was discovered and much became known about the dreaded disease. Six years later, the federal government took over financial responsibility for the lazaretto and conditions improved further.

Unlike penitentiaries, or orphanages and lunatic asylums, the lazaretto lacked basic health and medical requirements because people saw the lepers as social outcasts and refused to come into contact with them. Once the seven Sisters of Saint Joseph arrived and were willing to assist the victims of leprosy, the Tracadie leper colony quickly improved the treatment of its inmates.

1844
Perley's Indian Report

After the establishment of New Brunswick in 1784, the colonial government had little contact with the Aboriginal population and no policy for contact. Famine, disease, and population decline threatened the Aboriginal communities which had seen the boundaries of their land grants shrink because of white squatters. By 1840, the situation on the reserves was so desperate that the Colonial Office instructed Lieutenant Governor William Colebrooke to try and improve the lives of the Maliseet and Mi'kmaq.

Moses Perley was chosen to report on Indian affairs and became one of the few whites in nineteenth century New Brunswick whose interest in

114

Aboriginal affairs was not mistrusted but welcomed. As a young boy, Perley hunted and fished with Maliseet along the St. John River and developed a strong interest in their traditional skills and way of life. A tragic accident occurred in 1822 when Perley killed a Maliseet while target shooting. Considered an unfortunate accident by a Saint John court, Perley was fined £10 but never forgot the incident and attempted to advance Maliseet causes his entire life. A lawyer and businessman, Moses Perley was appointed Commissioner of Indian Affairs in 1841 with instructions to visit all Aboriginal settlements and report on their conditions and problems.

In his travels, Perley was shocked to find white squatters living openly on Aboriginal land, cutting timber and harvesting resources while infectious disease and dysentery threatened the indigenous population. White encroachment on reserves had seriously reduced the amount of reserve land, as well as the ability of the communities to sustain themselves. "The Indians of this Province" wrote Perley in his report to Colebrooke, "are among us, yet not of us; and it seems neither wise nor just to allow in our midst another race, to remain permanently inferior."

Named "Wunjeet Sagamore," Perley was declared a chief of both the Maliseet and Mi'kmaq for his on-site defense of their territory. He recommended that Aboriginal land be permanently held as reserves in trust for the people, who would be encouraged to form more centralized villages where education and medicine could be available. While not in favour of Aboriginal land sales, Perley recommended that any unneeded Aboriginal land that was sold should produce funds that benefit the community. While his report served as the basis for the New Brunswick Indian Act of 1844, Perley became unhappy with government policy since it allowed for the sale of Aboriginal land but did nothing to help the Aboriginal population or to check white encroachment. Without a special fund for Aboriginal affairs, Perley felt that little could be done to benefit the community. Substantial land sales did occur with little benefit to the Aboriginals, and by the 1900s, less than one-third of the original grants or about 17,600 hectares (42,000 acres), remained to form New Brunswick's twenty-six Indian reserves.

While still employed by the provincial government, Perley quarrelled with Lieutenant Governor Edmund Walker Head in 1848 and was dismissed for exceeding his authority. Commissioned to report on the province's fishery, as well as to serve as an immigration agent, Moses Perley remained an energetic supporter of the province abroad but his interest in the welfare of the Maliseet and Mi'kmaq remained with him his entire life. Perley's well meaning and insightful report into the desperate plight of these communities did not result in much enlightened government action, yet by drawing attention to the mistreatment and neglect, he did encourage whites to recognize the tragedy of the deplorable living conditions on the Maliseet and Mi'kmaq reserves.

While his accomplishments in improving the Aboriginals' lives were actually quite meagre, his special friendship with the Tobique Maliseet resulted in the adoption of his name by a Maliseet family. Perley's name is still associated with a number of upper St. John River Maliseet businesses. He died at age fifty-eight off the coast of Labrador while conducting a fishery inspection.

1845
The Celestial City

Fredericton's elevation to city status was due to an ecclesiastical need. Prior to 1845, all Episcopal churches in New Brunswick were part of the diocese of Nova Scotia with bishops rarely setting foot in New Brunswick. In order to create a new bishopric based in Fredericton, ancient ecclesiastic law required that the centre of the see be a city, yet Fredericton's population of four thousand was much less than the ten thousand citizens necessary for city status.

Nonetheless, Queen Victoria, on behalf of the Church of England, issued letters proclaiming that the town "henceforth be a city and be called the City of Fredericton." The city of Saint John was disappointed that they were overlooked as the provincial seat of the new diocese, and also that a beautiful new cathedral would be built at the provincial capital. Rivalry for dominance between Saint John, the commercial capital, and Fredericton, the political capital, was intense during the 1840s. Fredericton's tightly knit group of influential citizens were crucial to the city being chosen the diocese capital of New Brunswick.

Bishop John Medley arrived by steamboat on June 10 1845, and immediately began planning the construction of Christ Church Cathedral, which he copied from the architectural plans of St. Mary's Church in Snettisham, Norfolk. One of the finest examples of decorated Gothic architecture in North America, Christ Church took seven years to complete and featured exquisite stained glass art, and a magnificent spire that still is central to Fredericton's skyline. Characterized as the first new cathedral foundation on English soil since the Norman Conquest, Christ Church's location near The Green is often considered one of the city's most magnificent assets.

Fredericton became officially incorporated as a city in 1848 and despite its small size, its triumph as the Cathedral City firmly established the capital as the undisputed political centre of New Brunswick.

1845
The Early Steamboats

The first steamboat on the St. John River was the *General Smyth,* with a square stern, one mast and lug sail, complete with a side paddle wheel and sweep steer. The twenty horse-power engine, imported from Scotland, was fine for the initial bi-weekly service between Saint John and Fredericton where speed never exceeded eleven kilometres (seven miles) per hour. *General Smyth* was decommissioned in 1824. The next year, a new boat, the *Saint George,* under the same captain, Loyalist James Segee, began her maiden voyage to Fredericton and remained on the river for the next ten years.

Inventor Robert Foulis installed the fittings and engines of the *Saint George* and a larger steamboat *John Ward* at Market Slip. But despite a new circular wheelhouse and a more powerful sixty horse-power engine, the *John Ward* and later conventional steamboats were unable to run efficiently above Fredericton. The shallow flats made the trip to Woodstock and Grand Falls next to impossible, especially to navigate through the Meductic Falls. The first steamer reached Woodstock in 1837, assisted by horses, but the voyage did not result in a regular service because of water levels and insufficient steam power.

The *Reindeer,* launched in 1845, revolutionized steamboat service on the St. John, by establishing record runs to Saint John and allowing passenger service to run upriver to Grand Falls. Built and designed by another New Brunswick inventor, Benjamin F. Tibbets, the genius of the *Reindeer* was not in its design but its engine — the first compound marine steam engine.

Tibbets' invention was simply a device that was able to harness the new energy, steam, in an engine — first in a high pressure cylinder, and then again at a lower pressure. Tibbets had built the new steamer at the mouth of the Nashwaak River with assistance from Fredericton businessman Thomas Pickard. Its record run of just over six hours to Saint John was not broken for some time. A watchmaker by trade, Benjamin Tibbets' invention was of international significance to the development of steampowered engines for marine transportation. Tibbets built a second steamboat but, despite his genius, was not successful in business and died at an early age of tuberculosis.

1846
The Steeves' Dynasty

When Albert County was created in 1846, a Hillsborough lumber merchant William Henry Steeves, was elected one of the county's first two Assembly representatives. A descendant of Heinrich and Rachel Stief, who emigrated to New Brunswick in 1766 and changed their name to Steeves, William Henry aligned himself with the reform camp in provincial politics and was appointed to the Legislative Council in 1851.

Participating in the Smasher administration under Charles Fisher in 1854, Steeves became chief commissioner of the Department of Public Works. Having moved most of his business interests to Saint John, Steeves became involved in the New Brunswick lobby for aid to construct a railroad to central Canada. An advocate of Confederation, he supported Leonard Tilley at both the Charlottetown and Quebec Conferences, and was one of the original members of the Canadian Senate in 1867.

As one of New Brunswick's eight Fathers of Confederation, William Henry Steeves is best known for his work in convincing New Brunswickers to join Confederation. The local heritage association now operates a museum in his honour at his birthplace in Hillsborough.

1847
The Good Samaritan

The Miramichi was second only to Saint John in receiving Europe's unwanted and sickly immigrants during the 1840s. Facilities for receiving these poor and often diseased passengers were often less than adequate. The 1847 Irish famine caused a surge of immigrants to arrive and fear of typhus and cholera was so strong that most New Brunswickers, including many doctors, were unwilling to allow the immigrant ships to dock and discharge their passengers.

The immigrant ship *Looshtauk* left Dublin via Liverpool for Quebec on April 17, 1847. Within days typhus spread throughout the ship, killing more than one hundred passengers. Turned away at Sydney, the *Looshtauk* under Captain Thain was allowed to proceed to Middle Island in the mouth of the Miramichi River, where a make-shift quarantine station had been previously established. But authorities were unprepared and poorly equipped to deal with such an infectious situation, where both crew and passengers were too weak to even bury their own dead.

Finally, an Irish physician, Dr. John Vondy, who had opened a medical practice in Chatham the same year, volunteered to take charge of the

Looshtauk passengers. Despite poor shelter, few beds and little food, Dr. Vondy discharged the remaining 290 immigrants into quarantine on Middle Island, where he tried to administer to the sick and dying. With most locals terrified of the infectious disease, Vondy worked with only one non-medical assistant and without adequate supplies in an impossible situation of mass illness and death.

But the inevitable occurred on July 6 when the Good Samaritan died, despite being nursed on the island by his sister. Much praise and published tributes were heaped on the Irish doctor who gave his life attempting to help the typhus victims. Criticism was levelled at the local quarantine committee for not providing more assistance to the Middle Island immigrants; however, by the end of the summer, all remaining passengers had been discharged from the quarantine island and many remained in New Brunswick. Dr. Vondy's body was taken from the island in a lead coffin and buried in St. Paul's Church cemetery near Chatham, where a monument to his relief efforts was erected by public subscription.

1847
The Quarantine Island

Besides the site of New Brunswick's first lighthouse and the world's first steam fog horn, Partridge Island in Saint John harbour became one of the largest quarantine stations in North America during the Irish potato famine. The island's quarantine role had been established when Saint John was incorporated in 1785, and the island had known epidemics since the early 1800s when immigrant ships began arriving at Saint John. Cholera had broken out on many incoming ships during the 1830s, and Partridge Island had been used as a graveyard for the victims.

Hospitals had been constructed at the quarantine station to help separate the diseased immigrants but nothing prepared the small ten hectare (twenty-four acre) island for the massive invasion of starving Irish immigrants fleeing the Irish potato famine of the late 1840s. In the worst year, 1847, the Great Famine brought almost sixteen thousand refugees to Saint John, where an estimated two thousand victims died.

Dr. James Patrick Collins, a young Saint John doctor, began his practise in early 1847. He agreed to assist Dr. George Harding and his brother on Partridge Island during a typhus epidemic in May of that year. With almost 2,500 immigrants in quarantine, many in tents and others still on vessels in the harbour, the disease and its helpless victims overwhelmed the three doctors. Determined to help his countrymen, Dr. Collins continued to combat the dreaded fever but by early summer Collins and William

Harding had contacted the disease. Both Harding brothers survived but the twenty-three year old James Collins died and was buried in a lead coffin, after one of Saint John's largest funeral processions.

To acknowledge James Collins's sacrifice and short medical career, the provincial Legislature awarded his widow financial support until 1855. Since the majority of its 1847 victims were Irish, a Celtic Cross was erected on the island in 1927 and for its role as a quarantine station Partridge Island was designated a National Historic Site in 1974.

1847
The Woodstock Riot

Prior to 1840, Irish Catholic immigration to New Brunswick was largely confined to the ports of Saint John and the Miramichi. But a significant rise in the number of Irish Catholics entering the province during the early 1840s led to dramatic increases in their population in the interior settlements, especially Fredericton and Woodstock. This explosive influx of destitute Catholics escaping poverty and famine, together with a downturn in the province's lumber trade, set the stage for violent confrontations between these new citizens and the existing Protestant workers, farmers, and tradesmen of New Brunswick, who felt threatened by this turn of events.

The Protestant reaction to the new immigrants involved the expansion of the Orange Order. Established in 1795 in Ireland, the Orange Order pledged to maintain the Protestant supremacy in the British Isles and colonies. With secret traditions borrowed from fraternities, the ultra-Protestant order celebrated its xenophobia with paramilitary marches, especially during its most important annual event, the Glorious Twelveth. July 12, 1690, marked the defeat of the Catholic King James II at the Battle of the Boyne by William, Prince of Orange. By 1844, twenty-seven Orange lodges had been established in New Brunswick and two years later, Woodstock's first lodge, No. 38, was started with 110 members led by lumber baron and provincial legislator, Charles Connell.

On July 12, 1847, with tensions already high between the religious groups, several hundred heavily armed Orangemen marched in procession from Woodstock to the Jacksontown Baptist Church. Armed Catholics waited for the returning Orangemen on a hillside near the outskirts of Woodstock, while a British garrison of sixteen men intercepted the Orange procession and convinced the Protestants to temporally store their weapons in a trailing wagon. But both groups defied the law and refused to disband. Chaos broke out as the Orange and Green met. Later eyewitnesses,

120

who were sympathetic to the Orange Order, claimed the Catholics opened fire first. With superior weapons, the Orangemen quickly overpowered the Catholics, killing as many as ten Irishmen. Many of the fleeing Catholics were captured by the British garrison and other Woodstock citizens and held for trial.

With the local magistrates all Orangemen, or sympathetic to their cause, and the entire Woodstock establishment hostile to the Catholics, it is not surprising that only Irish rioters were tried and convicted in the Old Carleton County Court House at Upper Woodstock. Irish Catholics were not allowed to stand as jurors, and many of the convicted Catholics lost property and suffered discrimination. The massive religious battle at Woodstock resulted in Catholic deaths, Catholic arrests, and Catholic convictions. The Orange Order maintained Protestant domination in Carleton County and within a year twelve Orange lodges were in the county with more than 1,200 members.

On the same day, similar clashes occurred in Fredericton and Saint John but not on the same scale as Woodstock. The historic site of the violent battle on the edge of Woodstock became the victory site of a new Orange lodge that was dedicated in October, 1847.

1848
Responsible Government

After twelve years of intense agitation for political reform in New Brunswick, the Whigs came to power in Britain and Responsible Government came to the province. Two York County reformers, Lemuel Allan Wilmot and Charles Fisher played critical roles in pushing for the supremacy of the elected Assembly over the appointed Executive Council. Wilmot's 1836 voyage to London, to convince Lord Glenelg to surrender the Crown lands to the elected Assembly, resulted in the Colonial Secretary's decree that the Executive Council must be reassembled "to ensure the presence in the Council of Gentlemen representing all the various interests which exist in the Province." The old alliance between the colonial governor and the Family Compact of old Loyalist families appointed to the Council was now under attack. When Lieutenant Governor Archibald Campbell resisted Glenelg's move to open up the Council, he was replaced by Sir John Harvey.

Beginning in the late 1830s, Lemuel Allan Wilmot and especially the clever Charles Fisher fought the Council from the floor of the Legislative Assembly, aided by a loose alliance of Assemblymen. The House of Assembly was not formally allied into partisan groups, since political parties were still considered a strange British invention. Wilmot displayed great skills in speech-making, while Fisher was the undisputed constitutional expert who had adopted the main points of the Durham Report and its demand for full, Responsible Government in British North America.

Under a new provincial governor, Sir William Colebrooke, an all-factions Executive Council was appointed as a compromise solution in 1843, but Colebrooke's appointment of his son-in-law to the post of Provincial Secretary outraged the elected Assemblymen. Cries for change in the political system became even more pronounced. Responsible Government finally arrived in New Brunswick in 1848 with a new Lieutenant Governor, Sir Edmund Walker Head. His instructions from London were clear: to follow Earl Grey's dispatches to other colonial administrators in British North America that required all governing councils to be composed of "men holding seats in one or other House."

Sir Edmund Walker Head proposed a coalition of Assemblymen to form the Council. Amid cries of abandoning their principles, Wilmot and Fisher joined a number of their old political enemies and formed the first Executive Council composed entirely of elected members. Wilmot was appointed Attorney General but the coalition system of government proved unworkable, and in 1854 Charles Fisher formed the first government composed of a single political party.

Responsible Government did not come to New Brunswick without a price. British free traders cut the province loose from its exclusive access to Great Britain's markets, and the province was forced to seek markets in the United States and the Canadas. This break up of the old imperial system of protective tariff duties forced the province to become more self-reliant, increase its North American trade and, for the first time, seriously consider the idea of Confederation.

1849
First Female Educator

Women had been officially disenfranchised in 1843 by a provincial statue and attitudes towards any advancement for women were typically those of a patriarchal society. Even a role for women in the province's neglected education system was denied. Men alone were allowed to teach.

Martha Lewis, born at Lewisville near The Bend in 1831, was raised by her prominent Loyalist grandfather, Ichabod Lewis. Privately educated in Saint John, she tutored male students who attended the city's Normal School, which trained the province's teachers. Determined to attend the school herself, Lewis applied and was refused admission in 1849.

Edmund Head, an enlightened Lieutenant Governor and keenly interested in advancing the poor state of provincial education, argued her case before the Executive Council. The Council agreed with Head and passed an Order-in-Council allowing her admission to the school. Both the Council and the headmaster, Edmund Hillyer Duval, feared the community's reaction to a female student and imposed a most bizarre set of restrictions on her attendance. Ordered to appear ten minutes prior to class, Martha Lewis had to sit in the back, unable to speak and always remain covered in a veil. She was also made to leave early and ordered to avoid any contact with her male classmates.

After the historic first semester passed without incident, a second woman was allowed to attend and Lewis' pioneering efforts resulted in a sharp increase in female students and teachers. By 1852 over 50 per cent of the Saint John Normal School students were women and Lewis herself began teaching in 1850 in a parish outside Saint John. Lewis remained a pioneer educator and her daughter, Mabel Peters, became active in the women's suffrage movement in the early 1900s. But female teachers in New Brunswick still faced considerable prejudice.

The Provincial Schools Act of 1852 distinguished between men and women teachers in awarding salary grants, with woman receiving between £4 to £10 less than men, depending on their teaching certificates. But the most difficult condition imposed on female teachers in 1852 was the restriction of allowing only three women teachers per parish to be paid. Susannah Rodgers, a teacher in the Coverdale parish of Albert County, was out of luck when she attempted to receive payment for her teaching. As the fourth female teacher hired by the parish, she was refused her teaching grant from the Provincial Assembly. Not until 1920 did women teachers in New Brunswick receive equal pay with men.

1849
The Orange & Green Confrontation

New Brunswick's largest and most violent ethnic clash during the nineteenth century occurred in Saint John on July 12, 1849, the anniversary of the Orangeman's Glorious Twelveth. This date in 1690 became symbolic to the Order of the Orange after the Protestant Prince of Orange defeated the Catholic King at the Battle of the Boyne in Ireland. The Orange Order developed in New Brunswick as a Protestant response to Irish Catholic immigration, and by the 1840s, major clashes were occurring between the Protestant and Catholic population over jobs, housing, property, and other economic matters.

123

Religious fighting and rioting had occurred in Saint John in 1837, 1842, 1845, and again in 1847, but on the morning of July 12, 1849, an armed procession of Orangemen marched through the Catholic conclave of York Point, near present day Market Square, shouting anti-Catholic slogans. Accompanied by a band and colourful banners, one of the leaders of the Orangemen rode at the front on a white horse to represent their victorious William, Prince of Orange. Irish Catholics clashed with the marchers at a site where Catholics had erected a green arch to force the Protestants "under the Green," thereby symbolizing a Protestant defeat.

The Protestant marchers continued to Indiantown, where their numbers increased to six hundred, and headed back to York Point. Attempting to remove the Catholic arch, Saint John mayor Robert Wilmot was injured by Catholic defenders, and Wilmot searched in vain for city policemen who were suspected of having joined the Protestant march. A British regiment of sixty men was called out but they established themselves on the other side of the impeding confrontation at Market Square. Both sides refused to disband and the York Point clash involved more than a thousand people, resulting in at least twelve deaths and many injuries. The British garrison later sealed off York Point but violence did not spread, since the clash was essentially Irish Catholics defending their home turf from invading mobs.

While the subsequent coroner's inquests and magistrates' examination of the Orange and Green riot refused to lay blame on the Orangemen's vigilantism, for the first time riot participants from both sides were prosecuted on the insistence of Lieutenant Governor Edmund Head. But the Saint John grand jury was composed of Protestants, so the Catholics that were charged ended up being found guilty while the Orangemen were freed. However, the 1849 riot marked the end of large scale violence in Saint John because, for the first time, the investigation cited the armed procession of the Orange Order through Catholic quarters as contributing to the riot.

Orange marches were scaled back over the next twenty-five years, to avoid the negative effect that violence had on the Orange Order. The Order finally became respectable in 1875 when its incorporation was passed in the Legislature, yet the renewed processions produced none of the clashes that characterized the violent decade of the 1840s. Irish immigration continued to increase and soon the Irish became the largest ethnic group in Saint John, yet the Order of the Orange remained an influential force in New Brunswick life well into the twentieth century.

1850
Shipbuilding: The Golden Age

Almost six thousand wooden vessels were built in New Brunswick's shipyards during the nineteenth century. Shipbuilding became the province's first manufacturing industry, employing many New Brunswickers and using the most widely available local resource, timber.

Ships had been constructed at Saint John prior to the arrival of the Loyalists and the seaport remained the shipbuilding capital of the Maritimes, building and registering more ships than any other British North American port, with the possible exception of Quebec. The first major increase in shipbuilding began in the 1820s when British timber demands exceeded its shipping capacity. Timber merchants began building ships loaded with timber and cut lumber that they sold to British merchants, who often filled the vessel with immigrants and sent it back to the Maritimes pocketing a tidy profit.

British and American ships were usually made of oak and other hardwoods, but New Brunswick shipwrights used softwoods, especially tamarack, which was also known as hackmatack and was extremely buoyant for carrying heavy cargo. Local black birch was often used for the keel and floor timbers, with white pine for finishing, while black spruce was the choice for yards and top-masts. Once tamarack became scarce, shipyards turned to spruce and occasionally local oak, but salting and pickling the timbers to prevent dry rot often became necessary.

The early ocean-going vessels were around three hundred tons but became much larger as Pacific voyages to Australia, California, and other faraway destinations became regular ports of call. William and Richard Wright's shipyard at Saint John built the two largest ships in the mid-1850s. The full-rigged *White Star* weighed 2,339 tons while the *Morning Light* was 2,377 tons. *Morning Light* remained on the Saint John ship registry until Confederation when it was transferred to Liverpool, and finally, sailing under a German flag, New Brunswick's largest ship went down off the New Jersey coast in 1889.

However the most famous vessel to come out of New Brunswick's shipyards was the clipper ship *Marco Polo*. Built in 1851 by James Smith at Saint John's Courtenay Bay, the *Marco Polo* was described as a large and elegant ship at 1,625 tons. She earned the title the fastest ship in the world by completing the voyage from Liverpool to Australia and back in under six months. Quite remarkable for the period, the *Marco Polo* beat the steamer *Australia* by a week on the journey to Sydney, and averaged more than 576 kilometres (360 miles) a day, for several consecutive days on the return trip.

With gold fever in full swing in Australia, the *Marco Polo*'s notorious captain "Bully" Forbes had his crew of sixty men arrested on trumped-up charges in Sydney to prevent their desertion to the gold fields. When the ship was loaded for the return trip, the crew was released to the captain's custody, and the *Marco Polo* immediately set sail. While the clipper remained in the Australia trade for some time, it ran ashore in 1883 and broke up off Cavendish, Prince Edward Island.

1851
Grand Manan and The Fisheries Act

During the early nineteenth century, the New Brunswick fishery had some general laws but enforcement was the responsibility of the counties and their ineffectual Sessions Courts. By 1850, the inland fishery had been over-exploited while the inshore and offshore island fishery was finally beginning to be reclaimed from American fishermen.

Confirmed as British territory in 1817, Grand Manan Island was one of the most lucrative fish grounds along the east coast, with substantial quantities of lobster, hake, cod, pollock, and especially herring. By 1850, the island population of more than a thousand was entirely engaged in the fishery with a reported 120 vessels fishing constantly at Southern Head, the major spawning grounds for herring in the Bay of Fundy. As today, the unrestricted and intense fishing threatened the species, and with recommendations from naturalist Moses Henry Perley, who had conducted New Brunswick's first comprehensive fishery study in 1850, a Fisheries Act was passed.

By restricting herring fishing for three months each year along the spawning grounds, the 1851 Fisheries Act saved the infant Passamaquoddy Bay herring industry and established its long term viability. By 1884, the island's prosperity peaked as it became the world's major supplier of smoked herring. A million boxes of processed herring, weighing more than twenty thousand tons, were exported annually, mainly to the United States and the West Indies. Used to stimulate beer consumption with its salty or smoked flavour, the smoked herring industry had, at one time, over thirty operations around the island. It became concentrated at Seal Cove, where herring would be strung on sticks and loaded into smoke houses. A smoke tender would then cure the herring into hard-cured "bloaters" or mild cured "kippers."

Besides traditional fishing nets, herring were also taken by the famous weirs, which trapped the fish by means of a fence that forced the herring into the weir and held them captive. The first deepwater weir, named The Admiral, was built near Seal Cove which extended the range of

126

the weir out beyond the low tide mark. Weirs soon became so numerous that sites were named and registered, with restrictions established including distances between each weir.

While not the largest community in Grand Manan, Seal Cove is perhaps its most picturesque and, with its cluster of smoke houses, is certainly the island's most unusual looking village. And more than any other community, Seal Cove played a critical role in the nineteenth century Atlantic herring fishery. While shipbuilding and cannery operations played major roles in Seal Cove's past, the smoked herring business established the community's reputation and unique appeal.

1851
Madawaska Boundary Settled

Acadians fleeing the Loyalist invasion of the lower St. John River valley were the first white settlers to the Madawaska region in 1785. Governor Carleton attempted to administer the settlement that developed on intervale land around the junction of the Madawaska and St. John Rivers, granting land and organizing a militia. But French Canadian settlers also began to populate the region and three governments — New Brunswick, Quebec, and Maine — all claimed the territory. Beginning at Grand Falls, Quebec claimed the domain north of the St. John, and even prior to 1800 New Brunswick had arrested a Quebec lieutenant for attempting to execute a Quebec court order in Madawaska.

By 1820, approximately one thousand French residents of Madawaska were in the middle of a three-way quarrel that threatened to split the region and its rich timber reserves. New Brunswick chopped Carleton County out of York County in 1832, and the next year created Madawaska as a civil parish but by 1842, the territory south of the St. John River was awarded to Maine, and the single cultural community became politically separated. But a further separation seemed inevitable when Quebec and New Brunswick were unable to agree on the provincial boundary. New Brunswick separated Victoria County out of Carleton and defined its new county as the entire disputed region, but the Colonial Office disallowed the act, although the county was later allowed to exist with a more restricted boundary.

Finally a commission was set up in 1846 to arbitrate the quarrel. The panel recommended that the area in question, between the St. John and the hills south of the St. Lawrence, be divided approximately in half — with Quebec receiving 5,439 square kilometres (2,100 square miles) and New Brunswick 5,957 kilometres (2,300 miles). Quebec rejected the recommendation but a final decision was made in 1851 that approximated the original division. Quebec retained its claim over the Lake Temiscouata region but the New Brunswick portion of Madawaska was fixed nineteen kilometres (twelve miles) above the St. John River.

The bitter controversy affected relations between the two provinces for many years, but the selfish actions of the three governments left the people of Madawaska divided into three fragmented parts. Their ancestors had only wanted to farm the fertile region in peace but by the 1850s, the Madawaska colony had been dissected into three political jurisdictions. The New Brunswick territory became the County of Madawaska in 1873 and by 1900, only about 50 per cent of the entire population of the imaginary Republic of Madawaska was living within New Brunswick's boundaries.

At Saint-Basile the first French settlements were established and also in 1792, the first religious parish in the region. Called the cradle of Madawaska (Berceau du Madawaska), Saint-Basile's historic cemetery on Principal Street still reveals crosses with the names of the first Acadian families.

1851
The Railway Era

In *Railways of New Brunswick*, railway historian David Nason suggests that New Brunswick's early experiments with building rail lines were flawed because they were constructed in the wrong direction.

The first locomotive appeared in Britain in 1825 and four years later in the United States. With Saint John beginning to overshadow St. Andrews in growth, the idea of New Brunswick's first railway from Passamaquoddy Bay to the St. Lawrence appealed to the citizens of Charlotte County. In 1835, the St. Andrews and Quebec Railway Company was formed but its survey line was laid out through the disputed northern Maine territory. No investors were willing to fund a railway through lands that were part of an international controversy. After years of financial disputes and half-starts, the line was re-surveyed to Richmond Corner near Woodstock in 1850 and serious construction began, but financial problems appeared again, including a labourers' strike for more wages.

By 1853 the St. Andrews Railway had barely forty kilometres (twenty-five miles) cleared, with its locomotive only able to run to the town's outskirts at Chamcook; yet an American competitive line, the St. Lawrence and Atlantic Railway had finished its tracks, and was running freight and passengers from Portland, Maine, to Montreal. New Brunswick's first railway sputtered along and gradually made its way the full 112 kilometres (seventy miles) to Richmond Corner in 1862, but its route was indeed flawed since it ended in an empty field. Still a few miles from the St. John River and the town of Woodstock, the little railway was unable to recoup its investment since it was still hundreds of miles from the St. Lawrence or any major population centre.

The merchants of Saint John were equally determined to construct a railway to transport their imported cargo to inland markets. Yet British colonial interests and the politicians in Halifax were able to win the day. Instead of building north along the St. John River valley or south to New England, the European and North American Railway completed its Saint John to Shediac line in 1860 at an empty beach, overlooking the Northumberland Strait. At fifteen to twenty thousand dollars per mile, the Saint John businessmen were unable to finance such an investment without British help, which forced market considerations aside in favour of the more politically acceptable eastern route to connect with the yet-to-be-built Intercolonial Railway, between Halifax and the St. Lawrence.

Eventually railways were built in every conceivable direction throughout New Brunswick and into Quebec and Maine, but southern New Brunswick, and especially Saint John, did not receive the expected growth from the early railway lines. The first steam railways were not built to carry exports outside New Brunswick but instead, were constructed between sparsely populated locations within the province.

1853
The Milltown Timber Baron

One of New Brunswick's most successful nineteenth century entrepreneurs was James Murchie, a Charlotte County timber baron who rose from humble origins to control much of the lumber trade along the St. Croix River. Born in 1813 at St. Stephen, Murchie had few opportunities to acquire working capital and began his career cutting timber on his own land tracts but soon improved his fortunes by acquiring significant crown timber leases.

With capital of $20,000, James Murchie moved into the lumber business at Milltown in 1853, acquiring a sawmill and participating in the controversial truck system — where lumber employees were forced to work dangerously long hours to receive wages in credits against purchases. Of course, these purchases were only available at the timber bosses high-priced stores. A bitter strike against the timber barons broke out in Milltown over the truck system, low wages, and the mill owners insistence that during the production season employees work seven days a week. A union, the Work-ingmen's Society, had been established to protest the exploitation, and the town divided along economic and religious lines as the Wesleyan Methodist Church sided with the men in their demand for a non-working Sabbath.

The Milltown Methodist Church was burned during the conflict, and the timber barons quickly organized a Congregationalist Church, largely destroying the Wesleyan prominence at Milltown. A Methodist while at St. Stephen, James Murchie was foremost a man of self-interest and quickly became part of the Congregationalist community, expanding his milling operations and accepting appointments as a magistrate and militia captain of Charlotte County. Diversifying into shipbuilding, banking, insurance and railways, Murchie became one of the leading businessmen of Charlotte County.

Despite suffering negative publicity with his brother-in-law, John McAdam, over a Crown land scam involving fraud, James Murchie and his sons remained one of the leading corporate families of the St. Croix business community. Murchie became involved in provincial politics in the 1870s and survived the 1874 lumber collapse by going into manufacturing, including helping establish the second largest cotton mill in Canada, the St. Croix Cotton Manufacturing Company.

James Murchie died in 1900 at his estate in Milltown, with his lumbering operations the last major lumber business along the St. Croix River. His daughter, Emma Eaton, gave his handsome house on Milltown Boulevard to the town in 1928 and it was used as the Town Hall for forty-five years, before becoming home to the Charlotte County Museum.

1854
Reciprocity Begins

A mood of doom settled over New Brunswick in 1849 when the Whig government in London repealed the Navigation Act, effectively allowing any trading vessel to enter British ports. The abdication of Empire, as it appeared in New Brunswick, meant that the province's protected status as a colonial trading partner was no more. Since the Napoleonic conflict, tariffs had maintained New Brunswick's preferred position in shipping lumber, fish, and other goods to British markets.

Now that free trade had been forced upon them, New Brunswick's merchants began looking to the large American market where a 20 per cent lumber duty had excluded their exports. At first, lumber interests in Maine and other protectionists were able to hold off the appeal of reciprocity in the United States but American timber stands were mostly exhausted, and access to the Maritime inshore fishery had great appeal to New England

By 1851 there was still no reciprocal agreement with the Americans. Demand for lumber increased and New Brunswick merchants found they were able to compete with American shipping in the north Atlantic. The new prosperity cautioned British negotiators from giving in to American demands for trade concessions, and after New England fisherman began to be chased away from the Maritime coastline, Americans displayed a new interest in conducting a trade agreement.

Finally in 1854, British authorities concluded a treaty on behalf of the British North American colonies that allowed their natural resources including wood, fish, and farm products, free entry into the American states in exchange for American access to the coastal fishery of the colonial provinces. An export tax on Maine lumber on the St. John River was abandoned but American navigation rights on the river was denied, and New Brunswick's demand to be allowed into the American coastal shipping trade was also rejected.

Despite being excluded from the lucrative American coastal trade, New Brunswick's exports into the US fuelled a prosperity that for the next eleven years could well be described as New Brunswick's "Golden Age." As manufacturing industries such as woodworking, cotton mills, tanneries, canneries, and iron foundries began to appear larger ships were built to haul these exports to market. When reciprocity was ended in 1864 by the victorious American Union, which resented British interference in their Civil War, the thriving merchants of New Brunswick were now less concerned for their survival than in 1849. Yet the ending of the Reciprocity Treaty did hasten another agreement that was not an entirely attractive package from New Brunswick's perspective: the union of British North America.

1854 – 1864
Reform and Prosperity

1854
Rise of the Smasher Party

Until 1854, New Brunswick politics were dominated by Loyalist gentlemen, whose Family Compact party was more concerned with maintaining their traditional privileges than enacting self-government. Individual reformers had always fought the Compact establishment but in the 1840s a group of middle-class politicians, clustering around the leadership of Charles Fisher, began a loose association with the goal of attaining full Responsible Government for New Brunswick.

The "Smashers," as they became known for their attacks on the Lieutenant Governor and his appointed Council, had banded together while informally meeting at their favourite Fredericton hotel. Branded the "Barker House Conspiracy," the Smashers marked the beginning of New Brunswick's party system of government and also the origins of the Liberal Party. A typical Smasher-politician was of humble birth, native-born, usually a self-made man who had acquired wealth not through inheritance but from his own hard work and commercial instincts.

In 1854, the Family Compact government was voted down in the Legislature and Charles Fisher formed the first Smasher administration — composed of radical Albert Smith and lumberman William Steeves, both from the southeastern region, prohibitionist Leonard Tilley and hot-headed William Ritchie from Saint John, Charlotte County's James Brown, and Miramichi lawyer John Mercer Johnson.

Determined to attack the remains of the imperial system, the reformers challenged the Church of England's power as well as the prominence of King's College, but blundered by also insisting on enacting prohibition. Illegal liquor proved unpopular and led to the downfall of the Smashers in 1856. Returned to power the following year, the Smasher party introduced many sweeping reforms into New Brunswick's political process, including the secret ballot and an extended voter franchise. A period of unparalleled growth and prosperity, that began to transfer New Brunswick's economy away from lumbering and shipping into manufacturing, accompanied their administration. Remaining in power until Confederation, the Smasher reformers swept away the last vestiges of non-elected privileges, and completed the transfer of power from the British Colonial Office to the Legislative Assembly.

1855
New Brunswick's First Town

The roaring 1850s were strong years for New Brunswick's economy and also the decade that the little village at the bend of the Petitcodiac River grew significantly. As Saint John became a city in the 1830s, The Bend of Petitcodiac still had less than twenty dwellings. But strategically located on the Petitcodiac River where the Westmorland Road from Nova Scotia turned towards Saint John, The Bend began to thrive with the arrival of the mail coach line in the 1840s. Next came Joseph Salter's flourishing shipyard that employed a vast number of workers and the village enjoyed a construction boom in 1853 when the European and North American Railway began its line from Shediac to Saint John.

In 1855, the Provincial Legislature granted the petition for incorporation to town status, with three wards, six councillors, and a mayor. The boundaries of the new town included the river on the south, together with Hall's Creek providing the east and north line, and present day High Street approximating the town's western line. A clerical error omitted the "k" from General Robert Monckton's name but Mayor Joseph Salter and the citizens did not complain, so it remained as Moncton, except for a brief period of thirty-six days in 1930 when the "K" was officially used by city officials.

The growing community attracted many young entrepreneurs, such as Salter, William Sumner, and Charles B. Record. Record had become part-owner of the Saint John Stage Coach Company, opened Moncton's first furniture store, and in 1857 established the Moncton Iron Foundry. His new forging enterprise quickly cast rails for the new railway and also produced agricultural implements but Charles Record would establish his foundry's solid reputation as a stove manufacturer. His fourteen models soon became famous for their quality. After experiencing financial prob-

133

lems in 1882, he re-established the business as the Record Foundry on a large five hectare (twelve acre) site below Main Street.

Yet Joseph Salter's shipbuilding industry was the backbone of the town's economy, with more than a thousand men employed in the shipyard and surrounding woods. New Brunswick's first town was initially a one-industry community, with its health tied to the prospects of Joseph Salter. Salter served as mayor for three annual terms but his financial difficulties in the late 1850s would create havoc with the young town's municipal status.

1856
Prohibition Becomes Law

Like all frontier societies, the use of liquor in colonial New Brunswick was so widespread it was considered essential for everyday life. But concerns about crime, poverty, public drunkenness, and moral reform led people to question the use of heavy drinking, especially among the lumbering industry where each spring at break-up time, great crowds of inebriated lumbermen would descend on the river-towns and villages, creating chaos.

New Brunswick's neighbour, Maine, was also a lumbering region so it was not surprising that the temperance movement gained its first major foothold there in the early 1830s. Maine's crusade against alcohol had started as an evangelical religious movement but quickly became a powerful political movement by linking with anti-slavery forces to form the Republican Party of Maine. While a temperance society had sprung up in Saint John in 1830, the temperance movement in New Brunswick did not begin to achieve success until the 1840s when its religious leaders began operating the movement as a political organization.

Saint John druggist and future politician, Leonard Tilley became a member of the Total Abstinence Society in 1844 but the highly popular and ritualistic Sons of Temperance formed its first New Brunswick chapter in St. Stephen in 1847. The movement spread like wildfire and within six months, eight divisions were operating throughout the province in the form of a secret brotherhood with all family members involved in off-shoots such as the Daughters of Temperance and the young Cadets of Temperance.

Sir Samuel Leonard Tilley soon became the Sons of Temperance's most important advocate and in 1854, became its provincial leader and Most Worthy Patriarch. New Brunswick had strong anti-temperance forces as well, for provincial revenues were dependent on taxes on imported alcohol and liquor sales were vital to the business interests of many merchants — two hundred taverns operated in Saint John in 1852.

As a key member of the New Brunswick Legislature, Tilley was instrumental in passing a prohibition bill in 1852 but its enforcement procedure was flawed. Some taverns and breweries did close but underground drinking establishments flourished as The Bend of Petitcodiac reported an increase from three licensed sites to thirty-seven unlicensed liquor premises. Yet Maine had been effective in maintaining its prohibition law of 1851. In 1855 Tilley introduced a new prohibition act based on Maine's law, and the bill passed by a margin of twenty-one to eighteen. Maintaining prohibition in New Brunswick proved to be one of Leonard Tilley's most difficult tasks and the controversial and highly unpopular Prohibition Act led to a state of anarchy within the ranks of government.

The Legislature and the Executive Council were divided over prohibition but Lieutenant Governor Manners-Sutton opposed the bill. With the province facing a revenue loss of £25,000 from liquor taxes, and some counties in open revolt against the law, Manners-Sutton acted to repealed the new liquor law. When the Executive Council refused to grant his request, he called for new elections. Manners-Sutton had no love for his Council, so the charge of expediency was on the mark, but referring the question of prohibition to an election was also commendable since liquor continued to be sold openly throughout New Brunswick.

A bitter election followed with the outcome a disaster for the forces of temperance. Leonard Tilley was defeated and after only seven months in effect the prohibitory law was repealed. The "Rummies" had won the day while Tilley's radicals, the "Smashers," had suffered a setback. The voters of New Brunswick had firmly rejected prohibition but the temperance movement did not disappear. Drunkenness had been challenged as a social evil by the first non-ethnic mass movement in New Brunswick's history. Yet a total ban on liquor was not supported by a majority of voters, whose acceptance of rum drinking came from decades of direct experience.

1857
Collapse of the Moncton Shipyard

At age thirty-one, Joseph Salter came to The Bend from Saint John, where he and his brother ran a charter and chandlery business. Salter came to build wooden vessels since there was plenty of tamarack, black spruce, and birch, and the high tides were sufficient for launching any vessels of the period. An ambitious adventurer with plenty of sea experience, Salter knew shipbuilding and was hard-driving but well liked by his workmen. He employed many workers at his shipyard including hundreds of ship's carpen-

135

ters, blacksmiths, caulkers, and millwrights, as well as numerous men harvesting timber in the surrounding forests.

A keen negotiator, Joseph Salter granted a petition from his men for a shorter workday but insisted that the free time not be wasted in the surrounding grog shops. This date, April 11, was long celebrated as New Brunswick's first labour day. Salter also produced many innovations and improvements to shipbuilding techniques, including introducing the first steam powered mill in eastern New Brunswick. As a major shipbuilding centre, Moncton flourished for almost a decade producing twenty thousand tons of wooden ships, including many square-riggers for the overseas market.

Salter's troubles began in the midst of a prosperity that had been built on a speculative approach to shipbuilding. Instead of selling and delivering a vessel, Salter had built on the hope of selling overseas and had been surprisingly successful, due to the booming demand created by the Australian gold rush and the Crimean War. But in 1857, his agents were unable to sell a vessel on the Liverpool market. The same year a small wood-burning locomotive chugged into Moncton, perhaps a sign pointing to the town's future, but the tiny train was unable to affect the gloomy prospects of Salter's shipyard. With unsold ships in Britain, Salter was unable to pay his men and within the year was forced to declare bankruptcy.

The arrival of Moncton's first train had little immediate effect on the town's economy that had been badly damaged by Salter's failure. The town's first weekly paper, *The Westmorland Times*, also went under. Workers, unable to pay their mortgages and loans, destroyed the region's first financial institution. The Westmorland Bank of New Brunswick had opened in 1855 under local ownership with Oliver Jones as president. The bank's initial gold reserve was $30,000 but when it finally closed in 1867, its deficit was reported at $86,000. Taxes went unpaid and town services plummeted until a petition was sent to the House of Assembly in 1862, requesting permission to relinquish its town charter and revert to unincorporated status.

A difficult recession in the 1860s forced Moncton to maintain its unincorporated municipal status until 1875, when as headquarters for the Intercolonial Railway it began to again thrive. Joseph Salter remained in Moncton after his shipyard loss and attempted to regain his prominence. He became involved in oil-shale extraction in Albert County but was unable to rekindle his business acumen and moved to Cape Breton in 1870.

1858
New Brunswick's Last Duel

Gentlemen in colonial New Brunswick were very much concerned with honour. Personal honour meant that all insults must be challenged and challenges of duelling to the death were all too common. Among the most celebrated duels in the province's history was the Playhouse duel of 1800. Where the Playhouse now stands on Queen Street in Fredericton, pistol shots were fired on a cold January evening in 1800. Samuel Denny Street had challenged lawyer John Murray Bliss to a duel, based on Bliss implying that Street had lied to a jury during New Brunswick's most important slavery trial. After both shots missed, the hotheaded Street demanded to reload and have another round but Bliss apologized and they ceased the duel. The same trial so outraged slaver Stair Agnew, that he challenged Judge Allen to a duel but Allen declined his offer.

The most notorious duel in New Brunswick also involved the Street family and ended in death. In 1821, George Ludlow Wetmore, a young lawyer from a prominent Loyalist family, challenged George Frederick Street, Samuel Denny's son, outside the Fredericton courthouse. Since duelling was illegal, the two and their seconds met secretly outside Fredericton on an early October morning and discharged their pistols. Apparently Wetmore insisted on a second round and was shot to death at age twenty-six. Street and his seconds fled to Maine, and the "Hue and Cry" was issued for murder with a £30 reward for the capture of the accused. Street eventually returned and was tried for murder, while his father was indicted for tearing down the "Hue and Cry" sign.

Both accused and victim were from prominent Fredericton families and the picture presented by both the prosecuting attorney and the defense was that duelling was an unfortunate, but necessary, activity of the ruling elite. Judge Saunders acquitted Street. Duelling slowly began to lose public acceptance, yet the same George Frederick Street publicly challenged Henry George Clopper to a duel twelve years later.

The Street family seem particularly interested in duelling challenges. Another son of Samuel Denny, John Ambrose Street, struck the fiery Albert Smith during a heated exchange in the 1856 session of the House of Assembly. The remaining day was spent issuing and planning various duels and counter-duels. With the Smasher government in ascendency during the 1850s, public patience with gentlemen's honour and their fashionable privileges crumbled. The last duel was fought in 1858 in Fredericton between William Odell and a military officer, Lieutenant Jones. William Odell, the grandson of Loyalist Jonathan Odell, insisted on settling a private affair of honor and a duel ensued. No one was injured but this time the power of the church brought public scorn on the prominent judge, when Bishop John Medley excommunicated him before his parishioners in Christ Church Cathedral after Odell refused to apologize in public. Despite the scolding, Odell maintained his genteel reputation and was appointed to the Canadian Senate in 1867.

1858
Andrew Bonar Law

Britain's only Prime Minister to be born outside of the British Isles was Andrew Bonar Law of Rexton. The son of Rev. James Law, young Bonar Law at age twelve was sent to Scotland to be educated. He entered British political life to become a Minister of State during World War One. Victorious in the general election of 1922, Bonar Law was forced to resign as Prime Minister in less than a year due to ill health. He died in 1923 and was buried in Westminister Abbey.

In 1925 a memorial cairn was erected at Rexton to the memory of Canada's only British Prime Minister. Founded by shipbuilder John Jardine in 1825, the village of Rexton was called Kingston until 1901 when it was changed to avoid confusion with other locations of the same name. The house and farm of Bonar Law's boyhood overlooks the Richi-bucto River and has been preserved to depict the pioneer way of life on a nineteenth century New Brunswick farm.

1859
Steam Fog Horn Installed on Partridge Island

One of the most brilliant men to live and work in New Brunswick was artist, scientist, and civil engineer, Robert Foulis. Born in Scotland, Foulis arrived in Saint John in the early 1820s and soon was engaged in many business ventures, including starting New Brunswick's first iron foundry, installing engines in the early river steamboats, and conducting a survey of the St. John River above Fredericton for steam navigation.

Robert Foulis also lectured on chemistry and other subjects at the Saint John Mechanics Institute and established a Schools of Arts in the city. But the great invention that cemented his reputation, but not his fortune, was developed in 1853, and became fully operational six years later. Foulis' idea was a fog alarm operated by steam that automatically permitted compressed steam to escape at given intervals through a horn. When it was finally installed on Partridge Island in Saint John harbour, Foulis' alarm was the first mariners' automatic steam whistle in the world.

138

A controversial symbol of privilege during the Smasher era, the Old Arts
Building of the University of New Brunswick is the oldest university building
still in use in Canada. (NBPA)

Robert Foulis further developed his invention by establishing a coded
system of telegraphing directions to vessels. But his only patent protection
for his great invention was ensuring that the New Brunswick Legislature
recognize his efforts in 1864. Meanwhile a shrewd American patented the
concept and reaped the reward. Considered one of the most significant
navigational aids of the nineteenth century, the steam fog horn revolutionized marine transportation but its inventor died in poverty in 1866.

1859
The University of New Brunswick

Attacks on King's College became regular items of business for
Smasher politicians during the 1840s for two reasons. The public regarded
its annual £2,200 grant from public funds as payment for religious education, since King's was essentially an Anglican institution. Secondly, the eccentric and feeble principal Reverend Edwin Jacob, demanded a peculiar
classical instruction that was at best whimsical and certainly irrelevant to
the practical demands of the period. At one point only seven students were

enrolled, and in 1854 twelve students attended the college as Assembly-man Albert Smith introduced a bill to discontinue the annual grant.

The funding crisis especially concerned Lieutenant Governor Sir Edmund Head, who had attempted to advance the college by introducing the first astronomical observatory in Canada, as well as the first civil engineering course. Head convinced the Legislature to establish a commission to review the college and its standards. The Dawson Commission produced a report but no consensus, and in 1858 Mount Allison received degree-conferring status from the House of Assembly, while Orangeman Charles Connell introduced another bill to abolish all public funding to King's.

Hatred for the pompous Principal Jacob was as much the motivation for destroying King's College as was its Church of England status. Most agreed that a non-denominational provincial institution open to all students was acceptable. Connell's bill passed yet the leader of the Smasher government, Charles Fisher, was college registrar and much opposed to the bill. Together with Lieutenant Governor Manners-Sutton, Fisher acted to save the college by first appointing Charles Connell to the cabinet post of Post-master General at a salary of £600. During the next session in 1859, a bill drafted by Lemuel Allen Wilmot was introduced that transformed the college into a provincial, non-denominational university, governed by a Senate of eight laymen. Religious tests and the chair of Theology was abolished.

King's College was saved by being transformed into a public institution open to citizens of all religious persuasions. With its new president Joseph R. Hea, university courses began to reflect the educational demands of the era. Offered a pension, Principal Jacob refused to accept his fate and was finally evicted.

1860
The Face of a Cabinet Minister

By mid-century, Britain seem determined to withdraw her support from her North American colonies. Yet New Brunswickers still maintained much affection for the British crown, more so it seemed than for their own politicians.

Charles Connell was a Carleton County Orangeman, lumber merchant and politician, who served as Postmaster General in his brother-in-law's Smasher government of 1858. When Charles Fisher's administration replaced the British pounds currency with the decimal system in 1860, the Postmaster General began printing new stamps in the denominations of the new currency. A storm of protest erupted when the most popular five-cent stamp appeared imprinted with Charles Connell's face instead of Queen

Victoria's. Members of the Assembly cried foul and the political embarrassment did not go away until the stamps were withdrawn, and Connell resigned his position.

As collector's items, the rare stamps are worth a small fortune today. Charles Connell returned to politics and was re-elected in the provincial Confederation elections, and also represented Carleton County in the first Dominion Parliament. Although largely remembered for the stamp scandal, Charles Connell served Carleton County capably until his death in 1873. A typical lumber baron and politician of the era, his family home at Woodstock is now operated by the Carleton County Historical Society.

1861
Charles Fisher and the Crown Lands Scandal

Charles Fisher, a capable and talented lawyer-politician who led the fight for Responsible Government, also assisted the forces of Confederation. Fisher spent over forty years in public life and accomplished a great deal for New Brunswick but today is regarded by many as a less significant figure than his contemporaries, Samuel Leonard Tilley and Lemuel Allan Wilmot.

However, Fisher was the backbone of the reform movement that brought self-government to the province and the architect of the first non-Family Compact party that governed the province during the 1850s. Fisher's lack of recognition as New Brunswick's Joe Howe is partly due to his mild personality that tended to avoid outright confrontation and left the loud, hostile speeches to Wilmot and others. But Charles Fisher is also remembered as a corrupt politician, the one who got caught in the common nineteenth century practise of secretly acquiring public land.

About 1858 internal dissension, especially from Albert Smith and William Ritchie, seriously challenged Fisher's leadership of the Smasher Party. Several issues were at the heart of the discord including the attempt by Smith and Ritchie, supported by Leonard Tilley, to have the capital moved to Saint John. Personal antagonism between Fisher and Smith was especially bitter since the more radical Smith viewed Fisher as part of Fredericton's privileged elite.

In 1861, a campaign of insinuations began in a Saint John partisan newspaper, the *Colonial Empire*, that corruption was apparent in the Crown Lands Office. The old regulation that prevented individuals from owning more than one hundred acres for settlement purposes had never been enforced. The timber barons constantly had employees, some using fictious names, apply for timber leases to get around cutting restrictions.

141

Yet intense land speculation around the government's railway construction had forced the Crowns Lands Office to enact a regulation that restricted government officials from purchasing Crown land.

At Albert Smith's insistence, an investigative committee was formed and the public was shocked to hear that the chief clerk of the Crowns Land Office had confessed to being involved in secret purchases of more than 8,097 hectares (twenty thousand acres) in southeast New Brunswick. Fisher was implicated in the purchases and also accused of attempting a cover-up by trying to prevent the clerk from testifying. Despite the involvement of other members of the Assembly including Leonard Tilley, who at least knew of the secret affair, Charles Fisher alone took the fall for the scandal. Dumped as leader and eventually forced to resign as Attorney General by Leonard Tilley, Fisher's leadership days were over, although he retained his seat as a member for York County.

The ascendency of Tilley and Albert Smith coincided with Fisher's disgrace, but in 1864 Fisher was invited to join Tilley's pro-Confederation coalition. While Fisher was defeated in the anti-Confederation election of 1865, he did manage to contribute to New Brunswick's entry into Confederation. Left out of John A. MacDonald's first federal cabinet in favour of Tilley and Peter Mitchell, Fisher was appointed to the Supreme Court in 1868 — where he remained until his death in 1880. Chastised by the British authorities, the cloud of the 1861 land affair hung over Fisher's last days while the remaining members of the Smasher party were treated with great respect. Yet Fisher's contribution to New Brunswick's political maturity was, without doubt, the equal of anyone.

1864
Failure of Maritime Union

A union of the Maritime colonies had been discussed and promoted throughout the 1850s as a more practical merger than a confederation of the entire British North American colonies, especially since the Canadas were experiencing serious factional disputes. But Maritime Union involved real change as well as a threat to the power and pay of the assemblymen. Furthermore, a new administrative capital would most likely be situated in the Chignecto region, at the expense of the existing provincial capitals. Yet in the 1850s, Confederation and its promise of an Intercolonial Railway seemed even more remote.

New Brunswick's Lieutenant Governor Arthur Hamilton Gordon began pushing for the union as a solution to the parochial concerns of his Provincial Legislature. By 1863, with construction of the Intercolonial Railway

On board the steamer *Anna Augusta*, 1864. Leonard Tilley, William Steeves, Edward Chandler and other New Brunswick delegates leave Fredericton for the Charlottetown Conference. (NBPA)

in doubt, Gordon gained support from Leonard Tilley and Charles Tupper of Nova Scotia. Soon polite interest was expressed from Prince Edward Island, support was growing in Nova Scotia, and New Brunswick was at least not opposing the idea. Gordon and Tilley plotted a detailed picture of Maritime Union, with the first parliament to be composed of the three provincial legislatures which would decide the basis of the division of powers, while the Queen would decide the new site for the capital.

In 1864 all three provinces passed resolutions in favour of a conference to discuss the idea of a merger, yet Prince Edward Island was least in favour of the notion, while Nova Scotia seemed most willing to form a union. New Brunswick seemed only willing to listen to the merits of such a union. As no great demand existed to kick start discussions, the question of Maritime Union seemed to drift about without even an agreement for a conference site. Finally that summer, a dramatic new development occurred in the Canadas that forced Maritimers into a new dilemma.

Within eight days of John A. Macdonald and George Brown forming a grand coalition comprising the two former political enemies, the province of Canada asked to send an official delegation to the Maritime Union conference that was hastily set for Charlottetown on September 1, 1864. The conference convened with five New Brunswick delegates — Tilley, William Henry Steeves, John Grey, John Mercer Johnson, and Edward Barron Chandler. Maritime Union was quickly overshadowed by the Canadian proposal for a wider union of all British North America.

Strong pro-Confederation sentiment arose out of the Charlottetown Conference, especially from the New Brunswick delegates who saw more advantages to a Canadian proposal for union than a Maritime merger that guaranteed no such benefits. Besides the promise of an Intercolonial Railway, British assistance in forming the union, trade preferences and defense guarantees against US aggression, the Confederation proposal also called for each province to maintain their own legislatures. On the other hand, the call for Maritime Union had established the need for only one legislative centre, thereby reducing the demand for many of the very politicians who were asked to choose. The cry for Maritime Union would be heard again but the "let's go it alone" scenario was usually raised by malcontent politicians who saw the threat of Maritime Union as a way of extracting concessions from Ottawa.

1864
Father Lefebvre's College

The origins of the first French language, degree-granting institution in the Maritimes began in 1854 in the Memramcook Valley, where Father Stanislas Lafrance established a seminary. Saint-Thomas Seminary closed due to financial problems two years later, but in 1864 it re-opened as Saint Joseph's, a post-secondary college under the parish priest from Quebec, Camille Lefebvre.

Bishop Sweeney of Saint John, who wanted a college for all New Brunswick Catholics, assisted Saint Joseph's financially and initially more English-speaking Catholics graduated than Acadians. Father Lefebvre devoted his life to developing Catholic higher education in the Maritimes and his three decades at Memramcook saw great strides in Acadian higher education as well as the establishment of an Acadian national identity.

After the Common Schools Act in 1871 cut off provincial funding for religious institutions, Saint Joseph's was forced to operate without public aid. Despite the push from within the Acadian community to establish a French-language bishopric, Father Lefebvre managed to maintain good relations with both English-language bishops in New Brunswick — Bishop Sweeney at Saint John, and Bishop James Rodgers of Chatham both worked to obtain financial support the young college.

Throughout his career, Camille Lefebvre worked tirelessly for Acadians and even founded a religious facility for young Acadian women called Little Sisters of the Holy Family. But his vision of the new Acadia was a controversial one, and a vision ultimately rejected by Acadian nationalists. Lefebvre saw the struggling minority having a more viable future by joining a single French Canadian nationalism emerging out of Quebec. The young Acadian elite, largely educated at Saint Joseph's, chose to establish their own identity and symbols, distinct from Quebec. During this period, Lefebvre was often negatively portrayed as an agent of French Quebec's colonial ambitions towards Acadia.

However Lefebvre's value to the growth and survival of Acadian education has never been seriously questioned. As the cultural seat of the new Acadia, Saint Joseph's became the site of the first Acadian Congress in 1881 that defined the goals of the new Acadian nationalism. Lefebvre also established the first Acadian Museum in 1886 and his achievements at Memramcook have been recognized numerous times. The twenty-fifth anniversary of Saint Joseph's was marked with much appreciation for his work and after his death a monument to his work was erected beside the college. Monument Lefebvre became a celebration and testament to the renaissance in Acadian heritage that can trace its roots to his years at Memramcook.

1865 – 1879
The Confederation Era

1865
The Bull of Westmorland

Albert James Smith is best known for his anti-Canada stand that delayed Confederation by two years. He was also one of New Brunswick's most controversial, yet distinguished leaders. A brilliant lawyer both for his ability in front of a jury and his expertise in marine law, Smith had articled under Edward Chandler at Dorchester, and was well aware of the intimate connection between politics and a lucrative legal career.

In 1852, Smith burst on to the New Brunswick political scene representing Westmorland County but attacking his mentor Edward Chandler and the Family Compact system of government. Albert Smith quickly became known as a reformer, and the toughest Smasher, opposing all forms of imperial order and privileges, including the powers of the Lieutenant Governor, public money for King's College, and many other colonial traditions. His dark temper and sharp tongue made many enemies and contributed to at least two physical fights within the House of Assembly. He championed moving the capital to Saint John, a favourite issue. A few old Loyalist families from Fredericton the "oligarchy of privilege," became his special target, but by 1854 Smith, as part of the Smasher administration, experienced the pressures of governing a province with little direct knowledge of Responsible Government.

Smith retained his seat during the Smasher defeat in 1856 over Prohibition and earned the nickname "Bully Albert Smith," by his relentless attacks on the interim government. Returned to power in 1857, Smith developed a bitter feud with his Liberal leader, Charles Fisher. Despite travelling to London with Fisher to lobby Britain for railway funds, Smith

146

maintained his vendetta against Fisher until Fisher was ousted from leadership in 1861 over the Crown lands affair. Smith became Leonard Tilley's second-in-command, and virtually ran the government while Tilley became preoccupied with Confederation and the railway issue.

Disagreement over private versus public funds in the construction of New Brunswick's railways caused a falling out between Smith and Leonard Tilley. Smith's leadership ability became apparent in 1864 when he opposed both Tilley and the Lieutenant Governor in the Legislature and won. His tenacity and political talents surprised almost everyone in his handling of the question of Confederation. Out-manoeuvred by Tilley — who formed a coalition of pro-Confederation members from all sides of the political spectrum including Smith's Westmorland political rival, Edward Barron Chandler — Smith seemed to face certain defeat by opposing the federation of British North America.

Yet the "Bull of Westmorland" launched a campaign of letters and speeches questioning the wisdom of New Brunswick entering into a federation with large provinces that seemed intent on reducing it to a rump or municipality, with little power and almost 50 per cent less revenue. Fear of union was indeed the reason that Albert Smith carried the anti-Confederation election of 1865 that saw twenty-six of forty-one anti-union members elected. Smith formed a new government but British insistence on Confederation, a threatened Fenian invasion, and the United States rejection of a renewed reciprocity treaty, left Smith again out-manoeuvred. His party was defeated in 1866 and Confederation took place, but Smith was later elected as an independent for Westmorland in the first federal election of 1867.

Albert Smith's uneasy relationship with federal politics gradually changed as he began to be seen as New Brunswick's leader in the House of Commons. He became Minister of Marine and Fisheries under Alexander MacKenzie and succeeded in getting the United States to pay a huge fee in exchange for access to the inshore fishery. Smith declined the chance to become Lieutenant Governor but was the first New Brunswick native to be knighted. By 1882, he had served in public life for thirty years but appeared crushed by losing the election to a young Sackville lawyer. He died the following year at Dorchester. While not considered a Father of Confederation, Smith's radical views were often confirmed in later decades, and he remains one of New Brunswick's most powerful and controversial figures.

1866
The Fenian Scare

The ancient warriors of Ireland were called Fianna and in the spring of 1866, discharged Irish soldiers from the American Union Army were recruited into a Irish national movement called the Fenians. Formed in New York under the leadership of Bernard Doran Killian, and dedicated to the overthrow of British rule in Ireland, the Fenians set as their goal the invasion of British North America. The Fenians felt certain that Irish Catholics within the colonies would rise up and support the invasion, then with their colonies overthrown Britain would surely release Ireland.

Resembling a band of mercenaries more than a professional army, over one thousand of the Irish brotherhood arrived in April along the New Brunswick border from Machias to Calais. The banks in Saint John were thought to be their target. Three British men-of-war from Halifax under General Doyle, sailed into the St. Croix River while regiments of the New Brunswick militia marched to Charlotte County. While random crossings and occasional firings produced alarm on the border, little significant military action took place, although an invasion of Campobello had been planned.

Unwilling to suffer a breakdown of civil authority in eastern Maine, American authorities dispatched General Meade, of Gettysburg fame, to keep the Fenians out of mischief. Five Fenians managed to reach Indian Island in Passamaquoddy Bay where they burnt the Customs House, but General Meade's troops managed to convince the majority of Irish freedom seekers to return to their homes. The situation in Upper Canada became more violent as a force of Fenians invaded Fort Erie and Ridgeway.

However the impact of the Fenian Movement on the Confederation debate within New Brunswick was, without doubt, its most lasting effect. Bernard Doran Killian had declared in the streets of Calais that preventing the union of British North America would strike a blow for Ireland. Pro-Confederation sentiment on the eve of the crucial Confederation election was now being cast as demonstrating loyalty to Britain, while an anti-Confederation man was really a Fenian in disguise. In short, the people of New Brunswick could strike a blow for old Britain and against the Fenian threat by voting for Leonard Tilley's Confederation Party.

To clarify that being Catholic and Irish did not being mean pro-Fenian, the Bishop of Chatham, James Rogers, issued a public statement that it was the duty of New Brunswickers to vote for Tilley — and most Irish Catholics did, although the Acadian vote was still largely anti-union. Just one year earlier the majority of voters had been openly anti-Confederation, and had elected Albert Smith on an anti-union slate. The infusion of the Fenian Movement into the debate did more than any other single element to create the huge conversion of anti-Confederation New Brunswickers into Canadians.

1867
The Dominion of Canada

Sir Leonard Tilley is credited with skilfully bringing New Brunswick into Confederation, and also with coining the new union name of Dominion while reading his Bible one day. But many other New Brunswickers played important roles in the decision to join in an economic and political union with the other colonies of British North America. In addition to Tilley, New Brunswick's Fathers of Confederation are generally agreed to include Edward Barron Chandler, Charles Fisher, John Hamilton Gray, John Mercer Johnson, Peter Mitchell, William Henry Steeves, and Robert Duncan Wilmot. While Albert Smith played a key role in national affairs after Confederation, his strong opposition to union prevents his name from joining the list of pro-Confederation politicians.

Not all of New Brunswick's Fathers of Confederation were as strongly in favour of union as Leonard Tilley but all saw the inevitability of a union of the colonies, and sought the best possible deal for New Brunswick. The idea of British North American union had been seriously discussed since Britain had repealed the Navigation Act in 1849, yet the Canadian promise during the 1864 Charlottetown Conference of an Intercolonial Railway between Halifax, Saint John and Montreal soon had key Maritime delegates dropping the conference's theme of Maritime Union. Railways meant year-around trade, and with the abolition of the Reciprocity Treaty with the United States, trade with Canada seem vital to future prosperity.

Britain favoured union partly as a military response to American threats of invasion but also to encourage colonial self-reliance. A second conference in October, 1864 at Quebec ironed out some of the questions of retained provincial powers, but the defeat of Tilley in 1865 delayed the union by two years. However the Fenian raid into New Brunswick as well as powerful economic incentives convinced the voters of New Brunswick to chance union and they voted Tilley back into power in 1866. All counties — except Westmorland, Kent and Gloucester, where the Acadian voters remained against the federation — returned pro-Confederation candidates; forty-one members of the Legislature backed Tilley, while only eight were anti-union. The island colonies of Prince Edward Island and Newfoundland saw little advantage in railways and continental trade, and declined the invitation to unite.

149

On July 1, 1867, the British North America Act became official and New Brunswick became one of the four original provinces of a United Canada. Sixteen New Brunswick politicians attended the first National Parliament, with Leonard Tilley and Peter Mitchell appointed to John A. MacDonald's first Federal Cabinet.

1867
Leonard Tilley, Father of Confederation,

Samuel Leonard Tilley was New Brunswick's most important nineteenth century statesmen and the architect of the province's entry into Confederation. More than anyone in New Brunswick, Tilley planned the steps to Confederation and became the province's most vital politician at the national level. Born in Gagetown, Tilley began his business career as a Saint John druggist in a retail partnership called Peters and Tilley. He experienced a religious conversion in the late 1830s, and spent much of his early career working in the evangelical temperance movement.

Elected to the Assembly in 1850, Tilley is remembered as the one who introduced Prohibition to New Brunswick, and was burned in effigy as New Brunswickers rejected his call for temperance. In 1861 he replaced Charles Fisher as the leader of the Provincial Assembly and became committed to his two great obsessions — building the Intercolonial Railway and the union of British North America. Tilley attended all the pre-Confederation conferences, and seconded John A. MacDonald's motion for political union at the Quebec Conference. But Tilley remembered the rejection of his Prohibition Bill, and insisted on submitting the question of union to a vote. New Brunswick became the only province to reject Confederation, but a second election in 1866 confirmed Tilley with a mandate for political union.

While Leonard Tilley played an important role in the London Conference of 1866 that hammered out the details of Confederation and the future powers of the new national government, he was less than central to John A. MacDonald's first national government. Parochial concerns forced Mac-Donald to give Tilley the smaller role as head of the Customs Department, rather than the Minister of Finance post. Tilley seemed to have also lost the battle for locating the Intercolonial Railway along the St. John River. Isolated on the national front, he appeared without influence in the early days of Confederation. But in 1873, he was rewarded for remaining in MacDonald's cabinet by finally being named Minister of Finance.

The MacDonald government resigned in late 1873 and Tilley was appointed Lieutenant Governor of New Brunswick, where he immediately

Sir Samuel Leonard Tilley, 1818-96. Father of Confederation, Lieutenant Governor, and New Brunswick's most important political figure. Bust carved by Saint John artist John Rogerson.

banned wine from formal receptions. After his term expired in 1878, Leonard Tilley returned to federal politics, although he only won his Saint John riding by nine votes. He met his greatest political challenge by again becoming MacDonald's Minister of Finance with responsibility to enact the National Policy of tariffs and duties, designed to enhance Canadian manufacturing. Tilley also became involved in negotiations with Canadian Pacific Railway to complete the line from Montreal to make Saint John a winter port.

At age seventy-six, Leonard Tilley quit federal politics to become, for the second time, Lieutenant Governor of New Brunswick, a post he held until 1893. His public career stretched many decades as his pragmatic political wisdom and business skills transformed him from a provincial assemblyman to a first-class Canadian statesman. His contribution to Canadian nationhood was equal to any of Canada's other Fathers of Confederation, with the exception of John A. MacDonald. Tilley received many honours within New Brunswick for his extensive public career and was knighted for his efforts to unite Canada.

1867
The Struggle For Acadian Rights

For about a hundred years after the Expulsion, the Acadians of New Brunswick were silenced, routinely exploited or ignored by the ruling English-speaking majority. Voting rights for Catholics were only fully established in 1830, and the first Acadian to exercise political power was Amand Landry of Memramcook, who was elected to the Provincial Assembly in 1846. But by then, Acadians comprised more than 15 per cent of the total population, and slowly, during the 1850s with Memramcook as its undeclared capital, a new Acadia began to take shape.

The first Acadian college appeared at Saint-Joseph in 1864. In 1859, French scholar Rameau de Saint-Père published La France aux Colonies in Paris, the first study that affirmed Acadians to be a distinct cultural group from the Québécois. In 1867, while the province remained preoccupied with Confederation, two events occurred that signified a new pride in Acadian identity and demonstrated a determination to preserve the language and culture through more active involvement in the political process.

A petition signed by 173 French-speaking residents of Gloucester County was presented to the Assembly, requesting that all debates be available in French. A subsequent motion tabled in the Assembly called for all public notifications from government departments to be published in both

French and English. A growing number of Acadians were being elected to the Provincial Legislature. While the political realities of the day meant that the English-speaking majority had little difficulty blocking these Acadian demands, the simple use of French in the political process marked the beginning of a long struggle for linguistic rights in New Brunswick. When the first House of Commons opened the same year, Buctouche school teacher Auguste Renaud represented the people of Kent County and was the only French-speaking Maritimer in the federal Parliament.

The second important event for Acadians in 1867 was the establishment of the first French-language newspaper in the Maritimes. *Le Moniteur Acadien* was published in Shediac one week after the Dominion of Canada became official, and its banner read "Notre Langue, notre religion et nos coutumes." Started by Quebec native Israel Landry, who had difficulty locating French-language type, *Le Moniteur Acadien* was a weekly rallying force for Acadian efforts to improve their situation. Landry left after one year but Ferdinand Robidoux produced the newspaper for forty-seven years, championing numerous Acadian causes until ill health forced him to close the newspaper in 1918.

With a newspaper as well as an educational institution to serve their community, Acadians became enthusiastically involved in demands for political and linguistic rights that slowly evolved into a nationalistic movement during the 1880s.

1869
The Saxby Gale Disaster

On the evening of October 4, 1869, one of the worst natural disasters to occur in New Brunswick hit the Passamaquoddy Bay area of Charlotte County, and raged up the Bay of Fundy causing massive damages. The fierce storm was a southeasterly and, strangely, had been predicted by Lieutenant S.M. Saxby of the Royal Navy one year earlier. Saxby's interest in astronomy led to his prediction that one year hence, the moon's orbit would be closest to earth, rendering maximum tidal attraction at the same time that the moon would be situated over the equator, causing significant atmospheric changes.

Lieutenant Saxby's prediction was accurate to within ten hours yet few newspapers published his warning. The St. Croix River area sustained the most damage the hardest with two bridges knocked out, more than sixty vessels scattered along the shore, and more than one hundred buildings torn apart in the pitch blackness. St. Stephen's Christ Church lost its thirty meter (ninety-foot) steeple during a tremendous gust that witnesses swore caused the church's bell to toll twice before the steeple crashed. Numerous deaths were reported including a tragedy at New River where eleven lives were lost aboard the newly built barque, *Genii*. The St. Andrews-built vessel was loading lumber for Liverpool, tore loose from its mooring and broke up on the nearby rocks.

Further up the Bay of Fundy, the hurricane winds were less severe yet tides reached record heights of seventeen meters (fifty-seven feet) above the low water mark. At Moncton the tidal bore was reported to be in the range of three meters (ten feet), and the storm destroyed the new bridge that had just been built across the Petitcodiac River to Gunningsville. The raging storm flooded much of the Fundy marshlands causing a number of deaths, including those of several young children who had become stranded in the darkness.

1870
Peter Mitchell's Navy

A native of Newcastle, Peter Mitchell began his law career in 1847 and a few years later became involved in a lumber and shipping operation that built several large vessels on the Miramichi. Elected to the Provincial Assembly during the 1856 Prohibition controversy, he campaigned on the side of the "rummies," reportedly with a pistol for protection as he passed out rum on the Northumberland election trail.

A ruthless and bold politician, Peter Mitchell made enemies and allies in his early years in Fredericton, becoming known as one of the most capable Assemblymen. Appointed to the Legislative Council in 1861, he advised the Lieutenant Governor on measures that would advance the cause of Confederation. His clash over Confederation with Albert James Smith would make the two men life-long enemies. When Smith's anti-Confederation coalition party resigned in 1866, Mitchell became premier and led the pro-Confederation forces to victory.

At Confederation, Mitchell's popularity rivalled Leonard Tilley's and he received a cabinet post in John A. MacDonald's first federal government. As Minister of Marine and Fisheries, he organized Canada's first national policy on fisheries and marine matters, including establishing a fish hatchery program that saw the first successfully bred salmon released into the Northwest Miramichi River.

Peter Mitchell's years as a rough and tumble Miramichi politician came in handy in 1870, when he faced his toughest assignment. American fishing rights to Canada's inshore waters had terminated in 1866 with the lapse of the Reciprocity Treaty, yet the Americans continued to fish the waters without authorization. British warships patrolled Canadian waters but were reluctant to strongly enforce Canadian sovereignty. Determined to bring the Americans to the bargaining table, "Bismarck" Mitchell forced the issue with a gun-boat diplomacy strategy by creating his own navy. Consisting of six armed ships disguised as American fishing vessels, Mitchell's navy began arresting US vessels in Canadian waters threatening to protect Canadian sovereignty at all costs.

The next year under British leadership, but with the full participation of John A. MacDonald, the Treaty of Washington was signed as a result of Mitchell's actions. However the treaty was seen as a sell-out in the Maritimes, where Americans were given twelve years of access to the inshore fishery, in exchange for a price subject to arbitration. Mitchell's bitter enemy, Albert Smith, succeeded him as Minister of Fisheries and concluded a brilliant compensation package with the Americans, that awarded Canada $5.5 million in exchange for Americans being allowed to fish in Canada's inshore waters. In triumph, Smith was knighted while Mitchell, upset, complained that he deserved the credit and knighthood. He also felt that Leonard Tilley's role as New Brunswick's Father of Confederation should not have overshadowed his own, more forceful contribution to Confederation.

Peter Mitchell remained in politics for some time but drifted in and out of both federal parties, never again playing a crucial role in government. He published a newspaper in Montreal during the late 1880s that became a mouth-piece for his opinions, but Mitchell had become a bitter and somewhat tragic figure by his death in 1899. He seemed unable to accept his lack of recognition in the early years of Canadian Confederation. Yet Peter Mitchell's role in the formation of Canada was certainly recognized after his death. Considered one of the most important of New Brunswick's eight Fathers of Confederation, Peter Mitchell was honoured at his hometown of Newcastle where a plaque was erected to his memory.

1871
The Free Schools Act

Of the four partners in Confederation, New Brunswick had by far the most neglected schools since the ill-fated Parish Schools Act of 1858 had failed to improve conditions or better educational standards. The Protestant-controlled provincial Legislature blamed religious schools, mainly Catholic, for the province's meagre educational situation. And unlike Ontario and Quebec, New Brunswick's Catholics, with only 33 per cent of the population, had entered Confederation without constitutional guarantees for their schools, since education was prescribed in the British North America Act as a provincial matter

So it was not surprising that when New Brunswick's Methodist Premier George E. King introduced the Common Schools Act in 1871, establishing free public schools by direct taxation, Catholics felt excluded. Previously, all schools in the province had received a share of the small provincial educational allowance without restrictions on religious instruction, textbooks or teacher training. King's education bill established the right to free education for all children but insisted on a non-denominational curriculum, controlled and directed by the Protestant majority. Catholics were outraged when King appointed a Baptist educator, Theodore Harding Rand, as New Brunswick's Superintendent of Education.

English-speaking Irish Catholics composed the leadership of New Brunswick's Catholics, and Bishops John Sweeny and James Rodgers led the attack against the bill. They were supported in Ottawa by Irish Catholic MPs, John Costigan and Timothy Warren Anglin. For the next three years, little else seemed important as the Schools Act question divided the province along religious lines. Catholics refused to pay their school tax and their property was seized for non-payment, including Bishop Sweeny whose carriage was taken. But controversy reigned in the House of Commons where Costigan and Anglin appealed for federal assistance to help defend their right to operate separate schools.

The Supreme Court and the Privy Council maintained the province's right to educational control, but civil disobedience within New Brunswick was creating flashes of violence as the French-speaking Acadians became increasingly vocal in this dispute. Bishop Joseph Michaud was imprisoned for not paying his taxes, and while his release was granted after a public outcry he was arrested again. Besides the religious issue, the question of language and the lack of public funds for French instruction came out in the open. Tempers flared and provincial debates grew bitter as courts ordered more Catholic property seized. The impasse was temporally resolved when Bishop Sweeny and Premier King agreed to an accommodation in the spring of 1875, after the Caraquet riots convinced both sides that the violence would continue when a breakthrough occurred.

The compromise permitted teaching by members of religious orders, although they would be subject to the provincial exams. School textbooks would be edited to remove anti-Catholic bias, and Catholic schools would be leased to the school boards, while religious instruction could be taught after hours. Although the Common Schools Act did improve the quality of education by ensuring all students free access to improved basic teaching, education remained a flash point for religious and linguistic groups well into the twentieth century.

Immigration Building complete with root cellar. New Denmark, 1872. Photo by
G.T. Taylor. (NBPA)

1872
New Denmark

Almost halfway between Grand Falls and Plaster Rock on Route 108
is New Denmark, the largest Danish colony in North America. Spotless
white tiny farmhouses now dot the countryside. In 1872, the first of
twenty-nine Danish immigrants left Copenhagen on the promise of each
adult male receiving forty-one hectares (one hundred acres) in the province
of New Brunswick. But when they arrived by riverboat at Grand Falls and
journeyed through the Lucy Gulch trail by horse and wagon to their new
community, they encountered nothing but dense forest, and a small partly-
built government cabin called Immigrant House.

As European farmers accustomed to cleared pastures and farmlands,
the Danish settlers were later described in their own publication, *History of
New Denmark*, as "like children abandoned in the merciless woods." Like

157

the early Loyalists settlers at Fredericton, the first years forced incredible hardships on the Scandinavians. They were so close to starvation that they took seed potatoes out of the ground for food. Death from diphtheria and other diseases was common, as the early graveyards in the community still serve to remind visitors.

Yet New Denmark eventually flourished, especially in the   area around Klokkedahl Hill, largely due to the fortitude of the early Danish people. The original Immigrant House was destroyed by fire but a replica stands today.

1874
Decline of Shipbuilding

While large square-rigged vessels continued to be built in New Brunswick after Confederation, the recession of 1874 marked the peak period of shipbuilding and ownership in the province. Despite the new iron and steel steam vessels capturing much of the ocean-going cargo trade, the traditional full-rigged ships still seemed an attractive construction projection for New Brunswick shipyards well into the 1870s. The American Civil War had destroyed much of the American merchant marine and New Brunswick clipper ships were able to deliver American products to overseas ports at favourable freight rates. The inevitable decline was merely postponed.

From the outset of the shipbuilding boom in the 1820s, Saint John had remained in the forefront of ship production for the entire Maritimes. In 1865, twenty-seven shipbuilding firms were active in the port and six years later the city ranked as the fourth largest ship-owning port in the British Empire. Despite building more efficient ships with wire riggings, increased carrying capacity, and less need for sailors the decline of wooden shipbuilding was worldwide. Canada as a whole registered five hundred new vessels in 1875, yet twenty-five years later only twenty-nine vessels were built throughout the entire Dominion. Similarly, world shipping via wooden sailing ships declined from 84 per cent in 1870 to 38 per cent in 1900.

The Maritimes and New Brunswick were not well suited to build the new steel vessels since they had no significant steel-making capacity. Nor did freight rates for overseas shipping rebound after falling in 1874, so shipbuilders displayed little interest in examining the expensive new materials and methods for constructing modern steel vessels. In assition, the Great Fire of 1877 wiped out much of the shipbuilding capacity of Saint John. Finally Confederation had ushered in a new era where the old New Bruns-

158

wick firms were building factories to produce goods they hoped to ship by train to the new inland cities of Upper Canada and the west. John A. MacDonald's National Policy had turned New Brunswick's merchants and shipping entrepreneurs away from the waters that had sustained the province since its inception. The outcome of the gamble would not be known for several decades but by 1880 the sun had set on New Brunswick's golden age of shipbuilding.

1875
The Caraquet Riots

In January 1871, the Common Schools Act created a crisis among Acadians who had been denied their own schools and consequently had refused to pay the education tax. Unpaid school taxes meant the French-speaking majority of Gloucester County were ineligible to serve on the district school board. The census of 1871 reported only seventy-one English-speaking Protestants of the 3,111 inhabitants of Caraquet; yet two Protestants, Robert Young and James Blackhall, held economic and political control in the region, and fully supported the new Act that refused public funds for Catholic schools.

When Blackhall held a meeting at the Caraquet school to fill the school board with Protestants and impose a district school tax, tempers flared among the Acadians. They broke up the meeting and began demanding that all citizens of Caraquet have nothing further to do with enforcing the dreaded Schools Act.

Rum was never far from the scene as the Acadians threatened James Blackhall, forcing him to sign a pledge not to attend any future school meetings. In turn, a clerk of Robert Young's, Colson Hubbard, circulated a note promising to burn the Catholic priest's home if the Acadians didn't end their intimidating protest. Tension mounted again the next day when about a hundred men gathered outside Young's store with Young himself barricaded inside.

Sheriff Robert Vail of Bathurst arrived with a force of English-speaking Protestant constables and arrested several Acadians, and a group of twenty Orangemen from the Miramichi appeared and seized Acadians. Beatings occurred as Acadians resisted the Orangemen. On the evening of January 26, violence erupted as Young's gang of armed Protestants entered André Albert's house with a warrant for an Acadian, Charles Parisé.

Hearing noises in the attic, Constable Ramsay opened fire into the attic. More shots were fired; John Gifford died instantly from a bullet in the head, while Louis Mailloux was shot to death in the Albert attic. The next day, thirteen Acadian prisoners were taken by sleighs to the Bathurst

159

jail where some arrived seriously frost-bitten from the exposed trip in open toboggans.

The riots and death had shaken New Brunswick, but the previous year, a bitter election in Gloucester had maintained Protestant political power after a Catholic challenge centred around the school question. The English-speaking Protestant legal system soon investigated the tragic deaths and immediately determined that Mailloux's death was caused by unknown assassins, but John Gifford was killed by the Acadians held in the Bathurst lock-up. The first accused to stand trail, Joseph Chiasson, was found guilty but an appeal to the Supreme Court resulted in the charges being dismissed.

Despite the new public school system remaining non-denominational, accommodation with the Catholic minority began to occur as several educational concessions were granted that allowed religious instruction within the public schools. Twenty years later the educational compromises with the Catholic community would be challenged by a Protestant backlash at Bathurst, but a provincial inquiry ensured that the concessions remained intact.

The Caraquet Riots marked a turning point for the growing French-speaking population of eastern New Brunswick, who finally began to demand to share power with their English-speaking neighbours. While English domination of political life in New Brunswick would remain for some time, the riots of Gloucester County indicated a new reality within the province, a reality that demanded recognition for the Acadians and, henceforth, a role in decision-making in New Brunswick.

1875
Resurgo: Moncton Comes Back

"The Governor in Council, having approved the recommendation of the Commissioners, having selected Moncton as the most suitable place for the erection of the principal work shops for the Government System of Railways."

With this announcement in 1871 by the federal government, Moncton became the headquarters and repair centre for the Intercolonial Railway between Halifax and Quebec City. The struggling little community at the bend of the Petitcodiac River received its first good news in a decade. After Joseph Salter's shipyard collapsed in 1857, Moncton lost its town status, its bank, and many of its citizens, but railway commissioner Edward Barron Chandler had insisted that the new Intercolonial Railway be built through his community of Dorchester. That meant Moncton, and not Shediac, would be the natural centre for the interconnection between

160

the new line running north to the St. Lawrence and the European and North American Railway, which ran between Saint John and Shediac. Railway politics had given the little community of Moncton the nod.

Twenty hectares (fifty acres) for railway shops were acquired on Albert Street near Main Street. A construction boom began almost immediately as Moncton's population jumped from one thousand to five thousand by 1880, and doubled again the next decade to ten thousand in 1890. The same year, 1890, the town became New Brunswick's third incorporated city. But first Moncton had to reincorporate itself as a town, since it had lost its municipal status during the depressed years of the 1860s. Despite opposition from some powerful citizens — including Oliver Jones who had served as town mayor and first presdient of the Westmorland Bank — Joseph Crandall headed a petition to incorporate and convinced the House of Assembly to pass the Town Incorporation Act in 1875. Joseph Crandall had been mayor when Moncton became bankrupt in 1862, and again served as head of the new town, but received the title of chairman rather than mayor. Although now prosperous, the municipal council was cautious. Town spending restrictions were tight and taxes low, but the new civic government quickly established better law and order, fire safety, and other amenities.

The year 1875 also marked the completion of the Intercolonial Railway to Campbellton. Other industrial developments soon followed the railway, as entrepreneurs established a sugar refinery, a woolen mill, a cotton mill, a foundry and stove manufacturing company. Moncton's fortunes were strong throughout the late 1800s, as its position as headquarters of the Intercolonial Railway provided many commercial opportunities. While growth in Westmorland's more prominent places including Sackville, Dorchester, and Shediac stalled during the 1800s, Moncton continued to thrive and became one of the largest Maritime centres by 1900.

1876
Completion of the Intercolonial Railway

A British Army Engineer, Major Robinson, had surveyed a railway route from Quebec to the Maritimes in 1848 that ran through northeastern New Brunswick, in order to avoid the US border and the threat of potential military hostilities. With Britain still in control of the sea lanes, the Robinson coastal line was considered the best logistical route for any future railway, yet the majority of New Brunswickers were still situated along the St. John River valley. The route of an Intercolonial Railway to the Canadas became a controversial subject to the people of New Brunswick, especially during the 1860s, when it became obvious that provincial resources were insufficient to build such a line. The so-called "Lobster Act" of 1864 had provided incentives to build railways in all directions like a lobster's claw, but existing New Brunswick railways were just not profitable. Britain would need to fund the Intercolonial, and therefore would have a major say in its location.

In 1864, Sandford Fleming was hired to re-survey the line and recommend the best route. Fleming was reminded that Britain would still need to pay the major share of the construction costs, and the railway would need to serve British North America in time of war. Fleming preferred a short route north of Moncton through northwest New Brunswick, but British demands for security upheld the Robinson line through the northeast.

Rivière-du-Loup to Moncton would proceed in a straight line, without political interference. But south of Moncton to Truro, Fleming ran into local opposition when the most direct route threatened to bypass many small communities. Dorchester's Edward Barron Chandler, a member of the Intercolonial Railway Commission, succeeded in having the railway built an additional fourteen kilometres (nine miles) via the Memramcook Valley to Dorchester. North of Truro, a six kilometre (four mile) diversion into Londonderry was also constructed for political reasons. Fleming battled the politically-appointed commissioners to convince them to use modern rail construction methods such as standard gauge steel rails, and iron and steel bridges instead of the old, inferior wooden bridges.

Opened in stages, the final section of the Intercolonial through the Gaspé was completed in June 1876, with the entire eight hundred kilometres (five hundred mile) line from Truro to Rivière-du-Loup costing thirty-six million dollars. The first train from Halifax to Quebec arrived on July 6, 1876, and the Intercolonial is usually considered the first great experiment in Canadian public works. With headquarters in Moncton, the ICR seized control of most of the rail lines in New Brunswick, including the European and North American Railway and, by the early 1900s, employed several thousand workers. In 1917, the railway became part of Canada's national train system, the Canadian National Railway.

Begun as a dream in the early railway era, the Intercolonial Railway became the first all-Canadian line between the Maritimes and Upper Canada. At a cost of $72,000 per mile, Halifax, Moncton and the north shore benefitted from the new line but for most of southern New Brunswick the railway ran the wrong way. Within the first few years, the manufacturers in central Canada also benefitted from the new railway, as most east-bound trains were filled with manufactured products for Maritime consumers, while the west-bound trains carried little freight but were full of people heading west.

1876
Oldest City Hall

Erected on Phoenix Square in 1876, Fredericton's City Hall is the oldest city hall still in operation in the Maritimes. Designed by McKean and Fairweather (the same architects who created Saint John's city market), for many years it not only served as the city office and council chamber, but contained the jail, magistrate's office, a farmer's market in the basement, and a second floor Opera House that could seat eight hundred people.

Oscar Wilde was probably the most famous performer who appeared at the Opera House, sometimes called City Hall Auditorium. More typical of the period is photographer George Taylor's historic photograph showing a large number of hay wagons waiting to be weighed so the hay could be sold at the morning farmers market. Built at a cost of $32,500, the City Hall's most interesting feature is its town clock, made possible by Mayor George Fenety who donated his salary to purchase its three meter long (eight feet) dials. The clock still chimes today. However, a controversy developed in 1895 when the changeover to Sandford Fleming's standard time caused confusion and was voted down in a plebiscite. Fredericton did not officially accept Atlantic Standard Time until 1902.

The fountain in front of City Hall was constructed in 1885 with a horse-trough at its base but the three basins were eventually reduced to one, as spray sprinkled by wind soiled ladies' dresses on their way to the Opera House. To celebrate the two hundredth anniversary of Fredericton becoming the capital of New Brunswick, Gertrude Duffie and Dr. Ivan Crowell, two city artists, created a series of historical tapestries in 1985 that are displayed in the Council Chamber. The tapestries portray Fredericton's past as described in the late Austin Squires' book *Fredericton: The Last 200 Years*.

1876
Oldest City Market

The Royal Charter that incorporated Saint John into a city in 1785 also chartered a common-law commercial market that is among the oldest in North America. The first market was operated at the foot of King Street, and master builder John Cunningham designed and constructed the brick Market House at Market Square in 1839.

163

In 1876 the present City Market, which runs a full city block between Charlotte to Germain Street, was finished and miraculously survived the Great Fire the following year. The impressive Victorian structure was the result of a local design competition awarded to the firm of McKean & Fairweather. The floor slopes twenty feet towards Germain Street and the wooden rafters appear as an inverted hull of a sailing ship, recalling the city's glorious days as one of the largest shipbuilding centres in British North America.

1877
The Great Fire

"Black Wednesday" occurred in Saint John June 20, 1877 when, in the middle of the afternoon, a fire broke out in Fairweather's building at York Point, just behind Market Square. A fierce northwest wind quickly spread the blaze to McLaughlin's boiler shop next door, and within half an hour a dozen sites were in flames throughout the city.

Saint John had been built of wood and most homes had shingled roofs. Despite a number of early fires, the city displayed little regard for fire-proofing its buildings. In 1787, after the city's first serious fire, two fire-engines were purchased from London but the next year Benedict Arnold's store went up in flames. A large fire in 1837 destroyed 115 houses and caused over a million dollars in property damages. But nothing in the city's history compared to the 1877 tragedy.

Over 1,600 houses were burned, leaving more than fifteen thousand people homeless and eighteen dead. The destruction consumed sixteen kilometres (ten miles) of streets burning almost $30 million in property, much of it uninsured. The flames raged out of control for nine hours and destroyed virtually all property around the peninsula area south of King Street. Once Dock Street burned, merchants ran to the Bank of New Brunswick on Prince William Street with their currency, drafts and bonds to deposit their tin boxes into the fire-proof vaults.

The Mayor and council immediately formed a Relief and Aid Society, with assistance and advice from Superintendent Trusdell of the Chicago Relief Society since Chicago had also experienced a devastating fire a few years earlier. Large sums of money, food, furniture, and clothing were donated from Britain, the United States and the rest of Canada, including a $20,000 donation from the federal government. A significant number of engineers, carpenters, and labourers poured into the city as Saint John was rebuilt over the next five years. One eye witness wrote of the reconstruction, "To walk through the principal streets seems like inspecting a beehive."

Remains of the Bank of New Brunswick after the Great Saint John Fire, 1877.
From a photo by G.F. Simonson.

In August the Provincial Assembly passed a building regulation act that restricted where wooden structures could be built and their height. The Act also defined an area where only brick and stone could be used. As a result, the reconstruction produced a handsome new city flush with Victorian architecture that is largely intact today. The negative side saw Saint John stagnate and experience little growth during the next twenty-five years, as the city struggled to recapture its pre-fire economy.

By the time the city had completed its rebirth, the wooden ship industry had faded from its former prominence as the economic engine of the region. Hard times were common as the city's population decreased for the first time and labour strife, especially among the waterfront unions, became part of everyday city life. The shift to manufacturing and inland transportation was unable to replace the economic prosperity of the shipping industry since Saint John's factories were seen as too small and distant from their main markets in Central Canada and the United States.

While several prominent Saint John landmarks were destroyed in the Great Fire, a number of new architectural gems displaying outstanding Victorian elegance and workmanship soon graced the city's downtown. The city's oldest church, the Loyalist Trinity Church on Germain Street, was destroyed except for the old Coat of Arms that hung in the Old State House in Boston prior to the American Revolution. Rebuilt of stone in the English Gothic style, Trinity Church is now one of Saint John's most impressive structures.

The business district was rebuilt, especially along Prince William Street. The entire streetscape is still intact and an important part of the merchant heritage of the city and its architecture. To commemorate Saint John's many fires and the firefighters who gave their lives fighting them, a memorial now stands in King's Square. Called "They Answered Their Last Alarm," the memorial contains a fire alarm bell manufactured in Saint John in the year of the Great Fire.

1877
County Incorporation

New Brunswick's system of county government was weak and ineffective throughout its first one hundred years as a province. County seats of government did little more than organize elections and keep the peace, since the colonial governor had withheld all ability to generate revenue, and the Provincial Assembly continued the unfair system. Provincial authorities even insisted on appointing the local magistrates.

Prior to its birth as a province, New Brunswick had been designated Sunbury County of Nova Scotia. On becoming a province in 1784, it was divided into the eight counties of Charlotte, Saint John, Kings, Queens, Sunbury, York, Northumberland and Westmorland. A total of thirty-four parishes subdivided the province in 1784, and grew to one hundred by 1851. Twenty-six members were elected to the first House of Assembly including six from Saint John, four each from York, Charlotte, and Westmorland, and two each from the remaining counties.

As the northern and eastern regions grew, counties were carved up into more manageable sections, beginning with Kent and Gloucester which were divided out of Northumberland in 1827. Restigouche was created out of Gloucester in 1837, while Carleton was taken out of York in 1832, with Victoria carved out of Carleton in 1845. In the southeast, Albert County was created out of Westmorland in 1846 and finally, when the northern border with Quebec was established, Madawaska County was fused out of the remains of Victoria and Restigouche Counties in 1873.

County councils slowly began to form, with the first in New Brunswick meeting at the Old Carleton County Court House in the Carleton County shiretown of Upper Woodstock. But by 1875, only York, Sunbury and Carleton had incorporated. Two years later, Premier George Edwin King enacted the Municipalities Act, obliging counties to incorporate and thereby exercise control over their local affairs. Most importantly, the Act made the local councils directly responsible for county financial needs and allowed for limited local taxation. Towns and villages also incorporated, and this important new structure of municipal government remained essentially intact until the Louis Robichaud years of the 1960s.

1878
The National Policy

The decade after Confederation did not produce the renaissance in east-west trade that the union of 1867 had promised. A worldwide depression in 1873 hurt Maritime shipping exports of lumber and, while lumber markets would eventually bounce back, the outlook for the wooden ship industry was bleak.

All hopes for prosperity were placed on John A. MacDonald when his Conservative Party swept into power in 1878 on a platform of economic nationalism. With Minister of Finance Leonard Tilley in charge, the Conservatives erected a series of tariff barriers as high as 35 per cent on foreign manufactured items entering Canada. At the same time raw materials such as unprocessed sugar, cotton and hemp were allowed to enter

Canada duty-free. The goal of the National Policy was to encourage Canadian manufacturing and processing. The program became especially attractive to Maritime entrepreneurs when freight rates to central Canada, via the Intercolonial Railway, were reduced for manufactured goods.

The industrialization of the Maritimes in the 1880s that came about as the result of the National Policy was dramatic. Nova Scotia with its huge coal (and some iron) deposits led the way. In New Brunswick, Saint John, Fredericton, St. Stephen and Moncton all experienced manufacturing growth on a significant scale. Five of the eight cotton mills in the Maritimes were constructed in the province, with two immense structures at St. Stephen–Milltown and Marysville near Fredericton. Two sugar refineries in Saint John and Moncton were built, and soon foundries, ropeworks, leatherworks, nails, brass, soap, confectionary, and other enterprises appeared around the province. The New Brunswick Foundry, Rolling Mills & Car Works, established at Saint John, became one of the largest iron manufactures in Canada.

Many of the New Brunswick entrepreneurs involved in the new manufacturing economy were older businessmen from the wooden ships and lumber era who transferred their energies to the new challenge of factories and railways. Moncton's John Harris, Boss Gibson at Marysville, James Murchie along the St. Croix River, and John Parks in Saint John, had all been involved in lumber and shipbuilding in pre-Confederation New Brunswick. Low tariffs and transportation costs attracted these seasoned entrepreneurs to manufacturing and establishing the new enterprises.

Historians have debated throughout the twentieth century why the explosion of industrial growth throughout the 1880s could not be maintained in the region. Even by 1890 many of the new enterprises were in trouble, and by the turn of the century most of the major New Brunswick manufacturers were in the hands of Montreal capitalists. Nova Scotia with its vast supplies of coal and its access to iron deposits in Newfoundland, held out longer but by World War One, outside concerns owned most of the significant Maritime industries.

Whether the region's industrial development was defeated by geography, Montreal capitalists, manufacturing inexperience, lack of capital, overproduction or the loss of the freight subsidy, the net result of the National Policy was the transfer and consolidation of Canada's manufacturing facilities in central Canada by 1910. Whether the transfer was inevitable or caused by the economic nationalism of the 1880s is still unclear, and sure to be debated by generations to come.

1880 – 1899
The Challenge of Federal Union

1880
Poets Corner of Canada

With the release of *Orion, And Other Poems* by Charles G.D. Roberts, Canada's first distinctive literary movement began to take shape with Frede-ricton serving as the centre. The leading writers of this new English-language poetry and literature were three Fredericton born-and-educated poets, Charles G.D. Roberts, Bliss Carman, and Francis Joseph Sherman.

Roberts was a clergyman's son, born in Douglas in 1860 and educated at the University of New Brunswick. He taught for some time at King's College in Windsor, Nova Scotia, and along with his cousin Bliss Carman, established a unique Canadian style of poetic verse. Sir Charles G.D. Roberts was named Poet Laureate of Canada and in 1935 became the first Canadian poet to be knighted.

Bliss Carman, also born and educated in Fredericton, studied at Edinburgh and Harvard. While living in New England, he edited a num-ber of American literary magazines and continued to write passionately about na-ture and the Maritime landscape. Among his best known collections of verse is *Low Tide On Grand Pré*. Francis Sherman was also born and edu-cated in Fredericton. While maintaining a distinguished career as an inter-national banker, Sherman found time to pen a small collection of techni-cally superb poems that, like Roberts and Carman, reflected nature and spiritual themes inspired from living in Maritime Canada. As her literary sons became famous, Fredericton came to enjoy a reputation as Canada's literary capital.

1881
First Acadian Congress

The inspiration for a national convention of all Acadians grew out of the new French institutions, such as Saint Joseph's College and *Le Moniteur Acadien*, that had given expression to rising Acadian nationalism. However the idea itself came out of an 1880 Quebec City meeting of North American Francophone groups. Westmorland native Father François-Xavier Cormier proposed to the Acadians attending the congress that a special convention for Maritime Acadians be organized, and the next summer close to five thousand gathered at Saint Joseph's College in Memramcook to take part in this historic congress of Acadians from all over the Maritimes.

Prominent delegates included the new elite of Acadian society — Pierre-Amand Landry, first Acadian judge in New Brunswick; Pascal Poirier, who became the first Acadian Senator; Urbain Johnson, the Buctouche politician; Father Cormier; Father Camille Lefebvre; and the fiery Father Marcel-François Richard. The Acadianization of the Catholic Church received a lot of attention, but discussions also centred on agriculture, education, journalism, and Acadian political objectives. One decision symbolic of the new Acadian self-confidence, was the question of an Acadian national holiday.

Father Lefebvre, whose institution hosted the gathering, felt, along with a number of Acadians, that Acadia's future was tied to the French Canadian nationalism of Quebec, and therefore Saint-Jean-Baptiste Day was the natural holiday for all Canadian French-speaking persons. However, the majority of Acadians voted for the adoption of the Feast of the Assumption on August 15 to stress the uniqueness of Acadian culture.

Later Acadian conventions at Miscouche, Prince Edward Island, and Church Point, Nova Scotia, established further goals of the Acadian Movement, but a lasting accomplishment of the first congress was the founding of the quasi-political group, *Société Nationale l'Assomption*. This association of Maritime Acadians came under the direction of Pascal Poirier and Pierre-Amand Landry. The most important Acadian political organization, its mandate was to arrange future Acadian congresses and adopt policies that benefitted Acadians in all the regions of the Maritimes.

With headquarters in Moncton and later Shediac, the organization that grew out of the first historic congress remained central to Acadian political and educational development, although it became the *Société Nationale des Acadians* in 1957. At its 1960 convention, a recommendation urged the creation of a central Acadian university at Moncton and three years later Université de Moncton opened its doors.

1882
Chignecto Ship Railway

Canada had railway fever during the second half of the nineteenth century, building railways to almost every small town and village in the country. But during the 1880s, at the New Brunswick–Nova Scotia border, a Fredericton engineer attempted to build a very different kind of railway.

Henry Ketchum grew up in Fredericton and enrolled in civil engineering lectures at King's College in 1854. Eight years later, the educational institution issued Ketchum its first diploma in civil engineering. He worked in railway construction throughout New Brunswick and for a time in Brazil, earning a reputation as a skillful and energetic engineer. In 1865 he was in charge of constructing the eastern extension of the European and North American Railway, from Moncton to the Nova Scotia border.

While surveying on the Isthmus of Chignecto, Ketchum concocted his vision of the age-old dream that would allow ships to cross the Isthmus from the Bay of Fundy to the Northumberland Strait at Baie Verte. Instead of building a canal, Ketchum's idea was to build the first ship railway in the world, that would hoist fully loaded vessels by means of a hydraulic lift, onto double rail tracks where two trains would pull the ship the twenty-seven kilometres (seventeen miles) to the other shore. The merchants of Saint John would benefit the most from such a shortcut, that promised to save up to eight hundred kilometres (five hundred miles) between Montreal, Saint John, and Boston.

While the technology was untested, Ketchum the engineer felt that a ship railway was superior to a canal since it was cheaper to build and maintain, would allow paddle-wheelers to cross while a canal would not, and finally, would solve the tidal difference between the two bodies of water. In 1882, Ketchum formed the Chignecto Marine Transport Railway Company and raised £650,000 in Britain after the Government of Canada agreed to pay an annual subsidy of $150,000 for twenty-five years, once the project was completed. Cumberland County agreed to provide the land at no charge. When construction commenced in 1888, extensive docks were erected at Fort Lawrence near the entrance to LaPlance River and at Tidnish Bridge.

In 1891, nineteen kilometres (twelve miles) of track had been laid and three quarters of the entire project had been completed at a cost of $3.5 million. Yet the remaining $1.5 million needed to complete the ship railway did not arrive. The Canadian government had given additional guarantees but would go no further, and Ketchum's British partners could not raise more funds. Despite debates in the House of Commons and further attempts to complete the project, construction never resumed after 1891. The wood structures were reused in nearby farms and much of the heavy rock was recycled to maintain the Intercolonial Railway and to build the ferry terminal at Cape Tormentine that opened in 1917.

While K.C. Irving considered a canal for ship transportation at Chignecto again in the late 1950s, Ketchum's pioneering project probably failed because of the uncertainty surrounding the amount of ship traffic the crossing would eventually generate. His ability to build the ship railway was not in doubt but his enthusiastic estimates of projected tonnage was considered too optimistic, especially in the early 1890s when Maritime shipping was in decline. Building railways as public works projects was out of fashion by this time, and governments were simply unwilling to risk more public funds on uncertain projects.

Henry Ketchum died in Amherst of heart failure in 1896 and left instructions to be buried in the little graveyard at the Tidnish Anglican Church, near the site of his beloved ship railway. Funds from his will also went for the belfry and bell of the church but his widow later had him reburied at their joint site in the Sackville Cemetery.

1882
The Arrest of Oscar Wilde

In nineteenth century New Brunswick, celebrity status was usually reserved for royalty or sports figures who could perform great feats of strength or showmanship. Literary figures, though treasured by a small group of educated patrons, rarely achieved star status. The exception was Oscar Wilde, who arrived in North America in 1882 for a lecture tour on the Aesthetic Movement, and was immediately greeted with huge crowds and lots of publicity.

Oscar Wilde had agreed to tour North America as the spokesman for an artistic movement that had developed in England out of the writings of John Ruskin. The movement's chief aim was the elimination of poor taste in everyday life by instilling a cult of beauty into the drab, industrial society of Victorian England. Much of the inspiration for the Aesthetic Movement was the beautiful hand-made artifacts of medieval Europe, and the artistic mission of Wilde and others was to show how beauty could be incorporated into everyday life.

North Americans were now to hear from the notorious dandy of fashionable London. With his long flowing hair and his tight-fitting, colourful clothes, Oscar Wilde appeared to many hard-working New Brunswickers as a buffoon. He arrived in Fredericton from Boston on October 4 and, after meeting with Charles G.D. Roberts at the Barker House, delivered a lecture at City Hall entitled *The Decorative Arts*. But before the full house settled in, twenty-five university students created a commotion by parading into the hall in wild and ridiculous "aesthetic" costumes. Wilde was good natured about the spoof but it was typical of his lecture tour, in that large crowds, excitement and controversy seemed to follow him.

Wilde arrived in Saint John the next morning and was met by crowds, while newspapers announced his sold-out evening talk at the Mechanic's Institute. The audience was composed of curious onlookers, including one woodboatman from Grand Lake who described Oscar as the slickest looking man he had ever seen and afterwards named one of his scows the *Oscar Wilde*. Leaving the next day for Nova Scotia, Wilde had won over Saint John and agreed to deliver a second lecture on his return trip. That evening in Amherst, the trials and tribulations of being a hot property began to appear.

Two executives of the Moncton YMCA cabled to offer him $75 to appear in Moncton on the 13th, but his commitment in Saint John meant that the 12th was the only open date on his Maritime calendar. He wired Moncton that only the 12th was acceptable but not hearing back, he accepted another offer in Moncton for $100. Outraged at the turn of events, A.J. Williams and A.M. Hubly of the YMCA engaged a lawyer who obtained a writ to hold Wilde in breach of contract. When Wilde stepped off the train in Moncton on October 12, he was met by two very unhappy gentlemen.

The local sheriff served Wilde the writ in his hotel room but allowed the lecture to take place at Ruddick's Hall, where Wilde discreetly suggested ways the hall could be aesthetically improved. Afterwards, Wilde rejected a demand by the two YMCA executives for $100 in damages and ultimately his local sponsors agreed to post a $35 bond, which left him free to leave Moncton. Yet the arrest and attempt at blackmail had him accusing the YMCA of extortion, once he was safe in Boston; however, the main board of the YMCA had not authorized the move against Wilde and, once aware of its members' actions, it instructed the two men to withdraw the writ. Wilde's ten day lecture tour of the Maritimes was indeed eventful, and he seemed pleased with his attempts to bring aesthetic appreciation to the masses, although he did later complain of being poorly paid at small town talks. Yet his most fortunate incident was probably escaping the Moncton sheriff, since he would not be so lucky later in his career.

1882
Legislative Assembly Constructed

The first Assembly opened in Saint John in 1786 and, despite protests from the port city, the provincial capital was soon moved to Fredericton. Until the first Legislative Assembly building, called Province Hall, was completed in 1802, the Assembly met at the Lieutenant Governor's Mansion House, on the site of Old Government House, although some functions were thought to have occurred at the British American Coffee House on Queen Street.

Province Hall was described as cramped and too low to entertain a full council meeting. When it was destroyed by fire in 1880, the government had already announced plans to replace the old structure; however, while meeting at their temporary quarters in the Normal School Building, the Assembly became preoccupied with a proposal by the citizens of Saint John to transfer the capital back to the port city. For one hundred years, Saint John had mourned the loss of its status as the provincial capital, and tried numerous times to have the Legislative Assembly returned to its original location.

While a feeble proposal was also received from Moncton, Saint John offered to provide a site and erect the new Legislative Building. When the votes were cast on the location of the capital, both Premier John James Fraser and the opposition leader Andrew George Blair joined forces to defeat the Saint John proposal. The decision to maintain the capital in Fredericton and deny Saint John its bid was indeed determined by the parliamentary process comprised of a majority of the elected members of the Assembly.

The Legislative Assembly Building was completed in 1882, under the direction of architect J.C. Dumarsque. With its mansard roof, Second Empire style corner towers, and octagonal domed tower rising out of the roof, the Victorian era structure quickly became a city landmark. Built of Dorchester sandstone, the main interior hallway features portraits of the province's Lieutenant Governors, while the most interesting aspects of the building are the impressive Assembly Chamber and a famous spiral wooden staircase. The Legislative Assembly Building hosted its first session in 1883 and has remained the seat of government for New Brunswick ever since.

1883
Andrew Blair and the Liberal Party

Andrew George Blair is considered one of the most important premiers of the province — not only for his long tender in office, but also for his role in building the provincial Liberal Party. Born in Fredericton, Blair was elected to the Provincial Assembly in 1878 during the era when members still formed alliances on the basis of local interests or personal concerns. These loose coalitions functioned as political parties, but were rarely maintained as members moved their support back and forth to create temporary alliances.

Elected as a Conservative, Blair did not support the government and was chosen the leader of the opposition Liberals. Within three years, he had attracted a number of government members who crossed over to his opposition group. After the 1882 election had reduced the government party to a small majority, Andrew Blair succeeded in passing a non-confidence motion, and in 1883 assumed the premiership and the post of Attorney General in a new government. A skilled and unrivalled leader, Blair achieved many important government reforms during his twenty-five years of office including the abolition of the Legislative Council, and extending the voting franchise.

But his most important political initiative was the destruction of the coalition approach to governing and the imposition of party loyalty, which led to the establishment of the Liberal Party in New Brunswick. Blair used political power and patronage to impose party discipline on independent members, who gradually began to vote in blocks to support his policies. His success at consolidating both Irish Catholic and Acadian support led to the evangelical Protestant charge of Blair being the promoter of both "Rum and Rome." Yet in recognizing the growing Acadian population and its tendency to vote as a block on issues, Blair was able to broaden the base of support for his emerging Liberal Party.

Personally defeated at the polls in 1892, Blair was soon back in power after winning a by-election, and remained Premier until called to Ottawa in 1896 as Minister of Railways and Canals in Wilfred Laurier's Liberal Government. Blair resigned in 1903 and died in Fredericton four years later, a brilliant and relentless politician who brought New Brunswick politics into the twentieth century.

1883
The Departure of Timothy Anglin

In many respects, Timothy Anglin typified the Irish experience in New Brunswick during the nineteenth century. Although better off than most of his countrymen, Anglin emigrated to Saint John in 1849 in search of a better life. Within a month of his arrival in the city, he began publishing New Brunswick's first Irish Catholic newspaper, the *Saint John Weekly Freeman*.

Timothy Anglin quickly established himself as a leader in the Irish community, that then comprised about a third of Saint John's population. Defending Catholics against attacks by the Protestant Orange Order, Anglin also encouraged Catholic advancement through improved education and business opportunities. A vocal critic of the ruling Smashers during the 1850s, he first gained a seat in the Assembly in 1861, adopting an independent but pragmatic approach to provincial politics.

Anglin viewed the Confederation proposal as having negative economic consequences for New Brunswick and, in 1865, became one of the leading anti-Confederates that formed a government under Albert Smith. Yet his Irish heritage led to accusations of disloyalty during the Confederation election of 1866 — as the Fenian raids made a Catholic who took an anti-Confederation position also a pro-Fenian sympathizer. Going down to defeat at the hands of Leonard Tilley's pro-Confederation coalition, Anglin next ran successfully as a Member of Parliament for the Acadian region of Gloucester, and became a national spokesman on Catholic matters in the House of Commons.

Named the Speaker of the House of Commons under Alexander Mackenzie's Liberal Government, Anglin and fellow New Brunswick Catholic MP John Costigan fought the anti-Catholic New Brunswick Schools Act of 1871 from the House of Commons. A conflict of interest charge, the result of mixing government work with his newspaper interests, unseated him in 1877. His own base of support among French Catholics also began to weaken as the growing Acadian nationalism led to French-speaking candidates offering for political office.

Defeated in 1882 and with his newspaper in decline, Timothy Anglin did what many English-speaking Catholics did in New Brunswick during the late 1800s. With economic prospects dim, Anglin moved to greener pastures in central Canada where he died in Toronto in 1896. As the rest of North America continued to grow during the latter stages of the nineteenth century, New Brunswick suffered a population decline as a continued economic downturn drove thousands, especially English-speaking Catholics, to find better opportunities in the growing inland towns and cities of North

America. Timothy Anglin was one such Irish immigrant who quit Ireland for a better life, led the fight for Irish Catholic rights in New Brunswick, but left his first North American home for better prospects elsewhere.

1885
Boss Gibson's Cotton Mill

When it opened in 1885, Alexander Gibson's cotton mill in Marysville was the flagship enterprise of the largest industrial empire in central New Brunswick. The eighth cotton mill to open in the Maritimes, and the largest in Canada, the brick mill anchored the prosperous mill-town on the Nashwaak River. In full production, the mill employed five hundred people, most of whom lived in Boss Gibson's houses, shopped at his stores, and even attended his church. Gibson's industrial empire also included a foundry, leather works, a flour and grist mill, as well as railway and lumber interests, but how he got his start as one of New Brunswick's largest business tycoons is certainly interesting.

Born in Lepreau in 1819, Alexander Gibson worked in his early years in a lumber mill in the Saint Croix area and then operated a lumber mill at Lepreau with a family partner. In 1862 he moved to the Nashwaak valley, buying two lumber mills and almost 4,048 hectares (ten thousand acres) of timber reserves. The sawmills were the beginning of Gibson's rapid expansion that produced the milltown of Marysville, but the sale of his half interest in the Lepreau mill would not have been sufficient to establish his boomtown on the Nashwaak.

There is considerable speculation that Gibson's early funds came from the British brig *Plumper*, that went down close to Lepreau at Dipper Harbour in 1812 with £70,000 in gold and silver on board to help finance the British war effort. Fishermen were thought to have found gold coins around the shore, and Gibson reportedly hired divers to explore the wreck during the early 1860s.

Initially concentrating on lumber, Gibson's timber tracts became massive, including half the forests of York County, and he began building other mills, including one at Blackville on the Miramichi. Without rail connections above Fredericton, he began in 1870 to build a narrow gauge railway through his timber lands to Edmundston, and later, in partnership with Senator J.B. Snowball, built a railway to connect with the Intercolonial at Chatham.

In 1877 he built the first railway bridge across the St. John River at Fredericton but with MacDonald's National Policy in place promoting Canadian manufacturing, Boss Gibson turned to the production of cotton. The

Alex Gibson in his sawmill on the Nashwaak River. Gibson employed 1,250 men and 620 horses throughout his lumber operation during the winter of 1880-81. (NBPA)

company town of Marysville came to resemble a feudal village, in that all workers were totally dependent on Gibson for their livelihood. But Boss Gibson was a benevolent feudal baron who treated his employees with kindness and paid fair wages. Conditions and markets for cotton were inconsistent but the cotton mill operated profitably until the end of World War Two.

By 1900, Alexander Gibson's industrial empire was beginning to crumble, due to high debt and poor commercial prospects. The cotton mill was sold to Montreal interests in 1908, and the grand old man of the Nashwaak died at age 94 in 1913. But the fascinating Marysville architecture of Boss Gibson's era has remained largely intact, and is a rare remaining example of a complete nineteenth century industrial town in Canada.

1886
Exploitation and the Truck System

Systems of trade have always existed in pioneer societies where currency shortages were common but the truck system that developed in northern New Brunswick turned the region along the Baie des Chaleurs into a state of bondage. A truck system usually involves credits issued for payment of wages with the holder required to purchase at the company store. Around the Baie des Chaleurs, and indeed the entire Gulf of St. Lawrence, the fish merchants developed a truck system that resulted in virtual enslavement of the local inhabitants.

After the expulsion of the Acadians, French Protestants from the Isle of Jersey began to appear around the Gulf of St. Lawrence. In order to exploit the fishery, they recruited a sizeable number of Acadian refugees as fishermen. By 1800, the Charles Robin Company had established fishing stations throughout the Gulf region and had succeeded in trapping fishermen in a client indebtedness system of offering credits for purchases at their store, in exchange for the delivery of fish. Of course, the truck prices for goods at the company store were the cash price plus a premium charged by the firm of up to 40 per cent for issuing the credit.

Many Acadian fishermen, especially around the coastal areas of Caraquet, Shippegan, and the islands of Lamèque and Miscou, were trapped in irredeemable debt to the Jersey merchants, who had a monopoly in the Gulf fishery. With few roads or alternatives to purchasing at the company store, the exploitation continued as the merchants built fishing "rooms" or small company warehouses in the Gaspé and coastal Gloucester County, employing locals on land to process the fish but again, wages were paid in the truck system.

A challenge to the system appeared during the Reciprocity years of 1854 to 1866, when American fish buyers began paying "cash on the barrel head" for wet fish. But the Treaty was allowed to lapse and by the time of Confederation, the Jersey merchants, dominated by the Charles Robin Company, were back in firm control of the Chaleurs fishery. Non-Jersey merchants such as Robert Young and Kennedy Burns also used the truck system to pay wages — Young for road construction, and Burns paid his Acadian sawmill workers in paper bills that were only redeemable at his company store. Despite attempts by the Catholic clergy and government officials to change the status quo, the truck system remained firmly in place until the Robin Company went bankrupt in 1886, due to bank failures in Jersey.

The increase of Acadian political power in the 1880s, as well as the improvements in agriculture, roads, and land grants, reduced Gloucester County's dependence on the fishing firms. But the Robin Company was reorganized and remained in the fishery at Caraquet until 1958. The truck system gradually became unattractive and disappeared in the Baie des Chaleurs fishery during the late 1930s, when an American firm was established at Caraquet with a policy of paying fishermen for their catch in cash.

1887
L'Évangéline

In 1844, Valentin Landry was born in Gloucester County at Poke-mouche but moved to Westmorland County where he attended school in Moncton, and later enrolled at Saint Joseph's College. Landry spent ten years in Nova Scotia mainly teaching, then returned to New Brunswick in 1875 to teach French at the Fredericton Training School. In 1879, he was the first Acadian to be appointed a School Inspector. His responsibilities were in eastern New Brunswick where he encouraged young Acadians to improve their education and join temperance societies.

For reasons not entirely clear, Valentin Landry lost his government position in 1887 and turned to journalism to make his living. Perhaps his demands for more use of French in schools upset the Fredericton authorities, or patronage politics could have dictated that government jobs turned over when a new party arrived in power. What is known is that Landry returned to Digby with his Nova Scotian wife and at age forty-three, began *L'Évangéline* with "Religion, Langue, Patrie" as its motto. Since no French-language newspaper existed in Nova Scotia at the time, the modest four-page weekly with a subscription rate of one dollar per year was welcome news for Acadians.

Landry became immersed in the Acadian politics of Digby County and help established Collège Saint-Anne at Church Point. Landry's interests and the editorial direction of *L'Évangéline* was to promote nationalistic Acadian causes throughout the Maritimes, including the demand for a separate Aca-dian diocese. After eighteen years as a publisher in Digby, he moved to the rapidly growing city of Moncton where he felt more opportunities existed for promoting the Acadian cause. He fought the Irish Catholics and their Saint John newspaper, the *Freeman*, over their refusal to support a separate French diocese, and also quarrelled with the more conservative Acadian newspaper, *Le Moniteur Acadien.*

When his great cause was finally realized with the appointment of Monseigneur Edouard LeBlanc as the first Acadian Bishop in 1912, Landry had already been forced to sell his ownership of *L'Évangéline.* The Catholic establishment retaliated against his shrill attacks by urging Catholics to withdraw their support. Société l'Assomption withdrew its financial support in 1910, and Landry's newspaper career was over. Yet *L'Évangéline* remained the cornerstone of Acadian thought and communication, outliving its rival *Le Moniteur Acadien.* A great leader in the Acadian revival of the late 1800s, Valentin Landry died in 1919. In 1979, on the thirtieth anniversary of his newspaper's operation as a daily, a ceremony in his birthplace of Pokemouche unveiled a monument paying trib-

Valentin Landry, 1844-1919, the founder of L'Évangéline, the Maritimes first Acadian daily newspaper. (NBPA)

ute to this remarkable Acadian spokesman. *L'Évangéline* didn't quite last one hundred years for it ceased publication in 1982.

1889
Short Line to Montreal

The quest to establish an efficient rail link between Saint John and Upper Canada had begun well before the construction of the Intercolonial Railway, which took rail traffic away from Saint John along an eastern route to Quebec. The St. Andrews and Quebec Railway had ended in frustration and the Western Extension line from Saint John to Bangor had also proved inadequate, since it forced all traffic south to Portland before continuing to Montreal.

In 1870, Alexander "Boss" Gibson started building his New Brunswick Land and Railway Company line into his timber lands northwest of Fredericton. A government land grant of ten thousand acres per mile of railway was another incentive for Gibson to build into the upper St. John River valley. The line soon became known as the Patchwork Railway for its diversions and link-ups with small spur lines. Completed to Grand Falls and Edmundston in 1878, the New Brunswick Railway made no attempt to build into Quebec via Temiscouata and the St. Lawrence. Besides ending in Edmundston, the NBR had another shortcoming — its narrow gauge made it impractical for linking with other railways.

Gibson sold his railway interests in 1882 and the New Brunswick Railway eventually consolidated its tracks into standard gauge rails and acquired other railways in western New Brunswick. But its circuitousness route still meant that upper valley businesses had to first ship south in order to reach western Canadian markets. So by the mid-1880s, the western side of the province still did not have its railway link to Montreal, despite being much closer to Upper Canada than eastern New Brunswick.

Finally, with the village of McAdam designated a central divisional point, the Canadian Pacific Railway became committed to an eastern Canadian railway terminal, and began building from Quebec through Maine to New Brunswick. The "Short Line," with under eight hundred kilometres (five hundred miles) of track, carried its first passenger train from Montreal to Saint John in 1889. The following year, the CPR took over the New Brunswick Railway and its provincial rail lines.

While late (some would claim too late) to effectively compete with Portland, Maine, and Halifax as an ocean terminal for shipping Canadian freight overseas, Saint John and western New Brunswick had at last their railway northwest to the North American interior. More than a hundred men were employed at McAdam by 1890, where CPR trains could switch west to Maine, south to St. Andrews and Saint John, east to Fredericton, and finally, north to Montreal or Edmundston. As a major railway terminal, McAdam continued to grow substantially during the First World War.

1889
Tappan Adney and the Survival of the Birch Bark Canoe

Edwin Tappan Adney, born in Athens, Ohio in 1868, studied in New York, where he became interested in ornithology and natural history. On a trip to Upper Woodstock to visit New Brunswick's most famous orchardist, Francis Sharp, Adney met a Maliseet craftsman, Peter Joe. Joe's skill in birch bark construction so fascinated him that in 1889 he helped build a canoe and recorded each step in its construction.

The next year Tappan Adney published a story, with sketches, in *Harper's Young People* and later in *Outing* magazine. They are considered to be the first detailed, step-by-step descriptions for building a birch bark canoe. With an artist's eye and omitting few details, Adney's article became the definitive account for birch bark canoe construction and highlighted the superb Maliseet workmanship of Adney's favourite watercraft, the St. John River canoe.

By the late 1800s, much of North America's white birch had disappeared and few Aboriginal craftsmen were still building their traditional vessels. Tappan Adney devoted much of his life to detailing the various Aboriginal canoe designs and craft techniques, and almost single-handedly saved the ancient birch bark construction technology from extinction. When companies using white society's tools and materials, such as canvas, began mass-producing canoes in the early 1900s, the designs they used were taken from Aboriginal models. Using canvas and construction techniques pioneered by white canoe builders in Maine, Canada's best known manufacturer, the Chestnut Canoe Company of Fredericton, built many Maliseet-designed canoes. Even today, Aboriginal bark canoes are considered to be among the most highly developed watercraft ever produced.

Tappan Adney married Minnie Bell Sharp in 1899, and became a Canadian citizen serving as a lieutenant in the Canadian Army during World War One. He served as a consultant on Aboriginal matters for McGill University but returned to the Sharp family homestead in the early 1930s, where he compiled and edited his great collection of research on Aboriginal canoe construction and designs. An accomplished artist and craftsman himself, Adney built more than one hundred scale models of the various bark canoes that had been constructed in North America.

Adney's manuscripts and finely crafted canoe models were eventually deposited at the Mariner's Museum, Newport News, Virginia, and his great mass of research on the bark canoe was finally published by the Smithsonian Institution in 1964. Co-authored by Howard Chapelle, *The Bark Canoes and Skin Boats of North America* is still today the most enduring reference book ever produced on the history and design of Aboriginal watercraft. While few birch bark canoes were ever built in the 1900s, Tappan Adney preserved the fascinating and ancient technology and wrote that, in his view, the Maliseet craftsmen of the St. John River were among the finest canoe builders anywhere. The influence of the birch bark canoe on North American history was enormous as was Edwin Tappan Adney's role in uncovering the history of this remarkable vessel. Tappan Adney died in 1950 at Upper Woodstock, having discovered more about bark canoes than almost any white man, and was called "the most remarkable genius I have ever known" by noted New Brunswick author and historian, George Frederick Clarke.

1890
Early Catholic Churches

Civil and religious freedoms were strengthened in New Brunswick in 1810, when some restrictions against Catholics were removed by an act of the Assembly. Five years later at the intersection of Leinster and Sydney Streets in Saint John, New Brunswick's first English Catholic church was constructed. St. Malachy's, a small wooden Georgian structure, served Saint John's growing Catholic population well.

The province's first Catholic cathedral, St. Dunstan's, was actually built in Fredericton before the Protestant Christ Church Cathedral was finished. With Saint John experiencing a large influx of Irish Catholics during the 1840s, Bishop William Dollard moved his episcopal office out of Fredericton in 1848, and began building a new stone cathedral on Waterloo Street in the port city.

Architect Matthew Stead of Saint John, whose English Gothic Revival churches are spread across New Brunswick, began the Cathedral of the Immaculate Conception in 1853. Many of the most important artifacts from St. Malachy's were moved to the new cathedral in 1855, yet the cathedral was not completed until the spire was installed in 1871. Bishop Thomas Connolly, New Brunswick's second bishop, led fundraising efforts by local Catholics, including volunteer work at nearby quarries to acquire the stone foundation.

In the French-speaking regions of the province, pre-English chapels were constructed in a number of locations including Beaubassin and Burnt Church. The oldest existing Acadian church in New Brunswick, and among the oldest anywhere, is Église St. Henri de Barachois at Barachois near Shediac that dates from 1826. Many additions were made to this historic wooden structure including the present tower and spire. Today, this historic site serves as an important Acadian museum, auditorium, and art gallery in southwestern New Brunswick.

Not far from Barachois at Buctouche in Kent County, is another important Acadian Catholic church and provincial historic site. Église Ste. Anne de Kent was constructed of wood beginning in 1890, after the parish of Ste. Anne was established. Built in the neo-Gothic tradition by well known Acadian artist and architect Léon Léger, who designed or helped to build a number of Catholic churches throughout southwest New Brunswick, the interior of Ste Anne de Kent contains forty-eight frescoes on plaster and canvas by artist Édouard Gautreau, depicting religious imagery.

1891
The Acadian Judge, Pierre-Amand Landry

In 1846 Pierre-Amand Landry was born at Memramcook, the oldest son of Amand Landry, who the same year was the first Acadian elected to the New Brunswick House of Assembly. The young Acadian studied in Memramcook and Fredericton, becoming fluently bilingual at an early age. He trained as a lawyer in Dorchester, learning quickly from the Westmorland legal establishment of Albert Smith and Edward Barron Chandler. Soon young Landry was an important figure in Westmorland politics. Pierre-Amand became embroiled in the Common Schools Act controversy of the 1870s, and won Acadian admiration for refusing to support the anti-Catholic school bill in exchange for a government post as Public Works Commissioner.

Landry remained opposed to the school bill, petitioning the King government to offer the same privileges to Catholics in New Brunswick that the British North America Act offered to Quebec's Protestant minority. He organized the support group that assisted the defense of the Caraquet Acadians, accused of murdering an English deputy during the Caraquet riots of 1875.

A thoughtful and well-respected politician, Pierre-Amand Landry became an important minister in charge of Public Works in John James Fraser's government of 1878. This was the first New Brunswick government to give both Irish and Acadian Catholics representation in the cabinet. Landry also served in Ottawa as a Conservative federal Member of Parliament. Yet Landry was not deferential to English power nor hesitant to defend Acadian interests. He served as chairman of the executive committee for the first Acadian Congress and president of the Socété Nationale des Acadiens. Throughout his career, Landry earned the title of a champion of the Acadian people.

The English establishment in Westmorland did not welcome Landry's appointment in 1891 as the first Acadian judge of New Brunswick's Supreme Court. But Landry's reputation as a fair and patient legal arbitrator soon silenced any questions. He presided over many of New Brunswick's most celebrated criminal cases, including the criminal libel case of Henry Emmerson, and the manslaughter trial of Jane Stevens. Emmerson, a federal cabinet minister, sued J.H. Crockett and the Fredericton *Gleaner* for defamation after they reported an impropriety in a Montreal hotel room. The case ended in adjournment, after Judge Landry expressed the view that it was in the public's interest to encourage the newspaper's right to publish what it believed.

One of the most famous criminal trials in the history of Westmorland County was the case of manslaughter against Jane Stevens, the wife of Thaddeus Stevens who published Moncton's first daily newspaper, *The Times*. Jane Stevens was charged with the death of her adopted daughter, Mabel Glennie. Although she was found not guilty, Thaddeus Stevens described Justice Landry as a "French bastard" in reporting on the judge's conduct in his wife's trial and the eminent Landry threatened Stevens with a contempt of court charge.

While considered not militant enough for some nationalistic Acadians, Pierre Landry was also considered too radical by the English-speaking establishment of the province. Yet all groups saw Pierre-Armand Landry as an Acadian who could offer practical solutions based on compromise and consensus. In 1916, he became the first Acadian to be knighted.

1891
The Textile Wars: Saint John Fights Back

As the financial capital of post-Confederation Canada, Montreal's relationship with the Maritimes was uneasy at best during the later 1800s, as takeovers of Maritime industries became all too common. Yet not all incursions by Montreal into the east coast were seen as negative. For years, Saint John had demanded a rail link in order to replace Portland, Maine, as Montreal's winter port. However the clash between Montreal and Saint John capitalists over Montreal's attempts to gain control of Canada's cotton industry was especially bitter.

Maritimers had established eight of Canada's twenty-three cotton mills by the 1880s and New Brunswick was home to five mills, including two of the largest in the country at Marysville and St. Stephen–Milltown. William Parks had started the first cotton mill in the Maritimes at Saint John in 1861 and his son, John Parks, established a second mill in the city in 1881. Montreal textile manufacturers attempted to gain control of the entire Canadian industry by targetting New Brunswick, which had a significant amount of the country's cotton manufacturing capacity.

Early in 1891, David Morrice of Montreal's Dominion Cotton Mills Company travelled to the Maritimes with a $5 million war chest, offering to buy out the cotton producers. At Halifax, Windsor and Moncton, Morrice's offer was accepted, but John Parks refused the offer of consolidation. While not the largest producer, Parks' mills were efficient and quality conscious yet, like most Maritime firms, operating capital was hard to find. What happened next has been described in Saint John as the Montreal conspiracy. After refusing the Montreal offer, Parks' banker, the Bank of Montreal, demanded immediate payment of all outstanding debt.

Owing more than $100,000, the outraged Parks appealed to the Saint John business community for help to maintain the operation "free from all outside control." With the bank's foreclosure upon him, Parks received assistance from the New Brunswick Supreme Court, which placed the operations in receivership but insisted on the on-going operation of the mill — which was successful enough to repay the entire bank debt from the mill's profits. Such help was indeed rare in economic struggles, but it ensured the Parks' mills remained under local control for another decade. The Montreal initiative convinced all the other Maritime cotton mills to consolidate, except for a small operation in Yarmouth. Even the Marysville maverick, Boss Gibson, agreed to limit production and market his cotton under the Montreal consolidation plan. Consequently, by 1893 Canada's financial capital controlled the vast majority of Maritime cotton production as Montreal became the centre of Canada's textile industry.

1891
Official Abolition of the Family Compact

The long and inglorious tradition of non-elected officials influencing New Brunswick politics, while put to rest during the Smasher era of the 1850s, did not actually end until Andrew Blair's government finally abolished the Legislative Council in 1891. The history of the non-elected councils began in 1785 with Governor Thomas Carleton's arrival in the province. Despite witnessing the loss of the American colonies due to undemocratic regulations, the Governor was undaunted in declaring "I think on all accounts ... the introduction of acts of the legislature ..., the crown alone is acknowledged to be competent."

While Governor Carleton was not opposed to the Assembly having the appearance of authority, all power was to flow from him and his appointed council of twelve members of "substance." Only the Colonial Office in London could censure his absolute power that approved all political and financial decisions. Carleton's first Executive Council contained all four Supreme Court judges, as well as the Provincial Secretary, and this Council exercised both executive and legislative functions.

The early council met as an executive body to advise the governor and assist in the business of the province but once a year, while the elected assembly was in session, it met behind closed doors in a legislative capacity to pass, revise, or reject all bills passed by the assembly. The council could also originate bills which they would then send to the assembly for approval. Yet no one but the governor was allowed inside the council's chambers. The Family Compact label was soon applied to the governor's council since all new appointments were friends or relatives of those members already on the council. For example, the first Provincial Secretary Rev. Jonathan Odell, died in 1818, but was succeeded by his son who remained on the most powerful Council in the province until 1844.

Struggle for control of the province and its revenues between the elected assembly and the governor and his council, characterized the early years of the province. As the assembly began to wrest power away from the council, council members were encouraged to stand for election to the House in order to penetrate the assembly's ranks. Occasionally an assemblyman would be offered a council seat, but the two groups remained on uneasy terms.

In the early 1830s, colonial authorities insisted on a division of the Council into a legislative body, and a reduced, executive group of five members with the stipulation that some members of the latter should be elected Assemblymen. The Colonial Office was attempting to have all colonial councils reflect the upper chamber model of their own House of Lords, but the New Brunswick Assembly was unimpressed and only concerned with gaining control over all provincial revenues, especially the Crown Lands fund.

The Executive Council was eventually chosen from the Assembly in 1848, predating the modern cabinet system of government, but a unique situation arose with the victory of the Smasher Government in 1854. Rather than instituting an elected upper legislature like Nova Scotia and Canada, Charles Fisher's reform government decided to maintain the unelected tradition but agreed to broaden the appointments to include all regions and interests throughout the province.

Appointments now became the patronage of the ruling party and soon the Executive Council was reduced to a quasi-governing arm of the party in power. Weak and largely irrelevant, the Council limped on through the second half of the nineteenth century until the ultimate insult was arranged — each person appointed was obliged to pledge their commitment to vote for the abolition of the Council once the measure was introduced in the House. The 1891 session of the Assembly finally abolished the last remnant of the infamous Governor's Council.

1894
Women's Enfranchisement Association

In Saint John in 1894, eighteen women under the presidency of Sarah Manning joined together to form the first provincial association dedicated to extending the voting franchise to women. Universal suffrage for white men had been enacted five years earlier, but a majority of the House of Assembly members rejected reform to the 1843 statue that had specifically denied voting rights to women.

Most New Brunswick men endorsed the nineteenth century view that a woman was not a person and only "persons" engaged in politics. Accordingly, the 1843 enactment had only been stating the obvious for clarification purposes, yet New Brunswick society in 1894 was quite different from fifty years earlier. The women's franchise movement had grown out of the temperance and religious movements that began attracting women in the mid-1800s. As women became active outside the domestic sphere, groups like the Ladies Total Abstinence Society formed and petitions started to appear encouraging social and educational reforms. In 1870, the first YWCA in Canada was formed in Saint John to provide shelter and protection for young women moving into the city in search of employment.

Mount Allison educated women before Confederation and Grace Annie Lockhart received her Bachelor's degree in Science in 1875. Seven years later, Mount Allison also graduated the first woman in Canada with a Bachelor of Arts degree. Lockhart and Harriet Starr Stewart were among the many late nineteenth century New Brunswick women educated and socially engaged in the issues of the day. Yet social reforms without the vote and full political rights became unacceptable to an increasing number of women. Acadian women were also active in the women's franchise debates. Between 1895-98, sixteen letters by school teacher Émilie LeBlanc were published in *L'Évangeline* under the pseudonym Marichette. Threatening to set up her own paper if *L'Évangeline* refused to publish her letters, Mari-chette demanded that women be given the right to vote "to show the old codgers how to vote." LeBlanc also argued for an increase in educational opportunities for French-speaking children.

Within the Assembly, certain pro-women suffrage members lobbied in the 1870s for a limited extension of the franchise to unmarried female property owners. In 1886, the municipal voting franchise was granted to unmarried and widowed women with property, and in 1893 each school board was permitted one woman trustee. But further attempts to promote provincial female suffrage failed. However, women continued to petition for more substantial voting rights. In 1899 alone, twelve petitions were received by the House calling for voting rights for women. Despite continued calls for the full female franchise, women's voting rights were delayed for another twenty-five years after the historic formation of the Enfranchisement Association.

1895
A Winter Port

By 1879, the port of Saint John no longer exported vast amounts of lumber nor built a significant number of wooden ships. During the mid-1880s, the city became convinced that its future lay in becoming Canada's national winter port for exporting western grain and freight overseas. But when a federal government mail contract for winter service between England and Canada chose Portland, Maine, and Halifax as possible locations, Saint John was outraged. Its goal to be Canada's Atlantic winter port was now placed in doubt.

With the completion of the CPR in 1889, the disaffected port could boast an ice-free port and the shortest Canadian rail line to Montreal, Canada's largest city. Saint John's advantage over Halifax began to be promoted, as well as the political consequences of federal subsidies to steamships that shipped Canadian freight and mail through an American port. Portland had long been Montreal's winter port and the nearby Canadian port of Saint John had never been happy. Finally in 1895, with the expansion of port facilities at Sand Point on the west side of Saint John, a grain elevator was installed, and the Beaver Line of Montreal began a steamship freight service to Liverpool.

The early years as the eastern terminus for the CPR were boom ones for Saint John but local automony suffered as the federal presence became increasingly vital to the huge expenses necessary to carry out improvements to the harbour. An attempt by former mayor George Robertson in the early 1900s to establish a dry dock on the west side of the harbour failed, but the Saint John Dry Dock and Shipbuilding Company finally built one on Courtenay Bay in 1923. Thousands of vessels were constructed and repaired at this facility during World War Two.

As one of Canada's National Ports, the entire Saint John harbour was integrated and organized into part of Canada's national transportation system. By 1911, the city's Common Council and Board of Trade had deferred many critical harbour issues to the federal authorities and, with a downturn in the economy during the 1920s, the inevitable occurred. On August 1, 1927, the Harbour Commission of Saint John took over management of the port that had been nationalized the same year. The shift of responsibility would have occurred anyway but its acceleration was due to the city's inability to bear the financial costs of operating the system.

In 1931 a major fire destroyed most of the docking facilities in Saint John West and despite the Great Depression the facilities were rebuilt and expanded by federal efforts. The federal government poured millions into upgrading the infrastructure of the entire harbour, including a cofferdam from Saint John West to Navy Island, that allowed for the construction of new piers, huge grain elevators, and other improvements. Today, the Port of Saint John still annually exports millions of tons of cargo.

1899
Guides and Outfitters, The Wilderness Industry

By the late 1800s, the American wilderness of the northeast had been extensively explored and interest turned to the virgin Canadian outdoors. Northern New Brunswick had virtually unlimited hunting and fishing potential, and in 1899, nine men met at the York Hotel in Fredericton to form an organization which was then unique in North America. The charter members of the New Brunswick Guides Association included Harry Allen, Arthur Pringle, William Griffin, and "Uncle" Henry Braithwaite. The association lobbied government about game laws and license fees, but their main goal was marketing their services to American sportsmen.

The Maliseet and Mi'kmaq people had previously led hunting expeditions into the wilds but now whites were entering what they sensed would soon be a lucrative trade. Camps were built in the rugged Tobique and Mount Carleton area, where the first outfitters Adam Moore, Charles Cremin, and George Armstrong, provided "sports" with food, shelter, and guided excursions to hunt moose and caribou. In the off-season, displays were mounted at the American sport shows, especially in Boston, New York and Chicago, where New Brunswick was marketed as a sportsmen's paradise with guides in attendance, promising American sportsmen hunting and fishing success.

191

This early period of rod and gun tourism began in the Tobique River region but soon spread to the rest of northern New Brunswick including the Restigouche, Nepisiquit, and Miramichi areas. Many rich and famous Americans were attracted to the province, as were notable sports writers who wrote glowing accounts of hunting big game and catching the prized Atlantic Salmon. This wilderness industry grew in popularity and about 1910 a second wave of professional guides became active in the Tobique region, including the famous Ogilvy family who ran Gulquac Lodge near the Tobique River and also established lodges on the Restigouche River.

The three Ogilvy sons became legendary guides and so well-liked that bankers and Hollywood actors, such as John Barrymore, would only accept fishing advice from Jock Ogilvy. New Brunswick's famous canoe enterprise, the Chestnut Canoe Company, named some of their most famous models after the Ogilvy boys. The "Ogilvy Special" was produced in five lengths and widths, each named for one of the brothers, but all Ogilvy Specials were guide canoes with close ribs and flat bottoms, ideal for light draft that allowed for poling on New Brunswick's rocky salmon rivers. With abundant big game and incredible salmon runs, New Brunswick's reputation as a hunting and fishing mecca made the outfitting and guiding business a profitable industry throughout the twentieth century.

1900 – 1950
Modern Times

New Brunswick in 1900

At the turn of the century, New Brunswick ended the Victorian era a very different place than it had been in 1800. Although New Brunswick was still largely a rural province with over 70 per cent of its population living outside the urban areas, signs of industrial activity and commerce were everywhere. Farming was the leading occupation but the lumber trade was a close second as hundreds of sawmills and log operations dotted the province.

Railways were widespread in 1900 as the province contained almost 3,200 kilometres (two thousand miles) of tracks and one of the highest ratios of railway mileage per capita anywhere. About sixteen thousand kilometres (ten thousand miles) of dirt roads crisscrossed the province but the horse and buggy still reigned, as the Model A automobile was still a few years off. Most of the cities and towns had installed electricity that powered street lights and telephones, as well as the new streetcars in Saint John, Moncton, and St. Stephen.

The first sixty years of the nineteenth century had witnessed a tenfold population explosion in the province, as its leading city, Saint John, became a major centre on the North American east coast; however Saint John's growth had stalled after Confederation and the new railway city of Moncton experienced significant growth. After Confederation, New Brunswick's population had levelled off as migration due to uncertain economic conditions, more than offset the increased birth rate.

English-speaking New Brunswickers left for more prosperous parts of North American but the Acadian population grew considerably to make up over 20 per cent of the province's 330,000 residents. Acadians would

193

continue to increase to more than 30 per cent of New Brunswick's population by 1930. Immigration still came mainly from the British Isles and while the province continued to receive large numbers of immigrants, especially at Saint John, most of the new foreigners quickly left the province for the faster growing inland regions of North America.

1901
Oldest and Longest Covered Bridges

New Brunswick became famous in the nineteenth century for its beautiful and numerous covered wooden bridges. By 1944, there were 320 in existence but today there are only sixty-nine remaining, with the largest number in Kings, Albert, and Charlotte Counties. The oldest existing covered bridge was constructed in 1870 at Nelson Hollow near Doaktown, and is one of only two remaining bridges from the nineteenth century. Called Mill Brook No.1 (Nelson Hollow), it is one of only two hip-roofed bridges in New Brunswick, and was closed to traffic in 1938, but restored in 1977 by the Doaktown Historic Society.

Vibrations from trotting horses contributed to long term structural problems, so signs were posted on most bridges threatening fines unless one drove "no faster than a walk." The last covered bridge to be built in the province was the Shikatehawk River No.2 (Lockhart Mill) in Carleton County in 1954, since destroyed. Carleton County still has a number of the historic structures, including the longest covered bridge in the world.

Opened in 1901, the Hartland Bridge was built of Douglas fir and black spruce by a private firm called the Hartland Toll Bridge Company. The toll was abolished in 1906, as the province took over operation of the 391 meter (1,282 foot) structure that has seen fire, floods, rot, accidents, and even a proposal to rebuild in steel. Covering the bridge also became controversial as a petition circulated in Hartland questioning its effect on the morals of the local young people. Today, the famous covered bridge remains intact, although it is closed to heavy traffic.

Another covered bridge, the Coverdale River No.7 (Parkingdale) in Albert County was moved from its location in rural Albert County to become a tourist attraction at Moncton's Magnetic Hill. Built in 1915 by the province's best known bridge builder, Albert E. Smye of Alma, Albert County, the bridge was dismantled and reconstructed in 1982.

1903
The Pauper Contract System

New Brunswick had inherited the British legal system including the old Elizabethan poor law of 1601, that asserted civic responsibility for the destitute. The New Brunswick Poor Law of 1786 established that the relief of the poor would be financed and administered by the province's thirty-four parishes. Yet without significant taxing powers, many rural parishes could not afford to construct and maintain poorhouses

To offset the expense, a system evolved in New Brunswick whereby paupers were sold at annual public auctions to the lowest bidder, who then received payment from the parish. The contractor was then able to force the pauper to work. A parish overseer was responsible for ensuring humane treatment for paupers, but parish authorities were unwilling to pay any additional costs. Wilful neglect and physical abuse were common.

In 1887, the American crusader George Francis Train exposed this system of human bondage after witnessing the annual pauper auction in Sussex, where impoverished citizens were forced onto a station platform and sold. Despite numerous newspaper articles and speeches denouncing the practice, the annual auction was maintained in Sussex until the turn of the century, when a poorhouse finally opened in nearby Norton.

The inhumanity of the pauper system was revealed in 1903, when a contractor submitted a controversial bill to the Hopewell parish in Albert County after the death of a pauper. Alexander Hawks charged the parish $106.26 including board, lodging, medical costs, and even burial expenses for the upkeep, illness, and funeral of Paul Doherty. The parish attempted to avoid payment by citing the bill as excessive, and claiming the pauper's residence as the neighbouring parish of Harvey. Similar disputes while a pauper was alive would sometimes mean that the destitute person would be turned out if payment was in doubt.

Although the pauper auction and contract system was seen as cruel and inhuman, it continued to be maintained in some parts of New Brunswick until the late 1920s. By then, most counties had constructed poorhouses where the mentally ill, the sick, homeless infants, and vagrants were given permanent housing.

1903
Société Mutuelle l'Assomption

In and around Waltham, Massachusetts, a number of expatriate Acadians formed a financial institution that would eventually benefit almost all Acadians of New Brunswick. The idea arose out of a convention of American Acadians, with its stated purpose "to work by all possible and legitimate means for the advancement of the Acadian cause." The Assumption Mutual Life Insurance Company assumed the mandate of providing financial and business support to the growing Acadian community, and initially acted as a cooperative society, even establishing a scholarship fund for the education of promising young Acadians.

Acadian wealth was not great in the early 1900s, and with headquarters in the United States the Assumption's growth the first ten years was slow. After the Society's head office was transferred to Moncton, business began to expand. Except for Rogersville and Caraquet, the first twenty-one branches were all located in Kent and Westmorland counties, and by 1926, more than 4,800 Acadians were members. The 1920s saw the Assumption Company come under the capable leadership of former teacher Calixte Savoie, who further expanded the Society's presence in eastern New Brunswick, attracting more than ten thousand members. The Assumption Company continued to grow even during the hungry 1930s, and today is still a strong economic force in Acadian affairs with large modern headquarters in downtown Moncton.

1906
The Rectory Murder

A brutal murder occurred in the parish of New Ireland in Albert County in 1906, when Father Edward McAuley returned home to discover his sister dead in the church rectory. A young handyman Tom Collins disappeared, and was later apprehended near St. George on his way to the United States. He was in possession of Mary-Anne McAuley's gold watch.

Circumstantial evidence also pointed to Tom Collins as the one who bludgeoned Father McAuley's sister with an axe for a ten dollar watch. It took three long trials, all held in the Albert County Court House at Hopewell Cape, before Collins was found guilty of the murder of Mary-Anne McAuley. Held in the tiny stone jail next to the Court House, Collins was sentenced to hang and when the time came for the execution, his only request was to die in the daylight.

Albert County's first and only hanging occurred on a cold and wet day in 1907, on a make-shift gallows at the rear of the small jail. Within a month, Father McAuley was dead of heartbreak and sorrow from the long, drawn-out trials, and the people of New Ireland slowly began to move away as a result of the terrible event. New Ireland as a community is no more but the Albert County Museum displays details of the famous rectory murder.

1906
Women and the Law

A stumbling block in the advancement of women's rights in the nineteenth century was the question of whether a woman was in fact "a person in law." The issue arose in 1886 when Mary K. Tibbits wrote and passed the entrance exams to the University of New Brunswick. On the advice of her solicitor, she applied for admission but was not accepted even though the university's legislation for admittance stated that "any person who passed the exam, paid their dues ..." would be admitted. Certain members of the university's board were unwilling to see a woman enrolled in the university, and questioned the definition of a person as extending to a woman. However Mary Tibbits did gain admittance as the first woman at UNB, since university officials quickly allowed her entrance when John Ellis, a Member of the Legislative Assembly threatened to cut off their provincial grant. But the issue of "persons" was unresolved.

Throughout the 1800s, women had great difficulty owning property since their uncertain legal status made for a very unequal system of provincial justice. With the female suffrage movement agitating for women's rights, the issue of a woman's legal status came to the forefront in 1905 when Mabel Penery French graduated from King's College Law School in Saint John. French was the third woman to graduate but the first to apply for admission to the New Brunswick Bar.

In a stunning decision, even for early twentieth century jurisprudence, the Barrister's Society and the New Brunswick Supreme Court ruled that Mabel French was not a person as defined by law, and therefore unable to practise law in the province. Embarrassed by the ruling, the New Brunswick Legislature enacted a law in 1906 that clearly allowed women to study and practise law in the province. Mabel French was then installed as New Brunswick's first female lawyer and practised law and worked in the suffrage movement until her departure for British Columbia in 1910.

Yet change came slowly to the New Brunswick legal profession and it was not until 1934 that women were allowed to run for political office. Newcastle lawyer Frances Fish, who was the first woman to graduate from

Dalhousie University Law School, ran in the 1935 provincial election. Defeated, Francis Fish was also the first female to be appointed a deputy magistrate for Northumberland County in 1947. The first woman to be appointed a judge in New Brunswick was Muriel Fergusson, who became Judge of Probate in Grand Falls in 1935. But almost fifty more years would go by before a second woman was appointed to the bench in New Brunswick.

1908
John Hazen's Conservative Party

Like Andrew Blair before him, John Douglas Hazen realized early in his political career that loose coalitions of semi-loyal party members were ineffective in maintaining political power. He worked for nine years in opposition, building a political machine that became a credible alternative to the Liberal Party and, in doing so, established the roots of the modern Conservative Party in New Brunswick.

Hazen was born in Oromocto and studied at the University of New Brunswick. Like most politicians of his day, Hazen became a lawyer prior to his launch into politics, which began with a two-year term as the youngest mayor of Fredericton. Inheriting Hazen's Castle, his rich uncle's estate in Saint John, Hazen moved to the port city and was elected to one term as a Conservative MP in Ottawa.

John Hazen began his nine-year task of consolidating the provincial Conservative Party in 1899, and managed to include a number of dissident Liberals under his dynamic leadership. He finally defeated Liberal Premier Clifford Robinson in 1908, and governed with authority and ability until he, like many of his political colleagues, left provincial politics for greener pastures in Parliament.

Beginning in 1911, Hazen served as Minister of Marine and Fisheries in Robert Borden's federal Conservative government. While in Ottawa, Hazen remained the dean of the provincial Conservative Party, advising on strategic matters and exercising considerable influence over the party's reaction to Premier James Flemming's resignation over a campaign fund scandal. The founder of New Brunswick's Conservative Party spent his last years in public office as Chief Justice of the province. He died in 1937.

1912
The Father of Acadia

None of the seventeen Catholic bishops appointed in the Maritimes during the nineteenth century were Acadian. Anglophone Irish Catholics controlled the leadership of the church and conducted its affairs in English, yet many among their congregations were French-speaking. After Confederation, a new group of Acadian leaders emerged with nationalistic goals that included not just more use of French, but a new French-speaking diocese for New Brunswick. The move towards the Acadianization of the church meant that a clash with the Irish Bishop, James Rogers of Chatham, was inevitable. No one realized how long such a clash would last.

The first native-born Acadian to become a Catholic priest was François-Xavier Cormier, who was among the Saint Joseph's College priests who had become politicized while playing an active role in the Acadian nationalistic movement of the 1880s. But the most important Acadian priest to challenge the Catholic establishment in search of Acadian rights was Marcel-François Richard. Born in 1847 at Saint-Louis-de-Kent, Richard was ordained at age twenty-three, and assigned to his home parish where controversy seemed to always surround him. Bizarre circumstances had him in and out of the Dorchester jail over a protracted struggle with an unstable superior, but he emerged a popular figure, and was reinstated as the parish curé. A strong organizer with boundless energy, he founded Collège Saint-Louis before his thirtieth birthday.

Richard reported to Bishop Rogers. Tension began to mount between the two men in the late 1870s when the Bishop's English-speaking St. Michael's College at Chatham was forced to close for financial reasons, while Collège Saint-Louis in Kent County remained open. Bishop Rogers accused Richard of favouring French students and spoke harshly of the college administration being "too Frenchy," during his speech at the 1882 graduation exercise of the college. The Bishop was blamed when the institution closed later that same year. The rift between French and English Catholics widened as Bishop Rogers transferred Father Richard to nearby Rogersville, and denied his parish priest permission to travel or attend Acadian meetings. By 1891, the Bishop refused to travel to Father Richard's parish, as the determined priest began writing Rome for advice.

When Thomas Barry replaced Bishop Rogers in the late 1890s, Acadians were bitterly disappointed since they felt a French bishop was long overdue. Meanwhile Father Richard was busy lobbying for a French diocese in Moncton. After his third audience with the Pope in 1907, Richard returned to New Brunswick with a Pontifical promise to appoint an Acadian Bishop. Father Richard would travel once again to Rome, but in 1912 Edouard LeBlanc, an Acadian from Weymouth, Nova Scotia, was named the Bishop of Saint John and two years later a French parish, Notre Dame de l'Assomption, was established in eastern New Brunswick.

Failing health ended Father Richard's involvement in redressing Acadian grievances. But his life's work as a champion of Acadian causes earned him the title of Father of Acadia. In 1920, an Acadian bishop was appointed to the Chatham diocese but the Kent County priest had passed away five years earlier. Besides building a number of churches, schools and convents throughout Kent and Northumberland Counties, Father Richard assisted a religious order at his adopted village of Rogersville where his legacy has been honoured with a historic site.

1914
A Premier On Trial

A shocked and bewildered New Brunswick heard testimony in the 1914 session of the Provincial Legislature from Madawaska Liberal L.A. Dugal, that he had evidence linking the popular Conservative Premier James Kidd Flemming to graft and extortion. The charges centred around the claim that in conjunction with a provincial employee, Willard Berry of the Department of the Surveyor-General, the Premier headed a scheme that charged an extra $15 fee per square mile, to renew Crown land licenses. Dugal also claimed further evidence that Flemming received kickbacks from St. John River Valley Railway contractors, in exchange for government assistance.

Denying any guilt, the Premier did step aside. Attorney General George Clarke was chosen Acting Premier and appointed a Royal Commission headed by Supreme Court Judge H.A. McKeown to investigate the charges. Meanwhile the Conservatives received further bad news — one contractor claimed to have paid Flemming $70,000 but only $10,000 reached the Conservative Party. With intense public interest aroused by constant attacks from Liberal newspapers, New Brunswick's political trial of the century began to be played out in the historic Saint John County Court House.

Dugal's charges were supported by the best Liberal lawyers in the province and directed by well known Carleton County Liberal MP and lawyer, Frank Carvell. Flemming also had the support of Saint John's best legal minds. Besides Flemming, the key witness would be Willard Berry, but attempts to serve him a subpoena failed as he fled his Charlotte County home for the safety of Boston's Parker House. Although eventually served with the writ, Berry refused to appear before the commission.

Frank Carvell quickly established the existence of a large Conservative fund that had been run by Berry, who in turn reported to Premier Flemming. Flemming was then directly implicated in the scandal from testimony by John Brankley of the Miramichi Lumber Company, who claimed that he and Berry, along with Flemming and Tory bagman E.R. Teed, met at the Barker House in Fredericton where secret lumber funds were discussed, and later $60,000 was paid to a Conservative campaign fund.

James Kidd Flemming's testimony revealed a broken Premier barely able to deny his involvement in the kickback scheme, and a number of pro-Tory newspapers suggested he resign. As war broke out in Europe, the three-man Royal Commission delivered its report to Lieutenant Governor Josiah Wood, who delayed making the report public for six weeks until the government could agree on Flemming's fate. An impasse developed as Flemming resisted resigning and the Lieutenant Governor insisted he leave or be dismissed. Finally after receiving advice from ex-Tory premier John Hazen, Flemming resigned and the report was made public. Berry was found guilty of extortion and the report stated that Flemming was a likely co-conspirator, and guilty of compelling at least one railway contractor to contribute to Conservative Party funds.

A religious man who taught Sunday school, Kidd Flemming was now seen as sinful both by his Liberal critics and the Protestant and Conservative press, who had previously supported him. Yet his home town of Woodstock produced a crowd of more than a thousand faithful followers who gathered to rally their support around him. Flemming returned to his family sawmill business but ran successfully as a Conservative Member of Parliament in 1925. The most sensational political trial of the era made James Kidd Flemming somewhat of an outcast in provincial politics. However, in the 1950s, his son Hugh John Flemming became one of New Brunswick's most successful politicians and governed as premier for eight years.

1914
Saint John's Street Railway Strike

The early decades of the twentieth century were turbulent years for industrial relations as new unions challenged the autocratic ownership practices of the previous century. Saint John was the major industrial centre of New Brunswick with its union tradition dating well back to the 1840s, when Canada's first waterfront union was established.

But the militant labour groups of the early twentieth century were much better organized, affiliated with international organizations, and less

201

afraid to confront employers with strikes; violence and lockouts were common bargaining techniques of the period. Longshoremen, carpenters, textile workers, printers, even police officers formed union brotherhoods to further their interests, but the most violent union confrontation in Saint John's history occurred in 1914, when a dispute between the Saint John Railway Company and its workers erupted into a bloody riot.

Saint John's streetcar company was still a private syndicate prior to World War One. When its workers formed Local No. 663 of the Amalgamated Association of Street and Electric Railway Employees and demanded an eight-hour day, company officials rejected the request and hired private detectives to spy on the union. Union leaders were soon dismissed on trumped-up charges as the company ignored a conciliation board's recommendations and also ignored the workers' decision to prepare for a strike. Strikebreakers arrived from Montreal and on July 23 a confrontation became inevitable as striking workers and their large group of supporters took to the streets of Saint John.

Thousands were on hand as gangs of young men roamed the city intimidating streetcar passengers with rocks and bottles. The police force was overwhelmed and unable to prevent the mob from stopping the trolleys. The military was called in as Mayor James Frink stood at the SPCA foundation at Market Square and read the riot act to the swarming crowd. The mob seemed to calm down with the threat of life imprisonment, but panic broke out as Lieutenant Hubert Stethem and his Royal Canadian Dragoons charged down King Street on horseback with swords slashing, knocking down men, women and children.

The crowd reacted to the cavalry charge by fighting back. Lieutenant Stethem's face was smashed by a flying bottle while another trooper was knocked from his horse. Knives were drawn, slashing at troopers and horses. The Dragoons retreated but more violence erupted as the mob overturned stalled streetcars and set them ablaze. The mob attacked the railway company's powerhouse and forced it to shut down, but private detectives defended the repair barn by spraying rioters with buckshot.

The next day overturned trolleys and broken glass littered Saint John streets, as city officials attempted to break the stalemate between the union and the company. Peace was restored when suspended union leader Fred Ramsay accepted a lifetime position with the city's public works department, and the remaining dismissed workers were reinstated. Streetcar service was resumed a day later. While tensions remained high between the union and the Saint John Railway Company, war with Germany was declared in August and most unions temporally suspended their militancy to assist the Canadian war effort.

1916
Kent–Westmorland 145th Infantry Battalion

"For King and Country" was the rally cry of the First World War, and in the village of Dorchester during the winter of 1916 the motto of the newly formed all-Dorchester Platoon became "For King and Country and to Help Paint Dorchester on the Kaiser's Front Door."

Detachments of enlisted men were formed from towns and villages all over southeastern New Brunswick to make up the Kent–Westmorland 145th Infantry Battalion, Canadian Expeditionary Force. About 60 per cent of the eight hundred men were from Westmorland County but Albert and Kent Counties also contributed significant numbers, as did other regions of New Brunswick. Military parades together with patriotic music, supplied by the Battalion's own band, mustered the men in Sackville, Dorchester, Moncton, and other centres to waiting trains as the Battalion was shipped off to Valcartier, Quebec.

Arriving in June of 1916, the 145th trained as a unit over the hot summer where up to forty thousand troops were stationed in preparation for departure for overseas service. They lived in tents while conducting forced marches, rifle practise, and survival training; many of the original eight hundred men were discharged on medical grounds and the Battalion was reduced to about 525 men.

Due to a measles epidemic, the 132nd Battalion out of Chatham was quarantined, and the Westmorland 145th together with the Saint John based 140th Battalion, left Valcartier for Europe on September 22. Crowds so dense that the troops were barely able to disembark, met the 145th at Moncton, and as the Halifax-bound, overloaded train climbed the uphill section of the line between Dorchester and Sackville, five Dorchester men jumped off to stay the night with their families. The next morning, the AWOL men were quickly given fare and caught the next train for Halifax where they rejoined their battalion that evening.

Sailing aboard SS *Tuscania*, which was later torpedoed off the Irish coast, the Kent-Westmorland 145th Infantry Battalion quit Halifax on September 27, and cruised in convoy across the North Atlantic. Overcrowded, rusty and dirty, the SS *Tuscania* was at least fast, and while the men slept in hammocks, the vessel dodged German U-boats and despite an attack, actually survived and was able to dock safely in Liverpool on October 6. Assigned to a camp outside Folkestone in Kent, the 145th Battalion had set the goal of fighting as a unit in Europe, but it lacked the required strength of numbers with only about six hundred troops and was soon absorbed into the 9th Reserve Battalion.

By 1918 most of the original members of the 145th saw action as the 9th Reserve supplied reinforcements for front line fighting units. With the abolishment of the War Measures Act in 1920, most of the battalion was disbanded yet the surviving members of the 145th could proudly claim that they had upheld the old Battalion motto "For King and Country."

1917
Lord Beaverbrook

New Brunswick's favourite son, William Maxwell Aitken, grew up in Newcastle where he attended Harkins Academy in the late 1800s, and quickly became so successful in business that he earned his first million before the age of thirty. A son of a Presbyterian minister, Max Aitken sold eggs and operated a newspaper route as a child, displaying an entrepreneurial drive from an early age.

Aitken moved to England in 1910 where he was elected to the House of Commons under the Unionist Party and contributed greatly to the Allied war effort during World War One. Knighted and granted a baronetcy, Max Aitken was elevated to Baron Beaverbrook in 1917, a name he chose from a small stream near his boyhood home. Beaverbrook became a newspaper baron on London's Fleet Street but also managed to enhance his own literary reputation by writing a number of insightful books, including *Politicians and the Press, Men and Power,* and *My Early Life.*

During the Second World War he worked closely with his friend Winston Churchill, and became the British Minister of War Productions. Lord Beaverbrook is best remembered in New Brunswick for the many cultural gifts he bestowed on the province. Both the Beaverbrook Art Gallery and The Playhouse in Fredericton were built with his support, as well as many additions to the University of New Brunswick, including the law building, the gymnasium and a student residence. In Newcastle a public library, town hall, and skating rink were given as gifts, and he also made substantial improvements to the town square, where today a statue of his likeness graces the square along with his ashes that lie in the statue's base.

1917
Ten Years of Prohibition

New Brunswick had been unable to enforce its 1855 prohibition law but in 1878 the temperance movement succeeded in getting the federal government to attempt to regulate the liquor trade by enacting the Canada Temperance Act. Known as the Scott Act, it allowed city or county voters to ban by referendum all sales and public consumption of alcohol. First passed in Fredericton in 1879, and two years later in Moncton, the Scott Act was not adopted throughout New Brunswick since some counties chose to remain "wet." Nor was it consistently enforced in dry regions, because a number of legal loopholes and ambiguities allowed for the liquor trade to challenge the Act in the courts.

Initially Fredericton's efforts to enforce the Temperance Act was more vigorous than Moncton's. At one point during the 1880s, Magistrate Jacob Wortman dismissed the entire Moncton police force for their lack of enthusiasm in enforcing the Act. The dismissed Chief of Police, a bare-knuckle boxer named Ferdinand Thibodeau, eventually left law enforcement to open a hotel and tavern in Moncton that was frequently fined for liquor violations.

By 1890, municipal governments in New Brunswick were beginning to acquire significant revenues from liquor "fines," as a sort of quasi-licensing system developed where the major hotels and public houses paid regular fines to stay in business, while upstart groups were discouraged from entering the liquor business by police raids. The Scott Act became a way to regulate, but not outlaw, liquor consumption. Temperance organizations were not pleased with the outcome of the Scott Act but municipalities such as Moncton made thousands of dollars in liquor revenue during the 1890s, while the provincial government looked on in envy.

The War Measures Act of 1917 imposed Prohibition across Canada and on July 10, 1920, New Brunswick voted by a majority of two to one to prohibit alcoholic drink. All counties except 'voted in favour of Prohibition, yet importing liquor from outside New Brunswick was still legal. The Volstead Act had imposed Prohibition in the United States, and running European booze into the US soon became big business in New Brunswick. Besides bootleggers, druggists selling liquor by prescription also became rich, and with governments paying the high police costs of attempting to enforce the liquor ban, Prohibition became financially unattractive to the Tory government under John Baxter. By the mid-1920's, a cynical public had deemed Prohibition a great failure, and with the temperance movement in decline, repeal of the Temperance Act became inevitable.

205

In September of 1927, despite strong Prohibitionist attacks, Baxter's provincial government entered the retail liquor business and began selling booze to the public, arguing that the since the old Act was unworkable and disobeyed by most New Brunswickers, the government should at least regulate the liquor flow and earn a profit at the same time. And the people of the province seemed to agree because John Baxter and his Conservative government was re-elected to another term in office.

1918
First Department of Health

A unique development in the field of public health occurred in New Brunswick in 1918, when Dr. William F. Roberts succeeded in creating the first Department of Health in the British Empire. Representing Saint John, Dr. Roberts won election in Walter Foster's Liberal victory of 1917. The next year convinced the Liberal caucus to allow him to establish a Ministry of Health to control a deadly Spanish flu epidemic that had appeared in the province with the returning troops from the Great War.

A graduate of the Bellevue Hospital Medical College in New York, Dr. Roberts practiced in Saint John throughout his career. He became convinced that governments could play a larger role in improving public health, if special departments were established that were devoted to health issues. His bold move to prevent the spread of influenza by closing public buildings and prohibiting gatherings of five or more people, was credited with saving lives throughout the province. But Dr Roberts began to introduce an entire list of health reforms which New Brunswickers considered controversial, or at least too much too soon.

His mandatory vaccination against smallpox for children was cited as virtually eradicating the disease, but his insistence on wrapping bread and delivering milk in glass bottles meant price increases that proved unpopular with consumers. Compulsory pasteurization of milk became the most controversial legislation that Dr Roberts introduced, and the one that eventually led to his defeat in 1925. The dairy industry fought for retaining raw milk, and while Roberts went down to defeat, his legislation remained and the pasteurization of milk was eventually adopted throughout North America. Elected again to the Provincial Legislature in 1935, Dr William Roberts was appointed Minister of Health where he remained until his death in 1938.

1918
Riparian Rights & the Salmon Fishing Industry

The Atlantic Salmon has always been considered the king of all fresh-water fish and New Brunswick its rightful home. The Miramichi was known as the most productive salmon river system in the world with the St. John a close second. As New Brunswick's fame as a great salmon fishing region grew, sportfishing enthusiasts from all over the world began travelling to the province to fish.

A number of American sportsmen established the oldest known salmon fishing club in North America on the Restigouche River in 1880. The Ristigouche Salmon Club began as a group of wealthy New England and New York "sports," who sailed to the mouth of the Restigouche to fish for some of the largest salmon ever taken along the Atlantic coast. After purchasing tracts of land along the river, the group of about thirty-eight fishermen formed an association to help maintain the river's pristine state and to protect their riparian fishing rights.

As early as 1802, riparian fishing rights had been confirmed in New Brunswick as extending to landowners with property bound to any river or stream. The controversy that surrounded the question of whether the public could fish in Saint John harbour was not about rejecting the riparian rights of the adjacent landowners, but whether the harbour was part of the sea or the river. "All subjects" stated a bill enacted by the Legislature, "owning lands bounded on any river, cove, creek, or lake, should be deemed to have the sole and exclusive right of taking fish on or in front of the shores thereof."

By the early 1900s, much of New Brunswick's best salmon waters were leased to wealthy individuals or controlled by riparian rights owners, especially along the Restigouche watershed. In 1918, acting on the suggestion of celebrated sportsman and canoe builder, Harry Chestnut, the Liberal government of Walter Foster created the first public fishing water on the Restigouche. By reserving four miles of "Government Open Water" for New Brunswick residents, the government of the day established the principle that at least some public access was necessary to some of the best salmon fishing on the continent.

With an accommodation of six rods per day and operated by some of New Brunswick's most famous guides, including the Ogilvy Brothers, the Government Open Water stretch of the Restigouche became a legendary site for New Brunswick fishermen, including author George Frederick Clarke, who fished the water for over thirty years. Clarke's *Six Salmon Rivers And Another* praised the fishing program and described the angling stretch, now renamed Larry's Gulch Lodge and Pools, as excellent.

1919
Women's Right to Vote

"You might as well attempt to dam Niagara as to stop this agitation," said George Robertson, a Saint John Councillor in 1899. By the turn of the century, increasing numbers of women were demanding the vote. Yet without representation in the Legislature, women relied on pro-suffrage male legislators for support in their continued quest for the voting franchise. One of their strongest supporters was Henry Emmerson who became Premier in 1897. When told that a woman's place was not in politics but in the home, he replied: "But where is a man's place? In the vast majority of cases, his place is in the home too."

Despite being Premier, Emmerson's bill to grant full franchise rights to women was defeated by a vote of thirty-four to seven, and for a period in the early 1900s the women's movement died down. But Mabel French, New Brunswick's first female lawyer, prepared a new suffrage bill in 1907 and the Women's Enfranchisement Association attempted to introduce it in the Legislature. Deferred to the following year, a four member committee of the Association received a chilling reception from the anti-suffrage Premier John Hazen. Still another bill was introduced into the Legislature, but again to no avail.

In 1914 the suffrage movement began working for the war effort but the same year the first real breakthrough in thirty years occurred. A Saint John plebiscite granted married women voting rights in municipal elections, an extension of the 1886 declaration that had given unmarried women of property municipal voting privileges. Women were now 15 per cent of the New Brunswick workforce, and were working in the factories as men left for the European battlefront. With all provinces west of Quebec allowing the vote for women in provincial elections, voting rights for New Brunswick women were now inevitable. But again, Health Minister Roberts' franchise bill of 1917 was narrowly defeated, and it was not until April 15, 1919 that New Brunswick women were granted the right to vote in provincial elections.

The obvious question is this: why did it take so long? Many answers have been offered but political expediency is probably the most likely explanation, since there was little advantage for men to push the franchise issue, especially since so many of them felt that a woman's place was indeed in the home. The aftermath of 1919 was also disappointing for women — they had been given voting rights but were excluded from running for political office within the province. No such restriction was in place for federal elections, and Woodstock music teacher Minnie Bell Adney attempted to run for Parliament in Victoria-Carleton. After filing her nomination papers, her name was mysteriously dropped from the 1919 ballot list, apparently the result of a bribe. Adney managed to ensure that her name did appear on the 1925 federal ballot list and she received eighty-four votes. However it would be 1948 before a women would be voted into political office in New Brunswick, when Edna Steel became Saint John's first female city councillor.

1920
Moncton's Irish Home Rule Controversy

The granting of Home Rule to Ireland had erupted into civil war during 1920 over the exclusion of the six northern counties, and New Brunswick became swept up in the violent dispute. Lindsay Crawford was President of the Irish Self-Determination League of Canada, and became himself a source of great controversy for crossing over from his Protestant Irish roots in the Orange Order to the nationalist cause.

A journalist and fiery public speaker, Crawford began a cross-Canada speaking tour to promote Irish Home Rule, but his appearance in Moncton was challenged by a group of Protestant citizens that included the city's mayor. A resolution was passed opposing Crawford's appearance, and soon the Irish question became a Protestant-Catholic controversy, with Crawford's speaking engagement promising to explode into a bitter confrontation.

The evening of December 6, 1920, threatened to become one of the most violent in Moncton's history, as city hall quickly became overcrowded with partisan supporters. Before Crawford could speak, an Orangeman shouted "The King," and one side of the audience stood to sing *Rule Britannia*. Even the chairman, John Doherty, was unable to speak as disorder broke out, and Police Chief L. Hutchinson declared the meeting finished, ordering the crowd to disperse.

A mob attacked Crawford and his supporters as they attempted to leave the hall to catch a train out of town. Outside the railway station Crawford was roughed up and made to kiss the Union Jack. Crawford was unable to leave for Quebec City until the next day. Upon arriving in Quebec he was quoted as saying he felt his treatment in Moncton was not representative of the community, but the work of a small group of hotheads that were stirred up by professional anti-Irish nationalists. As the recipient of so many immigrants from the United Kingdom, New Brunswick could not escape the old hatreds and conflicts that continued to erupt in Europe.

Early twentieth century photo of Campbellton's Intercolonial Railway Station. (NBPA)

1920
Maritime Rights Movement

Tough times led to the near collapse of the Maritime economy in the early 1920s, and caused the rise of a protest movement that defended regional interests in a desperate struggle for economic survival. The 1918 integration of the Intercolonial Railway into the national railway system, and the transfer of its head office from Moncton to Toronto triggered this regional depression.

John A. MacDonald's National Railway, his "political consequence of a political union," was now simply a branch line, and freight rates to western Canada more than doubled, producing an abrupt crisis that threatened the Maritime economy. The crisis united a protest movement across all sectors of Maritime society. Yet the roots of the crisis and agitation were decades earlier in the post-Confederation era of the 1870s, when MacDonald's National Policy and railway interests forged a continental economic zone above the forty-ninth parallel.

To encourage trade within Canada and stimulate Maritime ports to focus on inland markets, import tariffs were raised and freight rates to central Canada were lowered, as the Intercolonial Railway became the engine for industrial development and nationhood. However a shift of power was occurring westward as every census after 1891 saw the Maritimes lose political representation: from 18 per cent of all seats in Parliament in 1890, to 13 per cent by 1914. Bursting with growth, western Canada would no longer tolerate unequal freight rates.

Just as the Great War ended and manufacturing enterprises were having to reinvest funds in order to retool for peace-time production, the government of Robert Borden cancelled the forty-year-old favourable Maritime shipping rate. As rates more than doubled, railway traffic slumped by more than 40 per cent. Further bad news appeared when a worldwide post-war recession developed, and central Canada began switching to hydroelectric power from Maritime coal. Investments in regional factories and industries were postponed, so by the mid-1920s few major Maritime industrial enterprises were still operating.

Despite deep divisions between employers and unions, Maritimers from all classes and occupations were unanimous in their protests. Railway Brotherhoods, farmers, fishermen, factory merchants, and shippers all demanded the return of the Intercolonial to independent control and management. New Brunswick Premier John Baxter, who assumed power in 1925, played a major role in the protest movement against federal transportation policy. The traditional Maritime reluctance to co-operate with each other was abandoned in favour of a Maritime-wide agitation for better federal treatment.

Prime Minister Mackenzie King appointed a Royal Commission in 1927 and the Duncan report succeeded in developing the Maritime Freight Rates Act, that restored a lower freight rate for Maritime shippers. But the limited success of the Maritime Rights Movement could not restore the industrial development of the pre-1920s period. By the late 1920s, trucking, capital shortages and an impending depression all contributed to prevent the re-industrialisation of the Maritimes. However, the Maritime Rights Movement did succeed in producing an awareness of the Maritime region as a single area within Canada and, once again, Maritime political union was considered but, in the end, rejected.

1920
The Return of John Clarence Webster

One of New Brunswick's most important historians was born at Shediac in 1863 and, although educated at Mount Allison, received a Doctor of Medicine degree from Edinburgh University. John Clarence Webster received a gold medal for excellence from Edinburgh, and also excelled in his medical career, pioneering the use of rubber gloves during operations while working at the Royal Victoria Hospital in Montreal. He spent the bulk of his career teaching and working in medicine at Chicago, but ill health in 1920 encouraged him to return to his boyhood home of Shediac.

Not content to languish in retirement, J. Clarence Webster became preoccupied with the forgotten historic treasures of the Maritimes, which had remained buried for years. He saw the stagnation of the Atlantic region as partly the result of this lack of understanding about the rich historic events of the past. In *The Distressed Maritimes*, his first publication after returning to New Brunswick, Webster argued for more knowledge and factual evidence about the earlier times. Such knowledge he felt could be a key to strengthen the region's culture and provide educational and commercial opportunities.

With help from his well-to-do American wife, Alice Lusk, a French-language scholar, Webster built one of the best collections of Canadiana in the country. During the last twenty years of his life, he self-published almost fifty, well-illustrated historical works about the region, including *The Forts of Chignecto*, *Acadia at the End of the Seventeenth Century*, and *Thomas Pichon, the Spy of Beauséjour*. His scholarship was unsurpassed, especially in his special area of interest — the French period in Acadia. Webster's interest was in popularizing history, and like William Raymond and William Ganong before him, saw his mission in the Maritimes as one of bringing history alive.

Webster's obsession became the establishment of historic sites, parks and museums. At these sites, while acquiring an appreciation of the past, the average person could experience history in an authentic setting. As New Brunswick's representative on the National Historic Sites and Monuments Board of Canada, he helped identify many of the more than sixty sites that are currently recognized in New Brunswick. He served as chairman of the National Board in 1943, and also served as president of the Canadian Historical Association. Yet his interest was clearly local, especially the Chignecto area, where he worked endlessly to have the old forts at Beauséjour and Gaspereau designated National Historical Sites.

As the driving force behind the establishment of the New Brunswick Museum in Saint John, Webster offered his historical collection to the Museum, and combined it with the Natural History Society's collection. The new institution opened its doors on August 16, 1934, one hundred and fifty years after Abraham Gesner first started the museum. The "Laird of Shediac," as Webster was called by his contemporaries, was instrumental in having a stone museum built at his favourite site, Fort Beauséjour. Having worked so hard to have the heritage of his province recognized, he died at Shediac in 1950. Reflecting on his life in his concise autobiography, *Those Crowded Years*, he wrote: "When I can no longer work, I have no wish to live."

1921
Game Refuge Established

In May of 1921, the provincial government became actively involved in wildlife management by establishing New Brunswick's first game sanctuary on the Canaan River in Westmorland County. An act of the Legislature two years earlier had authorized game refuges, and the 145 square kilometre (eighty-seven square mile) site, was soon doubled to 292 square kilometres (175 square miles), with no hunting permitted and only limited fishing.

"No person has the right to hunt or trap ... or travel upon it with either a gun or a dog at any time," stated the Act, which had a penalty for violation of $300 or a six month jail sentence. In all, six game refuges were established throughout the province by 1934, including the huge Kedgwick Game Refuge that covered 543 square kilometres (326 square miles) in Restigouche County. Lepreau, Becaguimac, Burpee, and Bantalor were the other early wildlife reserves. While hunting was outlawed, fishing was allowed with a permit between May 15 and the end of August, but restrictions were placed on fishermen that allowed only thirty fish per trip to be taken, and all were to be at least eight inches in length. Costs to fish on reserves were one dollar per trout license, with non-residents having to pay ten dollars, and wardens were hired to patrol for poachers and forest fires.

The era of wildlife protection and management had finally arrived in New Brunswick and, gradually, the large game refuges were converted to wildlife management areas with smaller refuges established for public education.

1923
P.J. Veniot, An Acadian in Power

Peter J. Venoit, the first Acadian to become Premier of New Brunswick, consequently came to symbolize the arrival of French political power in the province. While was born in Kent County in 1863, "PJ" was raised in Nova Scotia and graduated from Pictou Academy unable to speak French. Working as a reporter with the Moncton *Transcript*, his marriage to Catherine Melanson created a need to master the French language. In 1887, he moved to Bathurst to edit the French weekly *Courrier des Provinces Maritimes*. He later purchased the newspaper and won a seat in the provincial Legislature.

Peter Veniot took quickly to politics and became the undisputed leader of the Acadian faction of the provincial Liberal Party. His political partisanship also brought his newspaper into the Liberal Party orbit, as he championed the cause of Andrew Blair's Liberal Party. He organized the first Liberal convention ever held in Gloucester County but his promising future was threatened in 1900, when a serious accident forced his resignation from provincial politics amid personal financial difficulties.

A political appointment as a federal Customs Collector ensured his financial stability but the 1911 political defeat of the federal Liberals left him jobless, and he became a full-time Liberal organizer. Veniot himself won election in the Liberal sweep of 1917, and he played a major role in the victory by ensuring the overwhelming support of the Acadians. As Minister of Public Works, road building for the new automobile era meant hiring many pro-Liberal supporters. Under Premier Walter Foster and his government, Veniot won re-election in 1920, which included a vote for Prohibition. But as in the 1850s, Prohibition proved unenforceable.

In 1923 Foster resigned as Premier and the skillful Peter Veniot, now sixty, was selected his successor. The powerful foreign-controlled pulp mills challenged his decision to build the Grand Falls Power Plant with government funds. They threw their considerable support behind John Baxter's Conservative Party, which won the bitterly fought 1925 election. For an Acadian, and a Roman Catholic, to be elected to power was still too much for New Brunswickers — who finally did vote another Acadian into power in 1967, Louis Robichaud. Peter Veniot spent his remaining years in federal politics but his role as a Liberal and the first Acadian Premier firmly established the Acadians as a voting block of Liberal support well into the 1970s.

1923
The Pulp and Paper Industry

Within a single decade, New Brunswick's largest industry was radically restructured — from a traditional lumbering enterprise of sawmills and logging operations controlled by timber barons, to a small number of large pulp and paper mills owned by multinational interests.

Powered by hydro-electricity, the modern pulp and paper industry began around 1900 in central Canada and the United States. New Brunswick was late to enter the new use of forest products due to its lack of hydro development, and its Crown timber lands were also tied up in long-term lumber leases. By 1910, large amounts of pulp were being exported to paper mills outside New Brunswick. By the early 1920s, the lumbering industry that had driven the provincial economy for more than one hundred years was on its deathbed.

The province was one of the most enthusiastic Canadian governments to enact the 1911 Manufacturing Condition Act, that effectively outlawed the export of raw pulp from Crown lands. But without large-scale electrification, papermaking could not develop within the region. By 1918, six pulp mills were operating in the province but there was still no paper production, and the provincial government was fighting with the giant pulp and paper companies — especially the largest, International Paper — over illegal exports of pulp to their paper plants in the United States.

Small-scale hydro development by pulp companies did take place before 1920; for example the St. George Pulp and Paper Company built a hydro-power station on the Magaguadavic River for its groundwood pulp mill. But the large-scale pulp mills at Bathurst and Edmundston were still powered by coal-fired steam generators. In 1923, the first large-scale manufacturing of paper took place at the Bathurst Lumber mill, powered by a nine thousand horsepower hydro dam on the nearby Nepisiguit River. Demand for paper was rising, and the Fraser Company had also installed a hydro dam on the Madawaska River at Edmundston and began to produce paper. But without a large-scale hydro development, further expansion was limited.

As provincial revenues from the forests dropped in half during the 1921 recession, politicians became desperate to develop the pulp and paper industry and turned their attention to the Grand Falls site, where hydro electric plans had been in circulation for over twenty-five years. The 1925 provincial election was fought over the issue of whether the Grand Falls power dam would be built through public ownership or given to the private sector to develop. The Conservatives, under John Baxter, defeated Peter

The early days of New Brunswick's pulp and paper industry. The Edward
Partington Pulp & Paper Co., Saint John, 1910. (Isaac Erb photo)

Veniot's Liberals and handed the site to International Paper, the world's
largest producer of pulp and paper, to develop.

International Paper, along with the Fraser Company, acquired huge
tax concessions, unlimited water rights, and fifty-year timber leases, before
proceeding with the massive hydro project that was finally completed in
1930. By this time, the newsprint industry had replaced the sawmills as
the engine of the provincial economy. Two companies, International Paper,
who now owned the Bathurst Lumber Company, and the Fraser Company,
controlled the vast majority of papermaking in the province, and fully
two-thirds of all Crown timber leases in New Brunswick.

With transmission lines from Grand Falls north to Edmundston and
the north shore, New Brunswick had developed a capacity to produce
seven hundred tons of paper per day, when International Paper's huge mill
at Dalhousie opened in 1931. Most of the major lumber companies were
now out of business as the new industrial era had arrived in the province
— complete with New Brunswick's only central electric facility now
reserved for papermaking. As well, New Brunswick's vast Crown timber
stands were now in the hands of a few international corporations. Without
access to the new industrial power of electricity, other economic forces
were unable to develop, and the forest-dependent economy of the province
was firmly entrenched.

1925
K.C. Irving Arrives in Saint John

In September of 1925, New Brunswick's most successful entrepreneur, indeed Canada's greatest twentieth century industrialist, arrived in Saint John. K.C. Irving had left his home in Bouctouche, ready to make his fortune by taking over the city's Ford car dealership on Union Street. But Kenneth Colin Irving was interested in much more than simply selling cars, he also wanted to make money by keeping cars running.

Selling gasoline, oil, and repairing cars occupied his early years in the port city but Irving's business skills were already well developed from his boyhood days in Kent County. The son of a prosperous lumberman, K.C. had his own bank account at age five from his vegetable garden sales, spent a few years at Dalhousie and Acadia Universities, went overseas with the Royal Flying Corps near the end of the First World War, and ended up back in Bouctouche, selling Model-T Fords at only twenty-two years of age.

By 1927, K.C. Irving had Ford dealerships and gasoline stations in four New Brunswick towns, and the next year opened, in partnership with the famous speed-skating champion Charles Gorman, a service station in Saint John on the corner of Main and Portland Streets. Popular with city residents for years, the Gorman service station served as a flagship location for Irving's automotive business. In 1929, the Irving Oil Company was incorporated with Irving himself travelling the Maritimes, using his sales skills to convince many independent gas dealers to install his pumps and sell his products.

In spite of the Great Depression, K.C. Irving grew his business and flourished through a combination of hard work and entrepreneurial vision. In 1930 his revenues were $137,576. Four years later, they had increased to $570,410 with thirty service stations, and more than three thousand retail outlets selling his automotive supplies. While other New Brunswickers like Max Aitken and James Dunn left the province to seek their fortune, K.C. Irving remained in his native New Brunswick, creating wealth and opportunities.

Irving also acquired, or snatched, struggling companies and was absolutely ruthless against competitors. His transportation empire fought Nova Scotia's Fred Manning for control of the Saint John bus franchise and won, although the battle lasted more than ten years. During these halcyon years, Irving's headquarters were located in the five-storey Golden Ball Building on the corner of Sydney and Union Streets — it still serves as the head office for the enormous number of Irving companies and subsidiaries.

During the bleakest year of the Depression, 1933, Irving inherited his father's lumber business in Kent County. While other lumber operations were winding down, K.C. Irving took some of the profits from his oil business and began aggressively acquiring timber reserves. His greatest feat, one that provided him with extensive cash reserves to undertake his remarkable post-war expansion, was his involvement with Canada Veneers and the production of De Havilland's Mosquito aircraft.

The British company De Havilland had engineered a revolutionary airplane and by 1942 much of the plywood for the Mosquito fighter came from Irving's Saint John plant, which he had acquired in 1938 for next to nothing. Employment at the plant rose to more than five hundred people, as Canada Veneers became the world's largest supplier of hardwood veneer for aircraft production. Almost seven thousand units of the paper-thin plywood aircraft were produced during World War II. By the mid-1940s, K.C. Irving began increasing his business empire. Soon he controlled the daily newspaper business in New Brunswick, the New Brunswick Railway with its huge timber stands, a pulp and paper mill, and many more industries that all purchased from and sold to each other, allowing for a vertical integration of businesses never seen before in Atlantic Canada.

By the 1960s, Irving's three sons began to take on some of the daily responsibilities of running the various companies but continued expansion and growth of the Irving empire was Kenneth C. Irving's wish and command until his death in 1992 at age ninety-three.

1926
Grand Falls Hydro Project

Abbé Saint-Vallier gave the first written description of the twenty-three metre (seventy-five foot) falls on the St. John River in the record of his 1686 trip to Quebec and Acadia, entitled *Estat present de l'église et de Colonie Françoise dans la Nouvelle France*. Describing it as "a wonderful cascade," Saint-Vallier also named the Grand Falls site. About two hundred years later, the Maritimes largest cataract began to attract attention as New Brunswick's best potential site for large-scale hydroelectric generation. For the next forty years until the power station was completed in 1931, individuals, companies and governments fought for control of Grand Falls.

Electrification was really just an extension of waterpower that had fuelled industry in New Brunswick since the arrival of the first people into the region. But the transmission of power from a central electric station to a whole host of users held previously undreamed of promise for industry and modern living. Hydro development was to be the "salvation of the province" cried Peter Veniot in 1923, since it could provide power for all New Brunswickers and stimulate much needed economic development.

In 1920, Liberal Premier Walter Foster created the New Brunswick Electric Power Commission. Their first attempt at creating a central electric system for Saint John was plagued with problems — the wooden dam at Musquash burst after only two years. But the Liberals were committed to electricity and highways in the early 1920s, and under Premier Peter Veniot, public ownership and construction of hydro dams became a priority. The problem was that the province was nearly broke during this period, as de-industrialization was happening throughout the Maritimes. While the lumber and manufacturing industries were experiencing the worst recession in decades, the demand for paper was growing, and the powerful international pulp and paper companies wanted to build hydro dams for their paper mills.

Initially, public ownership of the Grand Falls hydro development was not considered an option, as International Paper in 1911 acquired the hydro rights for their future papermaking needs. But in 1923, the Veniot Government took over the Grand Falls site, and began building the hydroelectric dam that would be the central station in their plans for the electrification of the entire province. However, the Conservative Party led by John Baxter won the 1925 election, convincing the voters that mismanagement and revenue shortages meant that large-scale projects should be undertaken by private capital. Baxter halted construction on the project and dismissed most of the New Brunswick Electric Power Commission staff. Soon International Paper was back in charge of Grand Falls, with virtually all of the eighty thousand horsepower of electricity they finally generated by 1931 committed for pulp and paper use.

Unlike central Canada, where public ownership developed hydroelectric stations for a wide range of commercial users, the monopoly of hydro power for pulp and paper meant that New Brunswick's struggle to diversify and attract new industries became more difficult. Yet the New Brunswick Electric Power Commission recovered from its 1925 setback, and eventually, in 1959, took over the Grand Falls station — which finally did become central to a province-wide power delivery system that began to attract non-forest related industries to the province. Unfortunately, the provincial governments of the 1920s and 1930s lacked the financial resources, and the economic vision, to undertake hydro development to the point where they might have prevented the single industry domination that still remains today.

1927
Inventor Wallace Turnbull

Canada's most important aeronautical engineer was born in Saint John in 1870, and studied mechanical and electrical engineering at Cornell University and the University of Berlin. In 1902, Wallace Rupert Turnbull left his research position with General Electric in New Jersey and established his own laboratory at Rothesay, building the first wind tunnel in Canada.

Used to conduct some of his first aeronautical experiments in Canada, the wind tunnel was relatively small at two meters (six feet) long and fifty-nine centimeters (twenty-two inches) square, with a heavy four-blade fan at one of the open ends that drove air through the tunnel. Turnbull was able to regulate the speed of the motor driven fan, and discovered a number of important technical properties of aerofoils involving the structure and stability of aeroplanes.

Wallace Turnbull also pioneered the building of a private railway track for use in researching his greatest achievement in aeronautical research. The fixed-pitch propeller did not allow aircraft maximum efficiency or stability in flight, and Turnbull's genius was to develop a propeller that had variable pitch which adjusted the airplane's blades, allowing for increased efficiency, especially while taking off or landing. He tested the new propeller for over ten years, with the help of the Royal Canadian Air Force. Finally, in 1927, the variable-pitch propeller — which has been called the most important aeronautical invention — was declared a success.

Wallace Turnbull sold his invention to an aviation manufacturer in 1929 and stayed active in aviation experiments, but spent many of his remaining years working with a group of engineers and businessmen on a scheme to tap the huge tidal action of the Bay of Fundy for electrical power. He died in Rothesay in 1954.

1930
The New Brunswick Resources Report

The federal and provincial governments combined efforts to produce the first comprehensive study of New Brunswick and its natural resources. Compiled by L.O. Thomas and published in 1930 by the Natural Resources Intelligence Service of the Federal Department of the Interior, *New Brunswick, Canada, Its Natural Resources and Development* is a fascinating snapshot of the province's resource sector in the late 1920s.

220

The decade of the 1920s produced great change in the province as a 10 per cent growth had increased New Brunswick's population to 419,300, with 65 per cent claiming British ancestry and 30 per cent with French roots. But times had been rough, for both the 68 per cent of New Brunswickers who lived in the rural areas at the outset of the decade and for the residents of the cities and towns, where de-industrialization had produced a Maritime depression well before the 1929 worldwide stock market crash.

Agriculture remained the largest resource sector providing the leading source of revenue for the province, with a yearly income of more than $34 million with over half from field crops. Next came the forest industry which, when all its products where combined, contributed almost as much gross revenue to the economy as agriculture. Spruce was New Brunswick's major lumber export and, overall, forestry remained strong as a reduction in lumber exports were offset by the large growth and investment in the emerging pulp and paper industry.

Minerals were also important commodities that contributed to the provincial economy, including coal situated at the head of Grand Lake and gypsum, limestone, and even oil and natural gas at Stony Creek, Albert County. However, the large commercial finds of zinc and iron in the north were still years away. The fishery, especially lobster, smelts, salmon, and herring, were essential staples; more than thirteen thousand people were employed in the provincial fishery in 1928. Also important to the New Brunswick of the 1920s were fur bearing pelts, as both trapping wild animals and fox ranching were carried on in a significant manner.

The 1920s was also the decade of hydro-electric power as 112,131 units of horsepower from water-power installations was on-stream by December, 1929. The Beechwood site on the St. John River was already under consideration for future hydro-electric power. Another 100,000 horsepower units was cited as possible but most of the existing hydro power was committed to the pulp and paper industry. The report cited recreational resources as having great potential and the 1929 tourism industry was estimated to be worth $18 million to the province.

Manufacturing and industrial production had not increased during the decade, except for hydro-electric developments and the pulp and paper industry. Also revealed in the Natural Resources Report of 1930 was the status of the provincial taxes and debt. Taxation compared favourably with other parts of Canada, but even in 1929 running a deficit was considered normal government policy as the net provincial debt was pegged at $31,585,298.

1930
Prime Minister R.B. Bennett

Canada's eleventh Prime Minister was born in Hopewell Hill, Albert County in 1870, the son of a New England Planter who had moved across the Bay of Fundy from the Annapolis Valley. Richard Bedford Bennett became the leader of the Conservative Party in 1927, and at the start of the Great Depression in 1930 became Prime Minister of Canada.

Educated in Albert County, R.B. Bennett studied law in Chatham during the late 1880s in the office of Lemuel Tweedie, Premier of New Brunswick between 1900-07. After studying at Dalhousie Law School, Bennett practiced law with Lord Beaverbrook and eventually became a partner with Tweedie. He also became involved in municipal politics in Chatham in 1896.

In 1897, Bennet moved to the emerging western town of Calgary, where he practiced law and became involved in Alberta politics. He entered federal politics in 1911, serving as Minister of Justice in 1921. As Prime Minister, Bennett is best remembered as the leader who attempted to take the county out of the Great Depression by creating a massive public works program, but was defeated at the polls and spent his last three years in politics as leader of the opposition.

He spent his retirement years in England, where King George VI created him Viscount Bennett of Calgary and Hopewell — complete with a split coat of arms with a buffalo representing Alberta on the left, and a moose on the right to signify Bennet's home province of New Brunswick.

1933
Acadian Men of Letters

The early era of Acadian history and literature is considered to be the period between 1880 and 1933, when the first Acadian literature began to appear. The early years began slowly; the nineteenth century's sum total of Acadian publications was only twelve volumes. The number of Acadian books produced in the early decades of the twentieth century is considerably higher, but the number of Acadian writers remained small until after 1950.

Acadia's first era of self-discovery by its native sons officially ended in 1933, with the death of its most famous scholar, Pascal Poirier. The Shediac native was well known in Acadian literary circles but was also an important political figure who became the first Acadian senator. Poirier's first work, *Origine Des Acadiens*, published in 1874, is also considered the first native Acadian book. Like *Le Parler Franco-Acadien et Ses Origines*, his last book published fifty-four years later, it is an account of the history and development of the Acadian people. Despite his significant output of published material, a tragedy occurred in 1916 when one of his most important manuscripts of more than 1,200 pages burned in the Parliamentary Library fire. One of the most important Acadian leaders to emerge and advance the cause of French-speaking New Brunswickers, Poirier spent his entire life writing, speaking, and leading the Acadians to greater self-awareness and political power.

Placide Gaudet (1850-1930) was a contemporary of Pascal Poirier, and a Shediac neighbor, who wrote many articles and two books on the history and genealogy of the Acadians, including *Genealogies des Familles Acadiennes*. Gaudet became the Acadian Archivist in Ottawa, but is also considered an important Acadian literary figure for what he did not publish. Upon his death, a ten-volume scholarly manuscript on Acadian genealogy was left with his estate. Other important Acadian writers who made Shediac their home were Israel Landry, who began the first Acadian newspaper *Le Moniteur Acadien* in 1867, and Ferdinand Robidoux, who edited the pioneer journal for forty-seven years. In addition to the four Acadian literary figures, English-speaking Shediac native, J. Clarence Webster also contributed to our knowledge of the early history of Acadia.

1933
Maritime Advocate and Busy East

The first issue of *The Maritime Advocate and Busy East* appeared in August of 1933, and sold for fifteen cents a copy, or a dollar for a one-year subscription. Published by the Busy East Press and printed in Sackville by the Tribune Press, the new publication superseded the old *Busy East*, that had been first issued at Saint John in 1910.

Subtitled *"The magazine with faith in the future of the Maritime Provinces,"* the monthly magazine not only had a new name but a new policy. According to the magazine's editorial, the *Busy East* had been forced to change since now that the Maritimes were in the depths of the Great Depression, "there is no Busy East for the industries of the Atlantic Provinces have been on the down grade for some time." Without much advertising to support its pro-business orientation, the *Busy East* could not continue, and re-invented itself with a policy of advocating political reform while still championing the interests of the Maritimes.

With its first issue featuring a young Angus L. MacDonald on the cover with a caption that his mandate in Nova Scotia politics was to fight to regain responsible government, the *Maritime Advocate and Busy East* was soon perceived as a very partisan Liberal publication. But its well-known sense of humour and popular appeal was not lost, and the publication was widely read throughout the Maritimes. In New Brunswick, the magazine championed the opposition Liberal Party, to the extent of reprinting some of Albert Dysart's speeches from the New Brunswick Legislature. The Liberal Party under A.A. Dysart was swept into power in 1935, the first Roman Catholic to be elected Premier in the province, and the *Maritime Advocate* played a part in convincing New Brunswickers to vote Liberal.

After Newfoundland entered Confederation in 1949, the *Maritime Advocate* was superseded by the *Atlantic Advocate*, and under the new ownership of Michael Wardell, and later the Irving interests, continued to be published by the University Press of New Brunswick in Fredericton. A strong regional voice for Maritime interests, *The Atlantic Advocate* ceased publishing in 1991.

1935
Muriel McQueen Fergusson

Although women received voting rights in 1919, they were unable to run in political elections and were virtually excluded from serving in other forms of public office. More than any other individual in New Brunswick, Muriel McQueen Fergusson pioneered the entry of women into the mainstream of public life.

In 1935, Fergusson was appointed New Brunswick's first female Judge of Probate and acting solicitor for the town of Grand Falls. The Shediac native who had graduated from Mount Allison University in 1921, studied law in her father's law office and was called to the New Brunswick Bar in 1925. During World War II, she moved to Saint John and accepted a position as supervisor of the Wartime Prices and Trade Board. In 1947, she applied for a job as the Regional Director of Family Allowance and was told that it was an officially designated "male" position. With the support of a number of women's groups, Fergusson fought the discrimination of male-designated positions within the government, and was finally hired for the position.

During the 1940s, Muriel Fergusson began championing women's issues throughout New Brunswick. Living in Fredericton, she fought another battle with City Council who had barred women from sitting as councillors (nor could they vote in local elections if they did not own property). After convincing the provincial Legislature to change the law, Fergusson became Fredericton's first female Councillor.

Muriel Fergusson's campaigns for women's rights came to national prominence in the 1950s, after she was appointed to the Senate. "Women are People," her acclaimed program to educate people about women's rights, was quite successful in removing barriers for women, especially to allow women to serve in jury trials. During her extensive public career, Muriel Fergusson witnessed many advances in the status of women in New Brunswick, yet her role in these accomplishments has often been overlooked. The first woman appointed as Speaker of the Senate in 1972, she developed a new interest in contributing towards the many international programs for the advancement of women's rights worldwide.

1936
Credit Unions

The Depression era of the 1930s was especially painful for Canada's east coast provinces, and the principle of self-reliance and co-operation became slogans for Maritimers seeking to pull themselves out of the economic despair. In 1936, the New Brunswick Credit Union Societies Act was chartered under the Department of Agriculture's Co-operative Division. With a mandate to encourage and assist the formation of co-operative societies, the Act quickly resulted in credit societies springing up throughout the province, with New Brunswick's first in Northumberland County at Blackville.

Credit unions had their origins in Belgium more than 150 years ago. While Alphonse Desjardins of Quebec's La Caisse Populaire is usually considered the Canadian pioneer, Acadian communities have long had co-operative credit societies, beginning with the 1864 client-owned Farmer's Bank of Rustico in Prince Edward Island. In addition, much of the inspiration and organizing principles of New Brunswick's Credit Union Act came from Moses Coady's Co-operative Movement in Antigonish, Nova Scotia.

To assist rural communities to become self-reliant, the Co-operative Movement encouraged the accumulation of savings that would be pooled into a local resource of credit to be loaned to union members at reasonable rates. With one vote per member, instead of one vote per share, credit unions were able to maintain client ownership, and union membership mushroomed during the early years. From 1936 to 1944 union membership in New Brunswick grew to 27,558 members with almost a hundred rural credit unions with accumulated assets of about $2 million.

1938
Bilingualism and Acadian Education

New Brunswick's illiteracy rate was judged to be the highest in Canada during the early 1900s, and among Acadians, the per centage was even higher. One study in the predominantly Acadian region of Kent County, claimed that 47 per cent of all children never went beyond Grade Two.

While a number of problems contributed to New Brunswick's educational stagnation, including having the lowest paid teachers in Canada, the fact that French-speaking New Brunswickers could not receive instruction in their own language contributed to the inferior educational system of the early 1900s. After World War One, the struggle for French education began in Madawaska County where two key residents began lobbying for an overhaul of the school system for Acadians.

Dr. Albert Sormany was an Edmundston physician who served on the local school board, and Calixte Savoie was the principal of L'École Supérieure. Both were educational activists and spearheaded Le Petite Boutique, a local reform group devoted to improving educational conditions for Acadians. A small newspaper was also started and *L'Évangéline* in Moncton began reprinting a number of its articles on the public education system. The thrust of all the editorials was language rights. The demand for Acadians to be taught in their own language reached a climax in 1926, when school board officials voted down the Sormany–Savoie group. Branded a radical, Calixte Savoie was forced to resign as school principal, and left Madawaska County.

Savoie moved to Moncton, where his management of La Société l'Assomption reinvigorated the organization with over ten thousand new members. With Dr. Sormany as president, the Society helped convince the Tory government of John Baxter to adopt Regulation 32 in 1929, which recognized bilingual status for New Brunswick's public school system. But the breakthrough for the Acadians was not to last, as an English backlash led by the Orange Order caused Baxter to rescind the historic regulation. A Royal Commission on education produced a report in 1932, but it contained few recommendations concerning French educational needs.

A Liberal election upset under Albert Dysart in 1935 brought in a party more sympathetic to the Acadian cause, and a new lobbying group was formed to address French educational concerns. L'Association Acadienne d'Éducation gathered on August 30, 1938 at Université Sacré-Coeur, near Bathurst, and passed fifteen resolutions on the steps necessary to ensure that French-speaking students could be fully educated in their own language.

This gathering is often considered the most important educational conference in Acadian history, since the resolutions provided a basic document for the recognition of language rights in New Brunswick and the essential ingredients for French-language instruction. More years of struggle would ensue before the Louis J. Robichaud era enacted a bilingual educational system for New Brunswick, but the earlier Sormany-Savoie efforts provided the framework and support for the establishment of a French education system in the 1960s.

1939
The Age of Air Travel

Private air travel had begun over New Brunswick in the 1920s and by the end of the decade commercial air service started to appear in the Maritimes. In 1928, the first airmail ski-plane landed on the frozen city reservoir outside Moncton, and the next year, the southeastern region's first airport was established at Leger's Corner, now part of Dieppe. Nearby at Lakeburn, the Moncton Flying Club began holding air pageants by using their downhill runway to aid takeoffs. Yet during the early 1930s, the question of where to locate airports was really about what kind of airplane would eventually dominate the skies.

Shediac Bay was considered the nearest fog-free bay from the Atlantic, and ideal for landing seaplanes — which during the first years of overseas air travel was the favourite plane for ocean flying. In 1933, when the Italian air force used Shediac Bay as their stopover to an air exposition in Chicago, the *Moncton Times* predicted that Shediac would become the chief North American terminal for trans-Atlantic air traffic. And Shediac made the world air map for a time, becoming in 1939 the site of the first trans-Atlantic airmail terminal from Canada to Europe. By this time, landplanes began to replace seaplanes in overseas travel, and the Royal Canadian Air Force as well as Trans-Canada Air Lines, Canada's first major airline, decided to establish a major air base at Moncton as the airport hub for the Maritimes.

While the Eastern Air Command headquarters during World War Two was located at Halifax, Moncton's strategic location and better flying weather were determining factors in choosing the city to become the training, equipment, and repair centre for eastern Canada. As one of the Commonwealth Air Training Centres, Moncton became home to tens of thousands of British Commonwealth flight trainees. A flying field was also constructed at Chatham, but the Moncton region experienced the largest influx of personnel and equipment during the Second World War.

A construction boom strained the small city's resources as whole self-contained cities were erected almost overnight. The No. 31 Depot in the city's north end sprouted more than a hundred buildings in the summer of 1941, with facilities to accommodate up to ten thousand men. The city's transportation and entertainment facilities were also strained, and the thousands of airmen from various countries gave the city a new cosmopolitan air. While much of Moncton's wartime buildings were converted to civilian use after 1945, these structures are still visible today.

1939
The Industry of Handcrafts

The handcrafts revival in New Brunswick during the 1930s was the result of two factors, necessity and fashion. Mass production of cheap, but inferior quality, items in the latter half of the nineteenth century had destroyed the home-based craft industries. By the end of the First World War, public tastes for beauty and quality began to re-emerge. As the market for high workmanship and distinctive designs reappeared, old forgotten handcrafts experienced a renaissance. The other factor in the new popularity of handcrafts centred around the depression of the 1930s and the large number of unemployed people, who began to experiment with old pioneer crafts and hobbies. In the 1930s, rural New Brunswickers simply had to find ways to support themselves.

In 1939, two sisters in St. Leonard, Madawaska County, began hand-weaving scarves and ties that soon proved popular items in Montreal and other cities. Fernande and Rolande Gervais expanded their hand-woven enterprise to include many other items, and soon were shipping their products coast to coast as well as into the United States. When finding qualified weavers became a problem, the sisters decentralized their operation and moved weaving looms into women's homes in the countryside. By the 1960s, Madawaska Weavers was the largest home-craft industry in Atlantic Canada, with fifty-five employees. All products were still hand-woven.

Although the 1930s was the decade of the revival of handcrafts, the origins of the modern craft movement in New Brunswick dates from 1914 in St. Andrews. After studying and teaching art in England, New York, and Halifax, Grace Helen Mowat returned to her home in Beech Hill, St. Andrews. She began her craft business by shipping local hooked rugs to Montreal, where they fetched $15 apiece. As hand-looms and spinning wheels were brought down from the attics, Mowat encouraged the women of

Charlotte County to revive the old fireplace arts of spinning, dying, and weaving.

Using designs and colour reflective of the local area, Mowat's Cottage Craft Limited began turning out homespun fabrics, embroidered handbags, sweaters, and even table linens, which were sold in upscale craftshops throughout North America. With a highly successful tourist retail outlet on the St. Andrews waterfront, Grace Helen Mowat even expanded into producing pottery from local clay before retiring in 1945. During her retirement, Mowat wrote a number of local histories including her own story, *A Story of Cottage Craft*. She died in 1964.

1940
The Internment Camp

Canada established Second World War internment camps in 1940, after Great Britain decided that all its adult refugees from Germany and Austria were to be isolated from its civilian population. Fear of alien spies spurred the decision, and Canada agreed to accept a portion of the mostly Jewish refugees. Eventually forty thousand prisoners of war and civilians would be held in twenty-six internment camps across Canada.

Fredericton Internment Camp B/70 was hastily constructed about thirty-two kilometres (twenty miles) east of Fredericton at Ripples. It received its first 711 internees in August 1940, made up almost entirely of refugees from Nazi-occupied Europe. Internment Camp B had been constructed as a prisoner of war detention centre with barbed wire, sentry towers, and a 156-member Veteran Guard detachment. But instead of dangerous Nazis soldiers, the camp's internees were escaped Nazi victims who were happy to be safe in Canada. No escapes were attempted, and the most controversial incident was a hunger strike over a demand by Orthodox Jews for kosher food.

The following summer the foreign civilian internees were released, as most were not considered a threat to the Allied war effort. Some returned to Great Britain, while others remained in Canada or immigrated to the United States. Meanwhile a second camp was opened at Ripples that did contain more hostile internees, including enemy Merchant Seamen, German and Italian nationals, as well as Canadian civilians. Undoubtedly the Fredericton camp's most famous internee was the Mayor of Montreal, Camillien Houde, who was banished to internment for opposing Canada's national registration program of all citizens. Citing the law as a precursor to conscription, Houde refused to register and was held for two years, along with another famous Quebec politician, Adrien Arcand, the leader of the Quebec Fascist Movement.

Unlike the first camp, the second camp contained many prisoners of war who were interested in escaping, and made numerous attempts including the notorious tunnel escapade. As tunnelling efforts began underground, music would be played by other prisoners to disguise the digging noise. Finally the prisoners were caught and flushed out of the tunnel with a fire hose. Closed in 1945, and later demolished, the internment camp site is now covered in brush and forest.

1943
Social Security and the Marsh Report

A severe recession followed the First World War throughout Canada, but the Maritime Provinces were hit especially hard since the wartime economy failed to retool for peacetime purposes. This de-industrialization devastated the regional economy, well before the Great Depression hit the rest of Canada, and produced tremendous strain on the social welfare of Maritimers. During the 1920s, an exodus of more than one hundred thousand residents left for the United States.

During the Second World War, economists and social planners began preparing for the post-war recovery, where the emphasis would be on a comprehensive program of social security to offset the effects of a reconstruction period, where loss in employment and economic opportunities were considered inevitable. "Cradle to the grave protection" became the slogan, as social engineers were commissioned to map out Canada's future social programs.

In 1943, Dr. Leonard Marsh of McGill University issued his *Report on Social Security in Canada* for the Federal Advisory Committee on Recon-struction. Dr. Marsh's study became the cornerstone for a new social order for Canada that promised to guarantee national Canadian standards for social security and human welfare. Some national social insurance schemes had already come into effect, such as unemployment insurance in 1940. The Marsh Report was different — it recommended a series of ambitious steps to abolish poverty and provide universal social security for all Canadians.

A guaranteed annual income was rejected as too expensive, but "national minimums" for health care, social security, and education were adopted. By 1945, a number of national programs had been developed including old age pensions, housing, and (the most important new federal program) Family Allowance, which guaranteed every Canadian child un-

230

der sixteen between five and eight dollars per month. Health care soon followed, and the Maritime Plan for Hospital Care that began in 1943 as a group medical insurance plan by the Maritime Hospital Association, gradually gave way to early forms of today's Medicare.

With the post-war national standards came the National Adjustment Grants, which were early transfer payments to the poorer provinces to maintain the national programs. The Maritimes benefitted greatly from these programs, as it was estimated that 10 per cent of all the national funds were spent in the three Maritime provinces during the late 1940s, while only 3 or 4 per cent of the total tax revenue was collected from the same three east coast provinces.

1946
Campobello's Franklin Delano Roosevelt

James and Sara Delano Roosevelt first visited Campobello in 1883, with their one-year old son Franklin, and became so enchanted with the Outer Island that they purchased four hectares (ten acres), overlooking Friar's Bay. The wealthy Roosevelts spent their summer vacations amid their fifteen-room cottage, as Campobello became a fashionable resort island for well-to-do Americans.

The young Franklin grew to love the island as he spent his summers sailing Passamaquoddy Bay on the Roosevelt yacht, *Half Moon*. He became friends with the local fishermen, who loved to tell legends and stories about old Campobello. In 1905 Franklin married the shy and withdrawn Eleanor Roosevelt, a distant cousin, and five years later entered politics. Despite a fledging political career, the Roosevelts visited Campobello often and their son, Franklin D. Jr., was born on the island.

In 1921 aboard the yacht *Sebalo*, Franklin Roosevelt went fishing off Campobello, and fell overboard into the cold Fundy waters. Back on the *Sebalo*, Roosevelt remained in his wet clothes the rest of the day and within a week the athletic future President of the United States became stricken with polio. Barely able to walk, Roosevelt did not return to Campobello for twelve years, yet his will to overcome his disability allowed him to continue his political career with few Americans knowing the extent of his uncertain health.

In 1933 the President of the United States and his family sailed into Welshpool aboard his yacht *Amberjack II*, escorted by a United States Navy cruiser and two destroyers. Amid welcoming cheers from the wharf, Roose-velt had returned to his beloved Campbello Island, and an island-wide picnic was held the next day. Despite having to be lifted out of the

231

Fundy National Park, 1950, New Brunswick's first national park. (NBPA)

cockpit, the fragile Roosevelt made two more brief trips to Campbello before World War Two. Franklin Delano Roosevelt died in 1945 and the following year, due to the efforts of J. Clarence Webster, an international ceremony was held at Welshpool to honour this American President.

1948
Fundy National Park

In 1947, after years of searching, the province's first National Park site was chosen and the next year work began on returning a number of old homesteads and settlements back into wilderness. About fifty families within the parish of Alma were affected, and expropriation resulted in a number of buildings and homes being moved to locations outside the park boundary.

Situated in southern Albert County, Fundy National Park was opened to the public in 1952. While occupying a small land mass in comparison to many of Canada's national parks, Fundy's location near the world's highest tides makes it one of Canada's most unique and diverse natural landscapes. Although a park, Fundy was logged until 1965 to acquire large timbers for rebuilding the Fortress of Louisbourg in Nova Scotia. Today the 206 square kilometres (129 square miles) contains an intact Acadian forest, and remarkable waterfalls, back country trails, lakes, and thirteen kilometres (eight miles) of scenic seacoast.

Canada's first national park was created in 1885 at Banff, Alberta. In addition to Fundy, Kouchibouguac National Park became New Brunswick's second national park in 1969. Only truly unique areas of Canada have been deemed suitable for national park status, and Fundy is no exception. Situated near the head of the giant Fundy tides, Fundy's climate is profoundly affected by the tidal action which produces a Bay of Fundy weather system, distinct from the rest of New Brunswick. Where one hundred years ago farming, lumbering, and mining activities were evident throughout the area, Fundy National Park is today a natural preserve where flora, fauna, wildlife, and wilderness enthusiasts abound.

New Brunswick's first provincial park was established at Glenwood, west of Campbellton in 1935. From this humble beginning as a roadside picnic area for Model T motorists, a provincial park system was gradually developed to include rest areas, campgrounds, beaches and recreation parks, as well as a wildlife park at Woolastook, and the unique Mount Carleton Resource Park. A marine park in the Fundy Isles is also under consideration.

1950
The Last Log Drive

Around 1950, a way of life that had developed in the lumber woods of New Brunswick began to rapidly disappear. For almost 150 years, men had lived in wilderness log cabins during the winter months, where they cut the forest with their axes and crosscut saws and hauled the timber to the frozen rivers. Thousands of woodsmen headed to the forests each fall, where they were divided into cooks, choppers, teamsters, barkers, and yarders. Except for a brief stint at Christmas, most would live in the backwoods for four or five months.

After breakup, when the ice left the rivers in April, another crew of whitewater men were organized into river drivers, to ensure that log jams did not prevent the winter's timber from arriving at the river's mouth, where another workcrew stood waiting at the sawmills. Until 1860, rum was the daily drink of the woodsmen but poor working habits while under the influence, as well as the power of the temperance movement, led to a banning of liquor in the camps. But dry camps meant that liquor-hungry loggers sometimes invaded nearby towns and villages, where drunken brawls and destruction terrorized the community until sober heads prevailed.

The log drives usually began as branch drives on small rivers or streams. Often numerous small drives would take place before the logs were consolidated on the main river, where the "corporation drive" would begin, along with the assembly of a full crew of river drivers. Headed by a chief driver, or "the main walker," and armed with their peavies or canthooks as well as driving or spiked boots, the white-water men would climb onto a log jam, and attempt the dangerous work of prying the logs loose. The shanty where the loggers ate and slept became the centre of a male sub-culture that included songs and ballads, legends and folklore, as well as stories of brave deeds and strong drink.

The heyday of the traditional lumber industry in New Brunswick was the last quarter of the nineteenth century, but a number of factors led to the industry's gradual decline in the twentieth century. After 1950, few woodsmen slept overnight in log cabins, since improved roads and modern trucks meant that travelling distances of ten or more miles each day was not a major problem. The modern chainsaw had replaced the old hand crosscut saw, which meant that cutting trees took much less time and effort. With hydroelectric dams across many of New Brunswick's major rivers, log drives were no longer practical. With new portable sawmills and powerful log-trucks, sawing logs closer to where they were cut became an important option for the lumber industry.

The last major log drive on the Naskwaak River was in 1935 but extensive log drives lasted on the Miramichi for another twenty years and did not entirely disappear from the St. John River until 1966 when the Mactaquac hydroelectric dam was developed. While the lumber industry remained an important component of New Brunswick's economy throughout the twentieth century, the traditional method of harvesting the timber resource had disappeared by mid-century.

1950
The Social and Education Sales Tax

The first broad-based sales tax on consumer purchases was introduced in New Brunswick in 1950 and has remained a very lucrative source of provincial revenue. Commodity taxes were not new in 1950 since for years the provincial government raised revenue from the sales of liquor, gasoline, and other items. But for the first time, a four per cent surcharge was added to all sales transacted in the province to help pay for the spiralling

234

social and educational costs that had accompanied New Brunswick's post-war expansion.

The "equal opportunity" reforms of the 1960s were still well over a decade away, and local municipalities were unable to shoulder the increasing tax burden of providing additional social and educational services to New Brunswick's growing population. The Liberal administration under J.B. McNair attempted to assist the struggling schools boards and municipalities by taxing widely across the province and redirecting income back to the poorer districts.

Tax exemptions were issued almost immediately, and while churches raising funds for religious purposes were exempt, so were factories such as paper plants when purchasing capital equipment for production and distribution. The large paper mills in the north had already won so many tax concessions with low, fixed assessments and cheap timber rights, that municipalities with pulp and paper mills were the least able to pay for the social and education costs of servicing the mill's workers.

Almost 60 per cent of the first year's revenue of $2.8 million came from the three cities in southern New Brunswick. The new tax proved so unpopular that the Conservative leader Hugh John Flemming campaigned against the dreaded consumer tax in the 1952 election. Once in power, however, Flemming realized he needed the new revenue and promptly refused to cancel the tax.

1950
New Brunswick at Mid-Century

The rugged landscape of New Brunswick dominated by the St. John and the Miramichi Rivers had produced a hardy breed of settlers who realized limited opportunities for agriculture but managed to transform the well-forested region into a thriving timber colony.

Throughout its early years, the cost to New Brunswick for relying on forest exploitation was that the region would remain a marginal colony dependent on Britain's timber trade. With the collapse of timber markets in the mid 1800s, New Brunswick had little choice but to join a confederation of northern British provinces that would once again ensure her marginal status in a rapidly industrializing Dominion of Canada. The attempt to compete with the larger centres of North America for a significant piece of the industrial marketplace was not entirely successful and, by the turn of the century, New Brunswick had once again been forced to sell its natural resources at uncertain prices in exchange for imported manufactured goods. The Great Depression hurt the province immensely and sent many

New Brunswickers west and south in search of employment while a Maritime Rights movement sprang up to challenge federal policies and the region's weak position within Confederation.

Despite experiencing almost full employment during World War Two, the aftermath of the century's second great war had not been kind to the New Brunswick economy. By mid-century the province had once again become economically isolated as the new manufacturing and exporting industries of the post-war recovery avoided the region for the more prosperous centres of central Canada. Canada's national policies remained oriented in favour of the inland economies of Ontario and Quebec where a boom in industrial development was occurring. Almost one hundred years later, the promise of Confederation was largely unfulfilled as per-capita income of New Brunswickers lingered well below the national average.

As in the past two hundred years, the forest sector still dominated New Brunswick, although pulp and paper production had replaced the lumber industry as the engine of the provincial economy. Other enterprises that offered promising prospects were mining (especially in northern New Brunswick) tourism, fishing, and agriculture — especially the prospects for growing and exporting potatoes around the upper St. John River. The natural resources sector would continue to dominate the economy throughout the remaining decades of the twentieth century, although processing and refining the resource products would also begin to have a significant impact on the provincial economy.

Politically, the province had continued to lose power within the Canadian confederation as central and western Canada attracted the bulk of Canada's immigrants. And with only ten members in the House of Commons, New Brunswick's politicians had little influence and significance on the national scene. This had not been unexpected as New Brunswick had been dragged kicking and screaming into Confederation or, as Hugh Thorburn stated in *Politics in New Brunswick*: "New Brunswick had entered the new federation with the resignation of a sick man going to a quack, after he had tried everything else." Yet New Brunswick had one of its strongest leaders during the period in Conservative Premier Hugh John Flemming, who was able to convince the federal government to establish special programs to assist the Atlantic region in attempting to reverse the economic decline.

The post-war situation of the 1950s was not entirely bleak. While New Brunswickers had not become especially well-to-do, they had never been wealthy, didn't expect it, and despite significant religious and ethnic differences, had managed to create and maintain a functioning provincial democracy where these differences had been set aside in favour of equality.

Perhaps because of geographical factors, the northern regions of New Brunswick had remained politically isolated as well as more impoverished than the more populated southern areas where English-language New Brunswickers had long ago established strong links with the political institutions at Fredericton. With the arrival in the 1960s of Louis J. Robichaud, the province's first Acadian elected Premier, this north-south dichotomy would begin to collapse as Premier Robichaud instituted an ambitious program of political reform in order to provide equal access throughout the province to economic, social and political power.

By the 1970s Louis Robichaud's ten-year term had established the first fully bilingual province in Canada and, by the end of the decade, New Brunswick's first European settlers, the Acadians, had shed their second-class political and economic status and had finally come of age. Throughout the remaining decades of the twentieth century, Acadians would remain full and equal partners in the life of the province. The resurgence and empowerment of the Acadians would characterize New Brunswick during the latter stages of this century. Now in full effect, this respect for cultural and ethnic differences may well provide unique opportunities and great advantages for New Brunswickers in the twenty-first century.

Governors and Lieutenant Governors of Acadia and New Brunswick

Pierre du Gua de Monts 1603-1606
Jean de Poutrincourt 1606-1614
Charles de Biencourt 1614-1623
Charles de La Tour 1631-1642
Isaac de Razilly 1632-1635
Charles de Menou d'Aulnay 1638-1650
Charles de La Tour 1653-1657
Emmanuel LeBorgne 1657-1667
William Crowne 1662-1667
Sir Thomas Temple 1662-1167
Alexandre LeBorgne de Belle-Isle 1667-1670
Hector d'Andigne de Grandfontaine 1670-1673
Jacques de Chambly 1673-77
Cornelis van Steenwijck 1676-78
Francois-Marie Perrot 1684-87
Louis Alexandre De Friches 1687-90
Joseph Robinau de Villebon 1691-1700
Jacques-Francois de Bouillan 1701-1705
Daniel d'Auger de Subercase 1706-1710
Le marquis de Vaudreuil 1710-1725
Le marquis de Beauharnois 1726-1747
Le marquis de La Galissonniere 1747-1749
Le marquis de La Jonquiere 1749-1752
Le marquis Duquesne 1752-1755
Le marquis de Vaudreuil-Cavagnal 1755-1760
Charles Lawrence 1760
Jonathan Belcher 1761-1763

Mantaque Wilmot 1763-1766
Michael Francklin 1766
William Campbell 1766-1773
Francis Legge 1773-1782
John Parr 1782-1784
Thomas Carleton 1784-1817
George Stracey Smyth 1817-1823
Sir Howard Douglas, Bt. 1824-1831
Sir Archibald Cambpell, Bt. 1831-1837
Sir John Harvey 1837-1841
Sr. William MacBean George Colebrooke 1841-1848
Sir Edmund Walker Head, Bt. 1848-1854
Sir John Henry Thomas Manners-Sutton 1854-1861
Arthur Hamilton Gordon 1861-1866
Charles Hastings Doyle 1867
Francis Pym Harding 1867-1868
Lemuel Allan Wimot 1868-1873
Samuel Leonard Tilley 1873-1878
Edward Barron Chandler 1878-1880
Robert Duncan Wimot 1880-1885
Sir Samuel Leonard Tilley 1885-1893
John Boyd 1893
John James Fraser 1893-1896
Abner Reid McClelan 1896-1902
Jabez Bunting Snowball 1902-1907
Lemuel John Tweedie 1907-1912
Josiah Wood 1912-1917
Gilbert White Ganong 1917
William Pugsley 1917-1923
William Frederic Todd 1923-1928
Hugh Havelock McLean 1928-1935
Murray MacLaren 1935-1940
William George Clark 1940-1945
David Laurence MacLaren 1945-1958
Joseph Leonard O'Brien 1958-1965
John Babbitt McNair 1965-1968
Wallace Samuel Bird 1968-1971
Hedard Joseph Robichaud 1971-1981
George Francis Gillman Stanley 1982-1987
Gilbert Finn 1987-1994
Margaret Norrie McCain 1994-1996
Marilyn Trenholme Counsell 1997-

New Brunswick Premiers Since Confederation

Hon. A. R. Wetmore (Confederation Party) 1867-1870
Hon. G. E. King (Conservative) 1870-1871
Hon. George L. Hatheway (Conservative) 1871-1872
Hon. G. E. King (Conservative) 1872-1878
Hon. J. J. Fraser (Conservative) 1878-1882
Hon. D. L. Hanington (Conservative) 1882-1883
Hon. A. G. Blair (Liberal) 1883-1896
Hon. James Mitchell (Liberal) 1896-1897
Hon. H. R. Emmerson (Liberal) 1897-1900
Hon. L. J. Tweedie (Liberal) 1900-1907
Hon. Wm. Pugsley (Liberal) March-April 1907
Hon. C. W. Robinson (Liberal) 1907-1908
Hon. J. D. Hazen (Conservative) 1908-1911
Hon. James. K. Flemming (Conservative) 1911-1914
Hon. George J. Clarke (Conservative) 1914-1917
Hon. James A. Murray (Conservative) February-April, 1917
Hon. Walter E. Foster (Liberal) 1917-1923
Hon. Peter J. Veniot (Liberal) 1923-1925
Hon. J. B. M. Baxter (Conservative) 1925-1931
Hon. Charles D. Richards (Conservative) 1931-1933
Hon. L. P. D. Tilley (Conservative) 1933-1935
Hon. A. A. Dysart (Liberal) 1935-1940
Hon. John. B. McNair (Liberal) 1940-1952
Hon. Hugh John Flemming (Conservative) 1952-1960
Hon. Louis J. Robichaud (Liberal) 1960-1970
Hon. Richard B. Harfield (Conservative) 1970-1987
Hon. Frank J. McKenna (Liberal) 1987-1997
Hon. Ray Frenette (Liberal) 1997-

Ensigns and Provincial Symbols

The origins of heraldry are obscure. Within the European tradition, ensigns of arms dates from the Middle Ages, when ancient hoods and military helmets made emblems essential for waring armies to recognize their own men. New Brunswick's tradition of insignia dates from 1785 when the English Secretary of State Lord Sydney sent the "Great Seal For New Brunswick" to Governor Carleton.

The new province's sterling silver seal bore the British Coat of Arms with the Latin inscription *George the Third by the Grace of God King of the British Defender of the Faith*, while the reverse side revealed a settlement on the banks of a river beside large evergreen trees with a ship sailing up the river. Beneath the scene is the motto *Spem Reduxit* (she restored hope, or hope was restored) — which has always been taken to mean that restoration of good fortune awaited the exiled Loyalists in their newly created province, where huge pine trees would supply the King's navy with valuable masts.

The British Royal Arms was altered a number of times before Confederation, but only minor changes to the ship's sails were made to the provincial scene on the Great Seal. A number of Lieutenant Governors had their own privy seals, distinct from the Provincial Seal which was replaced after Confederation by a new seal about the same time that New Brunswick's first Coat of Arms was created. Added to a number of times, the original Arms for New Brunswick was assigned by Queen Victoria on May 26, 1868 and included a grant allowing the arms to be borne for banners and flags. The current seal of the province was issued a year later, in 1869, and is similar to the other provincial seals featuring the British Royal Arms and the motto *Dieu et mon Droit*. A small provincial Coat of Arms and the surrounding words: The Seal of the Province of New Brunswick are the only distinguishing features of New Brunswick's Seal.

The official heraldic description of the Arms of New Brunswick reads: "Or, on waves, a Lymphad, or ancient Gallery, with oars in action proper, on a Chief Gules, a Lion Passant guardant Or." The upper portion

241

of the shield is red and features a gold lion which represents New Brunswick's ties to Britain and the Duchy of Brunswick in Germany, King George III's ancestral home. King George III ruled England when the province was established in 1784. The lower part of the shield displays the ancient galley with oars in action to symbolize New Brunswick's shipbuilding and seafaring industries. The most recent version of the provincial Arms was adopted in 1966, when the crest of a royal crown was added above the shield and the Great Seal's motto *Spem Reduxit* was added below the shield.

The shield is supported by familiar icons from New Brunswick's past, two white-tailed deer wearing collars of Indian wampum. The Union Jack and the Fleur-de-lis are also displayed to indicate the province's two European traditions and the crest consists of an Atlantic Salmon leaping from a coronet of gold maple leaves and bearing St. Edward's Crown on its back. At the base is a grassy mound of fiddleheads and purple violets.

The official flag of New Brunswick, while authorized in 1868 as part of the Coat of Arms assignment, was not adopted until 1965 when the Lieutenant Governor finally proclaimed its use. The design is taken from the Coat of Arms and is displayed throughout on a banner of rectangular form of the proportions four by length and two and one half by width, with the upper one-third red portion occupied by the lion and the remainder of the arms occupying the lower two-thirds.

In 1936 by an Order in Council, the floral emblem of the province became the purple violet at the suggestion of the New Brunswick Women's Institute. A relative of the pansy, the marsh blue violet is found throughout eastern Canada and is especially prominent in New Brunswick's meadows and woodlands. Each spring the purple violet is one of the most frequently seen flowers.

Other important provincial symbols that have been adopted to signify the distinctive nature of the province and its traditions are the New Brunswick Tartan, New Brunswick's official tree, the Balsam Fir, and New Brunswick's provincial bird, the Black-capped Chickadee. The latter is a common year-round resident that is widely distributed over the province and is a favourite around winter feeding stations where its acrobatic feats are widely applauded. An interesting choice as the provincial tree, the Balsam Fir is common throughout the Maritimes and thrives best in New Brunswick's damp climate. A valuable softwood, the Balsam Fir is used for lumber, pulp wood and is now especially cultivated as a Christmas tree.

New Brunswick's armorial bearings assigned to the province by Queen Victoria
on May 26, 1868.

Bibliography

Acheson, T.W. *Saint John*. University of Toronto Press, 1985.

Bell, D.G. *Early Loyalist Saint John*. New Ireland Press, 1983.

Bryce, Douglas. *Weaponry from the Machault*. Parks Canada, 1984.

Clarke, Andrew Hill. *Acadia The Geography of Early Nova Scotia to 1760*. The University of Wisconsin Press, 1968.

Cook, Ramsay. *The Voyages of Jacques Cartier*. University of Toronto Press, 1993.

Cormier, Yves. *L'Acadie d'aujourd'hui*. Éditions d'acadie, 1994.

Durnford, Hugh. *Heritage of Canada*. Reader's Digest, 1978.

Finley, Gregg. & Wigginton, Lynn. *On Earth as it is in Heaven*. Goose Lane Editions, 1995.

Ganong,William F. *Historic Sites in the Province of New Brunswick*. Print'N Press, 1983.

Hamilton, W.D. & Spray, W.A. *Source Material Relating to the new Brunswick Indians*. Hamray Books, 1977.

Hamilton, William B. *Place Names of Atlantic Canada*. University of Toronto Press, 1996.

Hannay, James. *History of New Brunswick*. John A. Bowes, 1909

Hannon, Leslie. *Forts of Canada* McCelland & Stewart, 1970.

Leavitt, Robert M. *Maliseet Micmac First Nations of the Maritimes*. New Ireland Press, 1995.

MacBeath, George. *New Brunswick's Old Government House A Pictorial History*. New Ireland Press, 1995.

MacBeath, George & Chamberlin, Dorothy. *New Brunswick The Story of Our Province*. W.J. Gage Limited, 1965.

MacNutt, W.S. *New Brunswick A History: 1784-1867*. Macmillan of Canada, 1963.

MacNutt, W.S. *New Brunswick and Its People*. The New Brunswick Travel Bureau, 1964.

McCreath, Peter. and Leefe, John. *A History of Early Nova Scotia*. Four East Publications, 1982.

Milner, Dr. W.C. *History of Sackville.* The Tribune Press, 1970.

Murchie, Guy. *Saint Croix The Sentinel River.* Duell, Sloan and Pearce, 1947.

Nason, David. *Railways of New Brunswick.* New Ireland Press, 1992.

Pincombe, C.A., Larracey, E.W. *Resurgo The History of Moncton.* City of Moncton, 1990.

Raymond, W.O. *The River St John.* The Tribune Press, 1943.

Rees, Ronald. *St. Andrews & The Islands.* Nimbus Publishing, 1995.

Schuyler, George W. *Saint John Scenes From a Popular History.* Petheric Press, 1984.

Squires, Austin. *History of Fredericton The Last 200 Years.* City of Fredericton, 1980.

Thorburn, Hugh. *Politics in New Brunswick.* University of Toronto Press, 1961.

Trueman, Howard. *The Chignecto Isthmus and Its First Settlers.* Mika Publishing, 1974.

Tweedie, R.A., Cogswell, Fred, MacNutt, W. Stewart. *Arts in New Brunswick.* University Press of New Brunswick, 1967.

Upton, L.F.S. *Micmacs And Colonists.* University of British Columbia, 1979.

Webster, John Clarence. *Acadia At the End of the 17th Century.* New Brunswick Museum, 1934.

Wilbur, Richard. *The Rise of French New Brunswick.* Formac Publishing, 1989.

Wright, Esther Clark. *The Miramichi.* The Tribune Press, 1945.

Wright, Esther Clark *The Petitcodiac.* The Tribune Press, 1945.

Wright, Esther Clark. *The Loyalists of New Brunswick.* Sentinal Printing, 1955.

Wynn, Grame. *Timber Colony.* University of Toronto Press, 1981.

Index

M